GOVERNMENT BUDGETING

GOVERNMENT BUDGETING

A Practical Guidebook

GEORGE M. GUESS

Published by State University of New York Press, Albany

For information, contact State University of New York Press, Albany, NY
www.sunypress.edu

Production, Ryan Morris
Marketing, Michael Campochiaro

Library of Congress Cataloging-in-Publication Data

Guess, George M.
    Government budgeting : a practical guidebook / George M. Guess.
        pages cm
    Includes bibliographical references and index.
    ISBN 978-1-4384-5667-6 (hardcover : alk. paper)
    ISBN 978-1-4384-5666-9 (pbk. : alk. paper)
    ISBN 978-1-4384-5668-3 (e-book)
    1. Budget.   2. Finance, Public.   I. Title.

HJ2005.G86 2015
352.4'8—dc23   2014047304

10 9 8 7 6 5 4 3 2 1

Contents

List of Illustrations   vii

Preface and Introduction   xi

Acknowledgments   xvii

1. Budgeting and Public Financial Management   1

2. Analysis of the Revenue Budget   49

3. Budget Requests and Expenditure Analysis   85

4. Capital Planning, Budgeting, and Financing   129

5. Budget Implementation and Control   175

References   199

Index   207

Illustrations

Tables

1.1	Capital Budget in the Capital Plan	44
1.2	Budget for Code Enforcement	47
2.1	Alternative Revenue Options for Baltimore County, Maryland	58
2.2	Least Squares Regression of Whiskey Tax Collected Receipts, FY 2010–14	78
2.3	Whiskey Tax Receipts Forecast for FY 2015–16	79
2.4	Rockville City Property and Beer/Wine Receipts FY 2010–14	83
2.5	WMATA Ridership	84
3.1	Political versus Technical Budget Cutting Strategies	97
3.2	Allocation Criteria: Unit Measures and Investment Returns Treatment of Alcoholics: Cost Data	99
3.3	Treatment of Alcoholics: Data by Subprogram	99
3.4	Marginal Productivity Curve Schedule: Alcoholic Treatment Program	99
3.5	Rockville Municipal Orchestra Break-Even Analysis	102
3.6	Flexible Budget Example: Meals for Homeless	103
3.7	Analysis of the Salary and Wage Budget	109
3.8	New City Subway Flexible Budget	127
4.1	Present Value of $1	134

4.2   Undiscounted Payback Method of Project Appraisal   146

4.3   Discounted Benefit-Cost and Net Present Value Methods
       of Project Appraisal   148

4.4   Effect of Alternative Discount Rates on Project Efficiency   150

4.5   Weighting and Scoring Matrix for Three Health Investment
       Projects   153

4.6   Weighted Scores for Three Fire Engines   155

4.7   Rockville City Make-Buy Options Analysis: Animal Control   165

4.8   Budget Data for Two Sewerage Treatment Plants   166

4.9   Weighted Score for Purchase of Three Rail Cars   167

4.10   Summer Camp Van Lease versus Purchase Decision   168

4.11   Solution to Lease-Purchase Using Present Value of Annuities   168

4.12   Rockville City Medium-Term Expenditure Plan   173

5.1   Budgetary Control Using Encumbrance Accounting   182

5.2   Breaking Appropriations or Allocations into Allotments   184

5.3   Budget Line Item: Road Maintenance (Total Approved = $2m)   187

5.4   Original Budget versus Flexible Budget: Maintenance for March   188

5.5   Operating versus Cash Flow Budgets in Rockville City   198

Figures

1.1   Fiscal Transparency: Gaston County (NC) Readers Guide and
       Glossary   3

1.2   Leadership and Budget Priorities   7

1.3   Milwaukee 2003 Budget and Planning Process   11

1.4   Milwaukee Department of Administration   13

1.5   Financial Management Information Systems (FMIS)   14

1.6   Financial Condition Framework   16

1.7   Financial Condition Indicator for Gaston County:
       Revenue Shortfalls   17

1.8   Montgomery County (MD) 2010 GFOA Budget Award   20

1.9   Budget Pie Chart: Gaston County 2014   24

1.10   Budget Comparisons and Yearly Changes: Milwaukee 2002–03   25

1.11   Board of Elections: Budgeted versus Approved FY 10–12
       Budget: Montgomery County (MD)   28

1.12   Gaston County Proprietary Fund Balance: Solid Waste 2012–14   30

1.13   Debt Service Indicator and Debt Policies: Gaston County
       2006–12   32

1.14   Program Performance Measures: Public Transit   35

1.15   Public Transit Operations and Maintenance Expenditures   37

1.16   Functional Budget Format: Gaston County 2014   38

1.17   Program Cross-Walked to Objects of Expenditure   39

1.18   Linking Outcomes to Health Program Expenditures   41

1.19   Capital Planning Problems   43

1.20   Montgomery County 2010–14 CIP: Animal Shelter Project   45

2.1   The Consultant Forecasts Revenues   49

2.2   Revenue Policies: Gaston County 2014   55

2.3   Forecasting Model and Assumptions: Gaston County 2012–18   56

2.4   Milwaukee Tax Rate to Levy Conversion   63

2.5   Yield and Efficiency Responsiveness of Revenue Options   65

2.6   Cost Behavior in Relation to Volume   68

2.7   Price Elasticity of Demand   69

2.8   Natural Monopoly Cost Behavior   70

2.9	Income-Based Pricing	71
2.10	Revenue Assumptions	73
2.11	The Regression Equation	77
3.1	How to Meet Expenditure Targets	88
3.2	Program Performance Budget Examples	90
3.3	American University Budget FY 2012	92
3.4	Marginal Program Productivity: Effects on Three Sets of Beneficiaries	100
3.5	A Better Way to Estimate Pension Returns	112
3.6	How Not to Estimate Pension Returns	113
3.7	Subsidies and Contributions to Annual Budgets	118
3.8	Ft. Collins (CO) Debt Service Burden	121
3.9	Budget Transmittal Letter	123
3.10	Budget Message	125
3.11	Performance Measures Exercise	126
4.1	Capital Purchasing Made Hard	132
4.2	Needed: Alternatives Framework and Analysis!	135
4.3	Problems in Ordering Supplies	137
4.4	How Not to Estimate Project Costs	144
4.5	Profile of Project Cost and Benefit Timing	145
4.6	Project Information Should Be Organized for Decision Making	151
4.7	Milwaukee Capital Improvements Plan by Function 2003–08	157
5.1	The Chart of Accounts	180
5.2	Public Financial Management Transactions Using IFMS Support	181
5.3	How Not to Design IFMS	183
5.4	Gaston County 2014 Cash Management/Investment Policies	192

Preface and Introduction

Budgeting is the attempt to balance scarce means with public needs and ends. In the early twenty-first century, the context of scarcity looms large and government budgets reflect the pruning effects of this scarcity. Scarce tax receipts and fixed budget ceilings have meant cancelled transport infrastructure, public housing, school and health projects, and reduced spending for essential social services and programs, including facilities maintenance. At the international level, EU countries such as Spain and Greece debate the relationship between fiscal austerity and growth, that is, will greater fiscal austerity reduce deficits and debt but choke off growth? Will tight fiscal policies in contexts of high unemployment and high debts lead to even more reduced incomes and public revenues? Will they lead to more of the very problems that austerity was supposed to solve? At the U.S. national level the Great Recession of 2007–09 undermined state and local revenues while at the same time increasing state and local expenditure responsibilities to a far greater extent than recent recessions. The other crisis is the unsustainable trajectory of federal debt, which will grow faster than the economy even as the economy recovers (Rivlin, 2012, p. ix).

At the state and local levels, one fear is that, faced with an unsustainable federal fiscal path, the federal government might respond by pushing its deficit down to state and local budgets. In such a scenario, there could be fewer federal grants, more unfunded mandates (or "coercive federalism"), increasing federal preemption of revenue sources, and declining quality of services. Another fear is that a federal government bereft of resources and shorn of powers to govern effectively may fade away in importance, leaving the scope of the nation's governance increasingly up to the individual states to decide and finance (Ebel, Petersen, & Vu, 2012, pp. 4–5).

Consistent with these concerns, Congressional efforts have been preoccupied with budget cutting, reducing the size of government, and expenditure restraint. Despite the context of weak growth but ideally low interest rates on which to invest in energy, transport, and housing projects that would reduce unemployment, Congress is consumed with cutting spending and avoiding even the semblance of raising tax rates. "Fiscal drag" has been the predominant policy, with the exception of the 2009 federal stimulus program. Premature austerity starting in 2010, combined with constant brinkmanship, roils markets and saps consumer confidence (Milbank, 2013). While some states have taken up the slack by increasing taxes and fees, deadlock at the national level threatens U.S. defense, economic growth, and job creation. Even with the 2013 congressional agreement to increase "fees" slightly (not "taxes") and reduce the effects of the across-the-board 2011 budget sequester (freeing up funds for discretionary programs such as infrastructure and energy), the fiscal drag on the economy will drop only from 1.5 percent of GDP to 0.5 percent of GDP (*The Economist*, 2013).

The problem of balancing means and ends through subnational budget processes is urgent for many of the fifty states and ninety thousand local governments. States with declining manufacturing bases and heavily unionized public sectors such as Ohio, Wisconsin, and Michigan suffered severe fiscal crises from both losses in their revenue bases and high levels of mandatory expenditures. Other states with unbalanced revenue systems, such as Oregon (and four other states), that rely heavily on state income tax receipts paid the price during the 2007–09 recession, which destroyed incomes and jobs. Institutional settings also create constraints to effective budgetary policy responses at state and local levels. California, for instance, required supermajorities to pass taxes or approve budgets and consistently could not pass credible or timely budgets even in good years (Ebel et al., 2012, p. 8). Reduced availability of federal grant funds has forced subnational governments to rely more on their own revenue sources to deliver their needed services and invest for local economic growth. Depending on the programs, states receive on average about 30 percent of their funding from federal financing and localities receive about 4 percent. The tough balancing act is that they must satisfy current service needs, including pension payments for retired employees, and balance their current budgets by law every year.

Effective policy responses to these multiple fiscal crises require professional budget decision making. Staff must know the latest methods, systems, and skills that have worked in comparatively similar state and local contexts. They must also know what program and policy responses have not worked and why. Their task is to ensure that: budgets align with policy priorities, services are cost effective, and revenue sources meet the tests of efficiency and equity. Finance departments and legislative fiscal offices in many states have responded well by ensuring fiscal discipline through regular analyses of core expenditure programs and the debt sustainability implications of planned capital investments. To a greater extent than at the national level, perhaps, state and local fiscal officials have employed the latest analytic tools to control spending, allocate budget resources between sectors, and ensure funds for daily service and program operations. While the effects of the Great Recession will pass and growth will regain its momentum, albeit unevenly, across states and localities, fiscal challenges at the subnational level will recur.

This book provides examples of innovative responses to such challenges as pension and infrastructure financing, and how to reduce revenue losses through lower tax rates by expanding tax bases for such transactions as Internet sales purchases (Fox, 2012, p. 421). Needed is a cadre of highly skilled, well-paid public budgeting and financial management professionals at the subnational level that can respond creatively to conditions of permanent scarcity and create enough fiscal space to make ends meet. Budgeting is a field driven by practice and a number of current budget texts are based on extensive insider knowledge of their fine work. Consistent with this reality, this book targets two main audiences:

1. *Present and future MPA/MPP students with primary interests in public financial management.* The book might serve as a supplemental text or guide to basic budgeting for pre-service and in-service students. Since many MPP and MPA students are also "governing" in some capacity, they are sometime erroneously called "nonspecialists." Most are specialists in areas related to public financial management, such as real estate appraisals, nonprofit health care services delivery, or IT sales. The book might also serve MPA/MPP students with secondary or even limited interests in budgeting and finance. Often, students focusing on personnel or program evaluation end up writing grant or contract proposals. To perform these properly, they need to know how to tally up the costs of labor, supplies, and travel, and then add in indirect costs to the total. Similarly, they could work for a contractor attempting to win a local government contract to deliver such services as meals on wheels or public transit for particular routes. Here they must integrate their knowledge of program performance measures and local institutions by producing budgets that reflect efficient service delivery at least cost in order for their employers to win the contract and keep themselves on the payroll.

2. *MPA/MPP graduates that travel from one type of organization to another.* During their long careers, graduates work for multiple types of organizations. They move from local to state fiscal tasks; from local to nonprofit and private contractor work delivering public services or programs; from finance offices at the center of county or state government to departmental offices (e.g., transportation, education, health, social services); and/or from local or state fiscal offices to fiscal evaluation offices that assess program condition and fiscal transparency. For example, a number of private firms and nongovernmental organizations assess fiscal transparency for such uses as creditworthiness analysis. The International Budget Partnership of the Center for Budget and Policy Priorities examines national and subnational budget formats, systems and methods according to clear criteria for development of its annual Open Budget Index. The 2013 index can be viewed at: International_Budget_Partnership@mail.vresp.com or reply-7856b5bdb2-cb5084eeb8-f324@u.cts.vresp.com.

Those with primary interests in civil society and public policy, for instance, might work at *Revenue Watch* of the *Open Society Institute*, which consists of budget activists interested in monitoring the oil and gas revenues of firms in transitional and developing countries (Schultz, 2005). More information on OSI fiscal transparency work can be obtained from: mgreenwald@osiny.org.

Other students with interest in auditing service performance and obtaining value for money must understand budgetary basics as well. Units at the federal level such as the U.S. General Accountability Office or departmental inspectors general, or internal audit units at state and local governments require professionals with skills that can integrate public budgeting and public policy evaluation. Finally, credit rating agencies such as Moody's and Standard and Poor's need professionals who understand government operations, budgeting and financing.

Fiscal and policy work in these settings requires understanding of budgetary basics (both the revenue and expenditure sides of the budget) and the use of modern analytic techniques. Some of the basics can be obtained in books such as this one. More likely, this book will serve as a foundation on which to build new practical experience in the use of the latest techniques. As noted, unlike most fields, practice far outpaces the theory and research reported in the literature.

The organization of each chapter is as follows. The first part of each chapter subtopic will focus on (1) challenges faced by governments from the Great Recession of 2007–09 and ongoing fiscal crises related to tight fiscal policies, and (2) how fiscal officials responded to them; the strategies, methods, and tools used by them for mitigation. Second, each chapter will describe the value of the subject to budget practitioners and to the overall budget process. Third, each chapter will describe important tools, methods, and techniques used by practitioners in the field at state and local government levels. Fourth, each chapter will feature one or more hands-on exercise. The book consists of five technical chapters: (1) public budgeting and financial management concepts and practices, (2) revenue policy concepts and analysis, (3) current expenditure planning and analysis, (4) capital planning, budgeting, and financing, and (5) accounting, reporting and control over budget execution.

Acknowledgments

The author would first like to thank Michael Rinella at SUNY Press for his support of this project. He especially acknowledges the invaluable technical support of Tim Higashi, MPA student at George Mason University, in producing the figures, tables, manuscript formatting, and index for this book. The book was of course strengthened by the incisive questions and critical comments of his many former students from American University in Washington, D.C., and Georgia State University in Atlanta.

The author would also like to acknowledge the immense technical knowledge of local finances gained from his research projects and social interactions with a large number of friends who are also seasoned local government practitioners. These include: Earl Mathers, county manager of Gaston County, N.C., and former county administrator of Gallatin, County, Montana. Earl was also chief of party of the USAID/Development Alternatives, Incorporated (DAI) municipal reform project in Romania (2002–03) under whom the author served as the head of the budget and financial management reform team for ten cities. Thanks also to Ed Blackman, finance director of Gallatin County, for assistance with property taxation, and Bryan Morehead, budget administrator for Gaston County, for explaining the county's highly readable, comprehensive, and transparent annual budget to him. The author offers special thanks to other former colleagues: Tom Briggs, former CFO, City of Denver, for relating the challenges he faced in cash management for that city; Darlene Fairfax, director of OMB, Montgomery County, Maryland, for serving as gracious host for several of his classes; Sam Coxson, former city manager of Franklin, Ohio, and county administrator of La Plata, Colorado, for being a great colleague and friend both overseas in the field and in the United States; Bob Ebel of World Bank for his support during the author's three-year tenure at Local Government and Public Service Reform Initiative (OSI/LGI) in Budapest, Hungary; Ted Poister, his past boss and current friend at the Andrew Young School of Policy

Studies, Georgia State University in Atlanta; the late John Petersen, formerly of GFOA and later George Mason University; Bob Kehew, formerly of Associates in Rural Development (ARD) and currently with UNDP in Nairobi, Kenya; Ann Kinney, former director of the Budget Management Division at City of Milwaukee for demonstrating how results-based budgeting should and should not be done; Richard McCrillis, director of Treasury Services; Carroll Olson, head of the Budget Department, and Ken Gregor, general manager, all formerly with the Metropolitan Atlanta Rapid Transit Authority (MARTA), for hosting his research grants from UMTA (now Federal Transit Administration of USDOT); and Monty Josephson, Dona Turman, and Alan Wulkin, formerly of Metro-Dade Transit Administration (MDTA Miami), for their intriguing insights into the implementation of the large, complex capital project known as Metrorail. As always, he wishes to thank his wife Regula and their two sons Andy and Marty for their encouragement, patience, and understanding. Their continued support have made all things happen.

Budgeting and Public Financial Management

Challenges and Responses

Where the focus of the budget process is revenue, budgeters will be concerned with curbing the rise in expenditures and with finding revenues to fund current programs (Anton, 1966, cited in Wildavsky, 1986, p. 223). Participants respond to the certainties of reduced wealth and definite expenditure responsibilities with incremental changes and repeated budget revisions. "Revenue budgeting" describes the responses of budgeters at all levels of the U.S. government since about 2000. In response to the twin constraints of the 2007–09 financial collapse and recession and premature fiscal austerity imposed by the Congress, budgeters have had to cut programs, services, and projects.

To achieve fiscal discipline at the national level, cuts have been mostly crude, across the board with little concern for effects other than meeting legal targets of balance and political targets for deficits and debts. The tools used in response to such austerity requirements as sequestration involve simple attainment of percentage reductions. Decisions have been innovative to the extent that they used gimmicks to stave off reductions and achieve targets. In addition to controlling outlays, budgeting requires attention to allocation of resources between programs and competing claims in order to maximize results, including consistency with strategic planning objectives. Budget systems should encourage analysis of costs and consequences of each fiscal option selected. At the operations level, budgeting should also be able to ensure regular flows of cash to deliver services and predict costs and consequences on important variables such as demand, cost, revenues, and physical results for users. While value for money and performance-based budgeting systems have been installed formally in many jurisdictions, evidence of their use by elected officials to formulate fiscal policies is scant. Some exceptions will be noted. Nevertheless, further efforts are needed to find incentives to use rational budgeting techniques (for funding increases as well as decreases) that would appeal to both executive fiscal experts and elected officials.

The Budgetary Function

Budgeting is the art of using technical definitions to allocate and control resources. Retiring Washington, D.C., CFO Natwar Gandhi wants to be remembered as not just a "humble bean counter" or accountant but "as a poet" (DeBonis, 2013). Successful budget practitioners need to have enough artistic imagination to use the available technical methods and to employ fiscal definitions skillfully and creatively to improve the fiscal conditions of their jurisdictions. And to the bane of students and practitioners, definitions abound. General agreement exists on larger items such as budget formats. An object of expenditure budget looks the same regardless of level of government or difference in state or local jurisdiction. At the operational management level, however, definitions may be based on accounting and economic concepts or simply driven by politics. The latter often lead to deliberate obfuscation and use of "gimmicks." Definitional variation is useful when trying to maintain discipline and control budgetary balances. In a field drowning in data, through the skillful use of legal definitions, it is possible to hide expenditures and reduce the amount of fees and taxes required for balance. For instance, outlays might be classified as off-budget spending. They might have been made by a city or state enterprise and excluded from totals from a narrow budget reporting perspective. From a consolidated accounting perspective, though, they would have to be included and separated out by fund for audit and control. Similarly, distinctions between major and minor maintenance expenditures are flexible, often allowing minor maintenance to be financed with debt and excluded from the annual operating budget that must be balanced and state and local levels. More progressive jurisdictions respond to public doubts on budget figures as gimmickry with greater fiscal transparency. For example, Gaston County (NC) a smaller county of 208,000 population next to Charlotte includes a "reader's guide to the budget" and comprehensive glossary in its annual budget (Figure 1.1).

Reader's Guide

Welcome

Gaston County thanks you for your interest in your local government and encourages you to use this document to expand your knowledge about our community. Included on the following pages are descriptions of county departments, the services they provide, and how much it costs to provide those services. We hope this information is useful to you and answers your questions about your county government.

Feel free to contact the **Gaston County Budget & Purchasing Department** at (704)-866-3038 or via e-mail at bryant.morehead@co.gaston.nc.us with your budget questions, as well as your comments about how we can improve this document.

What's in Here?

This document is divided into numerous sections. The *Budget Highlights* section immediately follows. Here you'll find basic information on what's included in Gaston County's budget.

The *Budget Preparation & Amendment* section is next. This section outlines the planning processes, budget procedures, and official actions that led to the adoption of the FY 2013-2014 budget.

Following the *Budget Preparation & Amendment* section is the *Budget Summary* section. This section provides numerous schedules of revenues and expenditures for the current and several previous fiscal years.

After the *Budget Summary* section, you'll find sections describing the county's revenues and expenditures, personnel changes, capital requests, fund balances, financial policies, and debt.

Next, you'll find profiles of Gaston County's departments, which comprise the largest section of this budget document. Gaston County's departments fall into the following function categories, each of which is divided into several departments:

- General Government
- Community Services
- Human Services
- Education
- Public Safety
- Support Services

On each department page you will find a profile describing the department, along with tables listing the department's budget information.

Figure 1.1. ~~Fiscal Transparency~~: Gaston County (NC) Readers Guide and Glossary.

4

Reader's Guide

The **sources of funds** section of each department budget table identifies the amount of money received by a department from the federal and state governments, local, and other revenues. Local funds come from the property tax, unearmarked sales tax revenues, interest earnings, and so on.

The **expenditures** for each department are also presented in a summary format and include amounts budgeted for personnel costs, operational expenses, and outlays for major capital expenditures.

Figures in the *2010-2011 Actual* column and *2011-2012 Actual* column list revenues and expenditures received or spent by the department in the noted fiscal years. The county's fiscal year begins on July 1 of each year and ends on June 30 of the following year.

The next column, *2012-2013 Adopted* lists the budgeted revenues and expenditures as adopted by the Board of Commissioners for the 2012-2013 fiscal year. As of the date of publication, actual expenditures and revenues amounts for FY 2012-2013 were not available.

The *2013-2014 Requested* column lists the expenditure amounts requested by the individual departments. It is common for some amounts in the *Requested* column to be different from amounts in the *Recommended* column, sometimes substantially higher or lower. This is because the budget process is dynamic up to the date of the budget presentation. For instance, some requests such as fuel and utilities expenses and debt payments are calculated centrally by the Budget Department. Between the *Requested* and the *Recommended* phases of the budget process, projections for these expenditures are often refined and therefore changed in the *Recommended* phase to reflect the more accurate projections.

The *2013-2014 Recommended* column lists the expenditure and revenue amounts proposed by the County Manager for the 2013-2014 fiscal year.

The *2013-2014 Approved* column lists the expenditure and revenue amounts the Board of Commissioners adopted for the 2013-2014 fiscal year.

The **% Change** column indicates by what percentage the expenditures or sources of funds figures changed from *2012-2013 Adopted* to *2013-2014 Approved*.

Also on the department pages you'll find descriptions of the department, a discussion of the department's budget highlights, a list of goals and objectives, and a table showing performance measurement data totals for the past four fiscal years.

Finally, at the end of this document you'll find a glossary of technical terms used in this document, as well as the budget ordinance.

Figure 1.1. Continued.

Glossary

Accrual Basis of Accounting: The primary basis of recording assets, liabilities, revenues, and expenses for a government's business-like activities. Under the accrual basis, revenues are recognized in the accounting period when earned and expenses are recognized in the period that they are incurred.

Adopted Budget: The budget formally adopted by the Board of Commissioners for the upcoming fiscal year.

Appropriation: The Board of Commissioner's authorization, per the budget ordinance or a budget amendment, to spend money for a specific purpose.

Assessed Value: The value of real estate or personal property as determined by tax assessors and used as a basis for levying taxes.

Balanced Budget: According to North Carolina law, a budget is balanced when the sum of estimated net revenues and appropriated fund balance is equal to appropriations.

Basis of Accounting: This refers to the methods that determine when revenues, expenditures, and associated assets and liabilities, are recognized in the government's accounting system and reported in its financial statements.

Board of Commissioners: The elected governing body of a county in North Carolina. Gaston County has a seven member Board of Commissioners.

Bond Rating: A rating that indicates the credit worthiness of a government's debt. The major rating agencies, such as Moody's Investor Service or Standard and Poor's, are responsible for determining a government's bond rating. Governments with favorable bond ratings are able to obtain financing with low interest rates.

Bond: A written promise to repay a specific amount of money with interest within a specific time period, usually long-term.

Budget: North Carolina law defines a budget as a plan for raising and spending money for specified programs, functions, activities, or objectives for a fiscal year.

Budget Amendment: An adjustment to the budget ordinance made by the Board of Commissioners, or, in certain cases, the County Manager.

Budget Message: A message that North Carolina law requires the County Manager to include with his recommended budget. According to the law, the budget message should contain a concise explanation of the governmental goals fixed by the budget for the budget year, should explain important features of the activities anticipated in the budget, should set forth the reasons for stated changes from the previous year in program goals, programs, and appropriation levels, and should explain any major changes in fiscal policy.

Figure 1.1. Continued.

6

Glossary

Budget Ordinance: The ordinance that the Board of Commissioners adopts that levies taxes and appropriates revenues for specified purposes, functions, activities, or objectives during a fiscal year.

Capital Improvement: Major construction, acquisition, or renovation activities which add value to a government's physical assets or significantly increase their useful life.

Capital Improvement Program: A long term plan of proposed capital improvement projects which includes estimated project costs and funding sources.

Certificate of Participation (COP): A form of loan to a government where investors are entitled to a share in the periodic payments made by the government under an installment financing agreement.

Debt Service: According to North Carolina law, the sum of money required to pay installments of principal and interest on bonds, notes, and other evidences of debt accruing within a fiscal year.

Department: A basic organizational unit of the county that is functionally unique in its delivery of services. Some departments are divided into divisions.

Expenditures: Money that the government spends.

Fire District: Gaston County's unincorporated areas are divided into twenty volunteer fire districts. Each fire district has its own tax rate, which the Board of Commissioners approves. The tax revenues for each fire district support the volunteer fire department in each district in order to provide fire protection service for county citizens living in unincorporated areas.

Fiscal Year: The period that the government uses for accounting purposes and preparing financial statements. Gaston County's fiscal year starts on July 1 and ends on June 30 of the following year. The phrases "fiscal year 2013-2014," "FY 2013-2014," and "FY 2014" all refer to the period starting July 1, 2013 and ending June 30, 2014.

Function: A group of related departments. For instance, the General Government function includes, among others, the County Manager, Finance, and Human Resources departments.

Fund: An independent fiscal and accounting entity with a self-balancing set of accounts recording its assets, liabilities, fund balance, revenue, and expenditures

Fund Balance: The difference between a fund's assets and liabilities. Fund balance mostly includes cash and investments, but can also include non-spendable items, such as inventories.

GAAP: Generally accepted accounting principles. The standard accounting rules and practices used to record transactions and prepare financial statements.

Figure 1.1. Continued.

At the federal level, terms such as "tax expenditure" or "statutory revenue losses for a public purpose" are also subject to definitional alchemy and gimmickry. Elected leaders with a leftist bent view them as subsidy expenditures from the budget. If cut they could be viewed as an expenditure reduction. Elected leaders of a rightist bent often view their elimination as tax increases on beneficiary groups (e.g., property taxpayers if the federal mortgage interest deduction were eliminated) and therefore a violation of their antitax, antigovernment agenda. In fact, tax expenditures should be viewed as a transparency tool since they contain both expenditures and taxes. Without them, the taxpayer pays the tax but simultaneously receives a government grant equal to the amount of tax in that provision (Mikesell, 2014, p. 590). Given the definitional flexibility of the field, it is critical that students know the core concepts and definitions as well as how they have been used and misused in practice. Only in that way can public funds be allocated and controlled clearly and precisely.

To begin with simpler concepts and definitions, then, budgets have multiple purposes. Whether developed for individuals, firms, or governments, they are plans with accurate price tags; in addition, they express dominant political values and policy preferences; and they indicate in narratives and figures who gets what for what purpose and who pays (Axelrod, 1988, p. 1). Budgets record the annual outcome of political conflict between *guardian* roles who want to control spending, for example, to meet deficit and debt targets, and *advocates* who want to expand staff and resources to achieve more results for

Figure 1.2. Leadership and Budget Priorities. DILBERT © 2008 Scott Adams.

their departments, activities, or programs (Wildavsky, 1984, p. 160). How well budgets achieve any or all of these purposes depends on their transparency—how much relevant data and information they provide for analysis and conclusions by decision makers. In any jurisdiction, the quality of budgets depends in large part on the institutional and political process of making them. LeLoup notes that "[b]udgeting encompasses a range of decisions, participants and concurrent policy processes" (1988, p. 13). The annual budget process is the singular opportunity to compare means-ends for whole governments or their component parts as: departments, subnational governments, programs, projects by sector, and services. With comparative performance information from programs and projects in similar jurisdictions, the budget process is useful for highlighting the successes and failures of service delivery. In the last decade at the federal level, the budget process has accomplished few if any of these objectives and has not even produced an approved budget on time. Nevertheless, in many state and local jurisdictions, the process of analyzing the financial, labor, and material resources to be allocated for the year has worked well. The budget function continues to be carried out by professionals according to an annual calendar. How well or badly this process works affects the ability of the budget function to plan and control public spending.

The *budget process* consists of a cycle that covers about three years. Calendars vary, but the timing and sequence are the same regardless of governmental level. As is evident from the example of the U.S. budget *calendar,* and cycle below, the four phases of the cycle take place simultaneously, in what is known as a "scrambled cycle." For state-local governments, the importance of the federal process is to plan and gauge the levels of grants flowing to their core sectors, such as education, roads, bridges, water and sewerage, and public transit. Failure to anticipate cuts or delays in approval and release of these funds from Washington can disrupt state and local services.

U.S. Government Budget Cycle

1. Formulation: e.g., November 2013

FY '16 (preparation); FY '15 (approval); FY '14 (execution); FY '13 (audit). The formulation phase is called Spring Planning Review and takes place normally from March at the agency and OMB levels.

2. Approval

The president's budget is submitted to Congress in January and hearings-actions continue through September. Actions include the two-step authorization appropriation to produce *budget authority* (BA) for agency commitments. About 66 percent of budget authority consists of outlays outside the annual appropriations process. The forms of BA for this are: (a) *contract authority* or contracts that require BA for that fiscal year (e.g., multiyear sewerage project contracts that require contract authority later), (b) *borrowing authority* based on appropriations that require Treasury funds, sale of agency debt securities, or funds from the Federal Financing Bank through sale of agency securities, and (c) *entitlement authority* to pay for mandatory spending, the largest of which are Social Security, Medicare, and Medicaid (Mikesell, 2011, p. 119). The remaining 34 percent of the budget is funded by normal BA *appropriations authority* through the formal budget process. This portion is for *discretionary* funds; but roughly 16 percent of that is defense.

3. Execution (10/1–9/30 FY)

BA is allotted by the OMB, which allows departments to *commit* or *encumber* funds that turn into *outlays*. The OMB pulls control levers here to: vary rates of expenditures by:

a. Allotment: This process releases funds and transfers to departments and subunits. BA is then apportioned to agencies by time (i.e., quarter) and activity (i.e., project);

b. Pre-Audit: This ongoing phase controls the flow of commitments, outlays, and to maintain balances. OMB relies on departmental internal controls (rules and systems to safeguard spending), and inspectors general (IGs) that pre-audit compliance with appropriations acts.

c. Cash Management and Variance Analysis: are mechanisms through which the OMB monitors and analyzes outlays throughout the year and tries to ensure that sufficient funds are on hand to pay commitments.

4. Audit/Control

Postexpenditure audits focus on the legality and appropriateness of making payments, and the efficiency of operations. These activities take about one to two years beyond the end of the FY and are performed by state legislative audit units, local government auditors or private firms, and the GAO for the U.S. government. This phase completes the thirty-six-month budget cycle and results in an Annual Financial Report, which is a final audit of the two previous fiscal years.

To develop the annual plan and budget, it is critical that other policy documents must be used to estimate resource needs. At the state and local levels, these include the strategic plan, the land use plan, financial trend monitoring reports, and capital improvement plans (GFOA, 1994, p. 5). For example, the budget calendar that guides the annual process of the City of Milwaukee begins with budget formulation for about five months (January–May), and the fiscal year runs from January 1 to December 31. See: www.city.milwaukee.gov/budgetdocs/plan and the activity calendar for the annual budget in Figure 1.3.

Professional budgeting is needed to ensure accountability and control of the public finances and to link public funds with policy results. The *budget function* evolved from a diffuse municipal context in the nineteenth century where many directors had minimal responsibility for planning and managing core functions, to a more integrated model in the twenty-first century where a multiplicity of public financial management functions became the responsibility of a single department headed, typically, by a CFO. Public budgeting is considered one of ten core *public financial management* (PFM) functions including: accounting, cash management, debt administration, internal audit, procurement, capital investment, revenue collection, personnel, pensions, and payments or treasury. It is recognized that within PFM, the budgetary function should ensure (1) *liquidity* or availability of cash to meet obligations when due, (2) *cost control* or reducing the costs of internal transactions, services provided by state-local government, and interest burdens on borrowed money, (3) *productivity* or ensuring service efficiency and effectiveness and maximum socioeconomic returns on capital investments, and (4) *control of budget execution,* which means that budgeting is dependent on accounting for basic information (Lehan, cited in Petersen & Strachota, 1991, pp. 36–40). Because of the importance of these four requirements, budgeting is often considered the main PFM function. Past GFOA surveys have concluded that small to medium-sized cities integrate budgeting with the other PFM functions and have more centralized and vertical command structures under a chief finance officer or CFO (Lehan, cited in

BUDGET AND PLANNING PROCESS

City Strategic Plan

Citywide Objectives
Citywide Strategies

↓

Unified Strategic Plans and Budget

Department Objectives
Department Strategies
Department Performance Measures
Department Annual Budget

↓

Annual Budget

Executive Budget

↓

Adopted City Budget

CALENDAR DATE	ACTIVITY
January - March	Departments Prepare Plans, Objectives, and Performance Measures
Mid-March	Departments Receive Budget Materials
May 13*	Plans and Budget Requests Due
Mid-June	Mayor's Public Hearings on Plans and Budgets
July - September	Mayor's Executive Plan and Budget Review
September 24**	Plan and Budget Submitted to Common Council
Mid-October	Legislative Hearings
October 31 and November 1	Finance and Personnel Committee Budget Amendment Days
November 8***	Common Council Action on Budget

*   Second Tuesday in May
** Legal Deadline September 28
*** Legal Deadline November 14

Figure 1.3. Milwaukee 2003 Budget and Planning Process.

Petersen & Strachota, 1991, p. 33). Under this arrangement, those responsible for the various PFM functions report to a CFO. Larger cities seem to eschew the centralized and superdepartment model in favor of a more fragmented organizational structure.

The City of Milwaukee is a medium to large-sized city (population 597,000) and fits the hybrid pattern—the budgetary function is the sub-responsibility of a larger administration department. As indicated in Figure 1.4, the finance function is largely in the Department of Administration, whose overall responsibilities are: administration, budget analysis, capital financing and debt management, and purchasing (2003, p. 48). The Head of the Budget and Management Division reports to the Director of Administration; IT is a separate division; debt policy is shared between the Budget and Management Division and the Public Debt Commission; tax collections and responsibility for investments are with the City Treasury. Milwaukee includes departmental operating budgets (and their generated revenues) by object of expenditure and usefully breaks out personnel positions by main object of expenditure for additional transparency (see Figure 1.4).

One indicator of robust institutions is the functioning of checks and balances to prevent financial misbehavior and abuse of political power. Checks and balances are an important part of PFM effectiveness, and problems occur when, for example, internal controls and treasury payments are not clearly separated, resulting in uncontrolled and often illegal tax refund payments. Poorly designed and monitored PFM institutions can eliminate such checks. Fragmentation of vertical command authority and horizontal responsibility can wipe out firewalls and politicize the public finances. In Washington, D.C., the independent CFO office played an important role in restoring the city to fiscal health and producing a $1.5b fund balance for FY 12. Prior to CFO establishment in 1985, city finances were plagued by gimmickry and wasteful spending that led to the imposition of a federal control board (*Washington Post*, 2013). CFO resistance to 2012 mayoral intrusions to modify his department's revenue and expenditure projections resulted in the CFO's resignation. The mayor is now attempting to abolish the CFO office and return to the days when elected officials were directly responsible for the finance function.

Advances in information technology have made it more feasible to integrate PFM functions. In 1975 Moak and Hillhouse noted that "computer technology was 'forcing major changes in the organization of financial management'" (Lehan, cited in Petersen & Stachota, 1991, p. 30). Today it is clear that driven by the availability and high performance computerized PFM systems known variously as: Government Financial Management Information Systems (GFMIS),

BUDGET SUMMARY

	2001 ACTUAL EXPENDITURES	2002 ADOPTED BUDGET	2003 ADOPTED BUDGET	CHANGE 2003 ADOPTED VERSUS 2002 ADOPTED
PERSONNEL				
FTEs - Operations and Maintenance	78.05	81.60	75.43	-6.17
FTEs - Other	31.80	36.65	33.92	-2.73
Total Positions Authorized	135	132	119	-13
DLH - Operations and Maintenance	140,495	146,880	135,774	-11,106
DLH - Other Funds	57,245	65,970	61,056	-4,914
EXPENDITURES				
Salaries and Wages	$4,622,851	$4,669,776	$4,477,706	$-192,070
Fringe Benefits	1,560,436	1,587,724	1,656,752	69,028
Operating Expenditures	1,053,826	1,187,492	1,039,095	-148,397
Equipment	85,407	76,400	22,880	-53,520
Special Funds	951,268	1,166,615	1,301,836	135,221
TOTAL	$8,273,788	$8,688,007	$8,498,269	$-189,738
REVENUES				
Charges for Services	$3,646,215	$3,474,200	$3,605,500	$131,300
Miscellaneous	251,189	153,500	146,500	-7,000
TOTAL	$3,897,404	$3,627,700	$3,752,000	$124,300

CAPITAL PROJECTS - Includes $1,811,500 for the following projects:
    a. Technology Fund - $1,000,000
    b. Fire Suppression - North Computer Room - $153,000
    c. Air Conditioning - North Computer Room - $183,500
    d. Capital Needs Study - $50,000
    e. Uninterrupted Power Supply System - $425,000

ORGANIZATION CHART

Figure 1.4. Milwaukee Department of Administration.

Integrated Financial Management Systems (IFMS), or Financial Management Information Systems (FMIS), at all levels of governments, responsibility for core PFM functions should be under one CFO. These systems permit integration of all government finance operations vertically (from central to local government with real-time daily reporting of the fiscal position) and horizontally (across government departments to improve service efficiencies). Called Enterprise Resource Planning systems (ERP) by many IT specialists (Melbye, 2010), they have revolutionized planning and control of public expenditures. The various modules of FMIS's now have a lengthy performance in the United States at all levels and are also used in many countries to enhance fiscal transparency and accountability. (See: https://eteam.worldbank.org/FMIS). The relationship between PFM functionality and available modules for a comprehensive FMIS is illustrated in Figure 1.5 (Dener et al., 2011, p. 2); how GFMIS works to facilitate budgetary control will be explained in more detail in chapter 5.

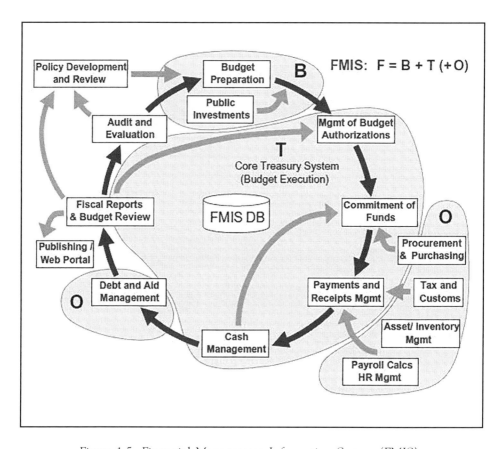

Figure 1.5. Financial Management Information System (FMIS).

Evaluation of Financial Condition

The thrust of this book is that practitioners need skills in three related areas: (1) budget and fiscal condition analysis, (2) problem spotting or gap analysis, and (3) critical evaluation of proposed or existing public expenditures. Before practitioners can analyze or evaluate expenditures or revenues, they must be capable of measuring them. Databases must be reliable and valid; measurement and analytic skills are needed for exercise of proper guardianship and advocacy roles as well as to improve the efficiency and effectiveness of public financial management. First, we examine the institutional *demand* for such skills; then we move to the *supply* side and to the topic of fiscal data and information.

The primary demand for fiscal analysis and evaluation is the need to ensure sound fiscal condition. This means determining whether a government can meet its financial obligations (Berne & Schramm, 1986, p. 71). Determination requires the skill to gauge how expenditure pressures relate to available resources. Expenditure pressures arise from the costs and demands for current services and from past commitments for debt and pensions. A government that has the *fiscal space* to raise additional resources to meet past and current spending obligations is in good fiscal condition. Revenue pressures derive from limited capacities to raise revenues from own-sources (e.g., property, sales taxes, and fees) and external sources such as the local economy and other governments (e.g., state or federal level grants or revenue sharing). They also arise from limits on internal resource liquidity, for example, low reserves, payables exceeding receivables, and poor investment performance of short-term assets (1986, p. 73). Additionally, if a government faces high costs in providing current services or excessive demands for service quantity or quality, it may be in bad fiscal condition if available resources do not permit response to these demands. The financial condition analytic framework is shown in Figure 1.6 on page 16.

Gaston County uses a financial condition framework to monitor solvency indicators. For example, one indicator is the ratio of revenue shortfalls to net operating revenues for the six period of 2006–2012 (Figure 1.7, page 17).

How to Read a Budget

Initiating fiscal condition assessment should begin with expenditure measures and classification (for the expenditure side of the budget). It is essential to establish a common terminology and conceptual baseline—budgetary classifica-

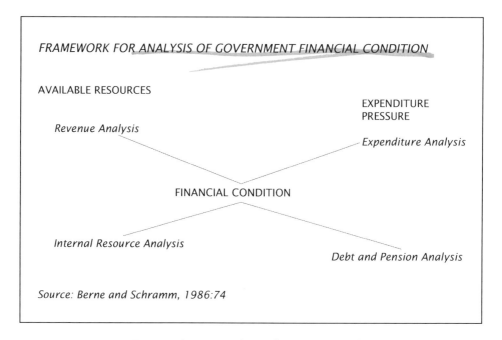

Figure 1.6. Financial Condition Framework.

tion serves this purpose. From item by item measurement based on valid and reliable figures, analysis can proceed and remain consistent with the needs of fiscal and policy decision makers. The importance of consistent nomenclature and fiscal definitions to avoid budgetary gimmickry was noted above. The level of wages/salaries paid, for example, can be measured in dollars, percentages of total expenditures, and per capita ratios. From here, analysts in the educational finance office, for instance, can zero in on particular issues such as the ratio of administrative positions and staff to teaching position or students. These can be compared to similar jurisdictions within states or between them to provide more comprehensive analysis. In chapter 3, we explore expenditure analysis for decision making in greater depth; in the next chapter, we review measures and method of revenue analysis. Budgets have been difficult to read and interpret intelligently because they are opaque, meaning vague, contradictory, or otherwise confusing. If budgets are opaque, it is difficult to assess the revenue and expenditure pressures faced by state and local governments; it is difficult to assess financial condition. Here are some common obstacles to comprehension:

Financial Condition & Outlook

of Deeds fees, Building Inspections fees depend on the real estate market, which has gradually started to improve in Gaston County since the last recession.

Revenue Shortfalls

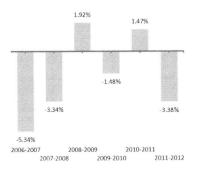

Description:

Revenue shortfalls as a percentage of actual net operating revenues

Calculation:

$$\frac{\text{Revenue shortfalls}}{\text{Net operating revenues}}$$

Warning Trend:

Increase in revenue shortfalls as a percentage of actual net operating revenues

This indicator depicts the differences between revenues budgeted and actually received during the fiscal year. Ideally, at the end of the fiscal year the government will have earned more revenues than budgeted. When the government earns less revenues than budgeted, then the government experiences a revenue shortfall. It is important to identify if the government is continually earning less revenues than budgeted, as this can indicate, for instance, unrealistic revenue forecasting techniques or the drying up of certain revenue sources.

This indicator is calculated as follows. The actual net operating revenues for a year are subtracted from the budgeted net operating revenues for that year. If the resulting number is negative, that means the actual net operating revenues for that year were higher than the budgeted revenues. If the number is positive, the opposite is true. This number is then divided into the actual net revenues for the year in question, which shows the revenue surplus or shortfalls as a percentage of actual net operating revenues. On the graph above, negative numbers indicate a revenue surplus; positive numbers indicate a revenue shortfall.

Gaston County's General Fund experienced revenue shortfalls for only two of the five years indicated on the chart. In addition, the amount of the shortfall was small. For FY 2009, the total revenue shortfall was 1.92% of actual expenditures, and for FY 2011 the revenue shortfall was 1.47% of actual expenditures.

The data for this indicator do not indicate a warning trend of persistent, or even growing, revenue shortfalls—a token of Gaston County's practice of generating conservative revenue projections.

Figure 1.7. Financial Condition Indicator for Gaston County: Revenue Shortfalls.

1. Sometimes there is too much *data* and not enough useful *information*. Finance offices might publish raw fiscal data online without breaking them down into percentages and ratios of total expenditures. It is hard to ask intelligent questions on raw data. Converting data into information through use of trends, ratios, percentages, and narrative indication of operating assumptions is very important for financial condition analysis. Examples include: expenditures/capita, debt service/net operating revenues, and personnel/capita.

2. Finance offices may not include interyear comparisons in the annual budget. The standard budget consists of planned allocations for the budget year. So, budget analysts might ask how this compares to the past two years of actual expenditures? This could give one an idea of expenditure trends by category and total. Since "people tend to think about what is put in front of them" (Lehan, 1981, p. 2), without this kind of basic information, there is little to be asked. As will be explained further below, "Budget classifications tend to define reality for budget-makers and reviewers, channeling their thoughts and attention" (ibid.). With interyear figures, they may now ask about trends and the reasons for shifts.

3. Operating assumptions are often not included. Budgeting is all about discerning what is included and excluded from estimates and why. For instance, most state-local budgets are in nominal or current terms. But both program advocates and budgetary guardians need to know proposed expenditures in real terms and inflation rates to be used for calculations. If inflation is increasing, nominal requests by departments may shortchange their service beneficiaries. Planning baselines and information on the accuracy of past revenue and expenditure forecasts need to be made explicit. These assumptions and definitions are often either missing or unclear. This requires time-consuming review by the media, legislators, public interest groups, and external auditors to reveal the basis of calculations. Only if this information is made explicit (even as footnotes in annual budgets) can intelligent inquiry begin on budgets at any of the four stages of the process noted above.

4. The budget often consists of several documents, making it difficult to integrate totals and track trends. For instance, the capital

budget is often separate; and there may be additional and separate budgets for city enterprises (e.g., Chicago Transit Authority). Indeed, the efficiency of the overall budget process is often affected by the fact that several separate departments prepare and monitor the implementation of these budgets, for instance, Department of Public Works. Since there are substantial interfund transfers between the general fund (including core government operations such as police and health) and special funds (including proprietary funds for enterprises such as water/sewer and public transit), these interfund flows need to be tracked and assessed. The financial condition risk is that city enterprises are like parallel governments and may be able to avoid direct controls from the city finance department despite receipt of substantial subsidies from the central budget. Since they are institutionally separate, it is important to examine the scope of central control over expenditures as well as liability for city enterprise debts.

5. Budget transparency only improves from the outside pressure of checks and balances. To counter institutional and political tendencies to hide assumptions and make totals serve in-house objectives such as maintaining balance, public interest groups, the media, and professional organizations monitor budgets and provide incentives for greater fiscal transparency. The Government Finance Officers Association of the United States and Canada (GFOA), for example, offers an annual award for the best presentation. Milwaukee (population 597,000) has a long history of public sector innovation, including the first school choice voucher experiment in 1990. The larger Montgomery County (MD) (population 971,000) has a similar type of fiscal administration: bold and innovative with high quality public services. Their GFOA award is indicated in Figure 1.8 on page 20.

GFOA evaluates budget quality on four criteria of whether: (1) the budget serves as an *Operating Statement* that includes activity measures and statistics; (2) it is useful for *Expenditure Planning,* including multiyear projections of both revenues and expenditures for critical items like debt and capital plans; (3) it is a realistic *Communications Device,* including clear narrative descriptions of issues faced and attempted remedies; and (4) it serves as a good *Policy Document,* setting out core programs and policies and activities in terms of problems

Figure 1.8. Montgomery County (MD) 2010 GFOA Budget Award.

faced, measures taken, and results in outputs and outcomes. GFOA also considers whether revenue, expenditure, and debt policies are formalized and publicly available. They also look for clear annual budget messages that relate policy needs and actions to fiscal data (Strachota, 1994, pp. 155–60).

Budget Classification

In common parlance, *budget* means planned expenditures and the breakout is by *line items* or *objects of expenditures*. All budgets are technically in line items, whether for objects, activities, or programs. The standard format and classification by economic objects of expenditure is simple to understand. Along with incrementalist budgeting, whereby participants consider small parts of budgets and make marginal adjustments to last year's base, line-item budgets are commonly badmouthed in the academic literature as an antiquarian brake upon measurement of what government could achieve through performance-based expenditure. In fact, objects of expenditure facilitate incremental budgeting and the normative wish is that participants would examine budgets by program, sector, service, or larger aggregates by relating their costs to actual volumes and services. But limited time, resources, adversarial roles, and specialization all act as incentives for the incremental method of budgeting (LeLoup, 1988:13). Moreover the critique of object of expenditure budgeting using incremental methods ignores the fact that the line-item budget was once a reform itself and developed to control misappropriation and theft of public expenditures. Line items are also a common political currency that legislators can use to allocate resources to their district-based constituents. For legislative logrolling, line items are the perfect political currency in a democracy. The object of expenditure classification, as will be discussed further under formats, can also be used for performance budgeting and efforts to assess the efficiency of public expenditures. Broken down by departments and subdepartments, the line-item budget also serves as a transparent control mechanism over the allocations and uses of public funds. In short, this classification is the foundation of public budgeting.

As indicated, government budgets follow a standard classification and rank order of line items:

Economic or Object of Expenditure Classification

1. Salaries: These are usually the bulk of government expenditures; about 30 percent of the USG budget is allocated to civil service salaries.

2. Employee Benefits: This consists of social security, group insurance, and retirement benefits; a growing liability for all governments, for example, 17 percent of the Illinois 2012 operating or current services budget; salaries and benefits amount to 83.3 percent of Milwaukee city expenses.

3. Operating Expenses: These are the running costs or operational procurements. Expenditures below a certain cash threshold and useful life are considered current; above that threshold they are classed as capital expenditures. Montgomery County (MD), for example, uses $5,000 and one year (2011, pp. 1–3) as the cutoff point between operating expenses, such as printing, motor pool, travel, and office supplies from capital items, such as computer systems and buses, police cars, and firetrucks.

4. Maintenance: These are expenditures for minor maintenance of facilities such as roads, bridges, ports, airports, some of which may be partly financed by fees; the rest of O&M funds flow from general fund appropriations. In many state-local governments, substantial amounts of O&M expenses are contracted out to save budget funds, for example, municipal refuse services and certain public transit routes. A useful measure of financial condition for this item is: maintenance level/unit of asset.

5. Subsidies: These are often uncalculated amounts spent for special interest purposes, for instance, to attract local investments with roads, tax breaks, and parking facilities that surround such private projects as convention centers and stadiums. At the national level, fuel and electricity subsidies are critical but also typically uncalculated and unreported by finance offices. For local governments, calculating the value of expenditures for businesses or special interests and revenues forgone from abatements, tax exemptions, and other incentives is often difficult to do.

6. Transfers: These are grants to other units of government such as from county to city, city to school districts, or the federal to local levels, for example, water facility grants from the EPA.

7. Arrears: These are the total amounts plus interest costs of unpaid or late bills owed to suppliers for unpaid invoices, taxpayers for refunds, and in some cases state or local employees for salaries. Despite the fact that arrears can be used to finance deficits by reducing outlays artificially, they are rarely included in state or local budgets.

8. Debt Service: These are annual payments of principal and interest on bonded indebtedness for general obligation and other debt incurred by departments agencies by special or enterprise funds. Despite their GFOA award-winning budgets, it is difficult to determine total debt service/total operating expense ratios in either the Montgomery County or Milwaukee budgets because they are in round numbers rather than ratios or yearly trends. In exceptional cities, such as Ft. Collins (CO), debt service is cited (25.1 %) and compared with a baseline measure (> 15% = high). (Strachota, 1994, p. 83).

9. Capital and Rehabilitation: This consists of construction, replacement, and major maintenance of assets, such as sidewalks, roads, sewers, bridges, transit systems, airports, and seaports. Montgomery County uses a $5,000 and one-year useful life threshold, which is quite low. Milwaukee distinguishes types of infrastructure: $25k for new or replacement construction; $50k for durable equipment; and $25k for renovation (2008, p. 4).

For maximum transparency, the percentages of total expenditures should be presented in one or more pie charts accompanying a simple three-year percentage table. Milwaukee includes a pie chart for some of the major object categories for general purpose spending (see Figure 1.9 on page 24).

The Gaston County (N.C.) pie chart indicates that personnel costs (wages and benefits) are 46.7 percent of general fund budget. Note that capital expenditures are only 0.16 percent of total expenditures from the general fund. But other capital expenditures occur from particular funds that are not financed by operating revenue (noted in the same chart). Also noted below is the City of Milwaukee operating and capital budget (see Figure 1.10 on pages 25–26). The capital budget is often termed "below the line" to distinguish its long-term purpose and to separate out its sources of financing. The Milwaukee budget in Figure 1.10 indicates all categories in round figures, which tend to cloud thinking with strings of zeros and numbers. Percentages and ratios should be included for basic measurement—for instance, the capital budget is 21.9 percent of total appropriations—which is quite high compared to most medium to large-sized cities. While readers can do it themselves with pocket calculators, including annual percentage changes in planned versus actual expenditures does add to fiscal transparency.

24

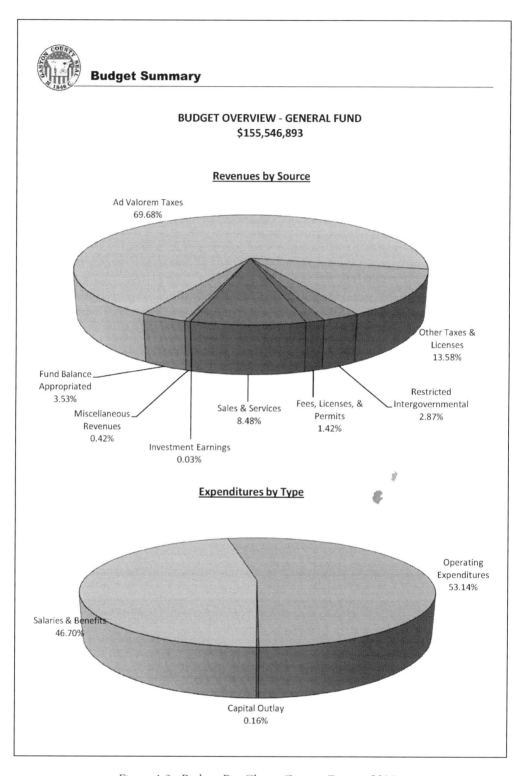

Figure 1.9. Budget Pie Chart: Gaston County 2014.

COMPARISONS BY BUDGET SECTION
BETWEEN 2003 ADOPTED AND 2002 ADOPTED BUDGETS,
REVENUES, TAX LEVIES, AND RESULTING CHANGES

	2002 ADOPTED BUDGET	2003 ADOPTED BUDGET	CHANGE 2003 ADOPTED VERSUS 2002 ADOPTED
A. GENERAL CITY PURPOSES			
Appropriations			
Salaries and Wages	$308,409,869	$309,455,851	$1,045,982
Fringe Benefits	93,830,102	97,517,405	3,687,303
Operating Expenditures	60,536,637	59,720,346	-816,291
Equipment Purchases	6,286,320	6,498,337	212,017
Special Funds	107,314,758	112,754,467	5,439,709
Fringe Benefit Offset	-93,830,102	-97,517,405	-3,687,303
TOTAL APPROPRIATIONS	$482,547,584	$488,429,001	$5,881,417
Funding Sources			
General City Revenues	$397,183,152	$394,394,620	$-2,788,532
Tax Stabilization Fund Withdrawal	11,000,000	9,300,000	-1,700,000
Potential Anticipated Revenues	0	0	0
Property Tax Levy	74,364,432	84,734,381	10,369,949
TOTAL REVENUES	$482,547,584	$488,429,001	$5,881,417
B. EMPLOYEE RETIREMENT			
TOTAL APPROPRIATIONS	$63,770,867	$66,634,994	$2,864,127
Funding Sources			
Non-Property Tax Revenue	$25,680,658	$25,697,662	$17,004
Property Tax Levy	38,090,209	40,937,332	2,847,123
TOTAL REVENUES	$63,770,867	$66,634,994	$2,864,127
C. CAPITAL IMPROVEMENTS			
TOTAL CAPITAL IMPROVEMENTS PROGRAM			
Appropriations	$102,842,313	$107,128,383	$4,286,070
Funding Sources			
1. BORROWING (General Obligation)			
a. New	$63,790,401	$64,985,180	$1,194,779
b. Carryover	(58,740,643)	(60,768,188)	(2,027,545)
2. BORROWING (Tax Incremental Districts)			
a. New	$14,500,000	$14,000,000	$-500,000
b. Carryover	(14,734,180)	(15,629,180)	(895,000)
3. SPECIAL ASSESSMENTS (Internal Borrowing)			
a. New	$4,936,093	$7,955,400	$3,019,307
b. Carryover	(16,599,821)	(17,320,926)	(721,105)
4. CASH FINANCED			
a. FROM REVENUES			
1. New	$9,600,000	$9,600,000	$0
2. Carryover	(0)	(0)	(0)
b. FROM TAX LEVY	10,015,819	10,587,803	571,984
c. TOTAL CASH FINANCED	$19,615,819	$20,187,803	$571,984
TOTAL REVENUES (Capital Improvements)	$102,842,313	$107,128,383	$4,286,070

Figure 1.10. Budget Comparisons and Yearly Changes: Milwaukee 2002–03.

	2002 ADOPTED BUDGET	2003 ADOPTED BUDGET	CHANGE 2003 ADOPTED VERSUS 2002 ADOPTED
D. CITY DEBT			
TOTAL APPROPRIATIONS	$113,987,651	$118,803,887	$4,816,236
(Includes borrowing for Milwaukee Public Schools)			
Funding Sources			
Revenues	$28,814,582	$35,411,106	$6,596,524
TID Increments	12,885,445	15,653,716	2,768,271
Delinquent Tax Revenue	13,371,861	12,976,832	-395,029
Property Tax Levy	58,915,763	54,762,233	-4,153,530
TOTAL REVENUES	$113,987,651	$118,803,887	$4,816,236
E. DELINQUENT TAX			
TOTAL APPROPRIATIONS	$1,000,000	$1,000,000	$0
Funding Sources			
TOTAL REVENUE (Property Tax Levy)	$1,000,000	$1,000,000	$0
F. COMMON COUNCIL CONTINGENT FUND			
TOTAL APPROPRIATIONS	$5,420,458	$5,000,000	$-420,458
Funding Sources			
TOTAL REVENUE (Property Tax Levy)	$5,420,458	$5,000,000	$-420,458
SUBTOTALS (ITEMS A THROUGH F)			
CITY BUDGET APPROPRIATIONS	$769,568,873	$786,996,265	$17,427,392
(Excluding Special Revenue Accounts)			
Less: Non-Property Tax Revenues	581,762,192	589,974,516	8,212,324
PROPERTY TAX LEVIES	$187,806,681	$197,021,749	$9,215,068
SPECIAL REVENUE ACCOUNTS (ITEMS G THROUGH M)			
G. PARKING			
TOTAL APPROPRIATIONS	$40,206,098	$42,387,797	$2,181,699
Funding Sources			
Current Revenues	$15,095,035	$16,434,597	$1,339,562
Capital Improvements from Reserves	5,000,000	5,000,000	0
Withdrawal from Reserves	0	0	0
Parking Enforcement Offset	0	0	0
Citation Revenue and Processing	19,289,063	19,292,200	3,137
New Borrowing	822,000	1,661,000	839,000
Other Funding (Carryover Borrowing)	(0)	(200,000)	(200,000)
Property Tax Levy	0	0	0
TOTAL REVENUES	$40,206,098	$42,387,797	$2,181,699
H. GRANT AND AID			
TOTAL APPROPRIATIONS	$81,534,000	$83,572,350	$2,038,350
Funding Sources			
Grantor Share	$81,534,000	$83,572,350	$2,038,350
Out of Pocket Current Year	0	0	0
In Kind-City	0	0	0
Property Tax Levy	0	0	0
TOTAL REVENUES	$81,534,000	$83,572,350	$2,038,350

Figure 1.10. Continued.

Budget Coverage

To ensure transparency and comprehensiveness (where all expenditures and revenues are visible in the annual budget), the object of expenditure budget by appropriation is normally disaggregated into departments and special funds. An example from the Montgomery County Board of Elections is provided in Figure 1.11 on pages 28–29, which includes changes and adjustments from the original appropriation. Notice that funding for election operations, work years, and personnel expenditures is dropping significantly. This suggests diminished interest in election administration at a time when the issue is becoming more important in other cities and states. Analysts might examine the basis of the new budget composition.

Government budgets are divided into many separate funds, which often confuses outside reviewers. A problem with early–twentieth-century government budgeting is that jurisdictions could hide expenditures (and revenue losses and liabilities) in off-budget funds. This violated the basic norm that budgets be comprehensive, that is, contain *all* revenues and expenditures. Effectively, the availability of extrabudgetary funds narrowed coverage, since the totals available to the public and most reviewers excluded substantial amounts of revenues and expenditures. This kind of coverage gimmick has been used to make government financial conditions look better. Generally Accepted Accounting Practice (GAAP) standards now ensure (if applied) that government budgets are comprehensive and that expenditures through all funds are transparent. *Funds* are self-balancing sets of accounts segregated to carry out specific activities (Coe, 1989, p. 14). All government funds are (1) *governmental* or *general*, (2) *proprietary*, or (3) *fiduciary* in nature (1989:14). Governmental funds consist of the bulk of governmental operational expenditures. The governmental funds category also includes special funds targeted or restricted for uses such as: debt service, capital projects, bond proceeds, and special assessments for such items as sidewalks. Proprietary funds consist of enterprise-type operations. They include fees or user charges for operations such as: transit, utilities, and golf courses. They also contain internal service funds for internal government-wide services such as the motor pool and printing. Fiduciary funds are banking-type operations where the government holds funds in trust for particular beneficiaries, for example, refunds, social security or pensions, and highway users (Coe, 1989, p. 15).

	Expenditures	WYs
Decrease Cost: Operating Expenses Directly Related to Election Day and Canvasses	-3,010	0.0
Reduce: Local Conference Related Education, Tuition, and Training	-6,000	0.0
Reduce: Other Education, Tuition, and Training	-14,380	0.0
Reduce: Sample Ballot Printing	-30,210	0.0
Reduce: Sample Ballot Postage (Other - Mail)	-30,400	0.0
Decrease Cost: Annualization of FY11 Operating Expenses	-33,670	0.0
Decrease Cost: Election Cycle Changes - Legal Services and Advertising	-47,000	0.0
Decrease Cost: Sample Ballot Printing Contract	-52,500	0.0
Decrease Cost: Sample Ballot Postage	-80,000	0.0
Miscellaneous adjustments, including restoration of employee furloughs, employee benefit changes, changes due to staff turnover, reorganizations, and other budget changes affecting more than one program	-84,120	0.0
FY12 CE Recommended	**991,270**	**7.0**

BUDGET SUMMARY

	Actual FY10	Budget FY11	Estimated FY11	Recommended FY12	% Chg Bud/Rec
COUNTY GENERAL FUND					
EXPENDITURES					
Salaries and Wages	1,858,751	3,067,140	3,330,810	2,077,620	-32.3%
Employee Benefits	502,839	632,500	788,220	482,570	-23.7%
County General Fund Personnel Costs	*2,361,590*	*3,699,640*	*4,119,030*	*2,560,190*	*-30.8%*
Operating Expenses	1,015,080	4,272,040	3,772,950	2,330,970	-45.4%
Capital Outlay	0	0	0	0	—
County General Fund Expenditures	*3,376,670*	*7,971,680*	*7,891,980*	*4,891,160*	*-38.6%*
PERSONNEL					
Full-Time	28	28	28	28	—
Part-Time	0	0	0	0	—
Workyears	46.2	43.9	43.9	40.3	-8.2%
REVENUES					
Publication Sales - Board of Elections	6,587	2,500	2,500	2,500	—
County General Fund Revenues	*6,587*	*2,500*	*2,500*	*2,500*	—

FY12 RECOMMENDED CHANGES

	Expenditures	WYs
COUNTY GENERAL FUND		
FY11 ORIGINAL APPROPRIATION	**7,971,680**	**43.9**
Changes (with service impacts)		
Reduce: Canvass Expenses [Administration]	-800	0.0
Reduce: Local Conference Related Education, Tuition, and Training [Administration]	-6,000	0.0
Reduce: Other Education, Tuition, and Training [Administration]	-14,380	0.0
Reduce: Sample Ballot Printing [Administration]	-30,210	0.0
Reduce: Sample Ballot Postage (Other - Mail) [Administration]	-30,400	0.0
Reduce: Electronic Pollbook Computer Equipment Repairs/Maintenance [Election Operations]	-63,340	0.0
Reduce: Part-Time Temporary Election Aides [Election Operations]	-72,070	0.0
Reduce: Election Overtime [Election Operations]	-182,490	0.0
Reduce: Temporary Office Clerical [Voter Registration Services]	-296,250	0.0
Other Adjustments (with no service impacts)		
Increase Cost: Annualization of FY11 Personnel Costs	33,670	0.0
Increase Cost: Restore Personnel Costs - Furloughs	33,670	1.8
Increase Cost: Printing and Mail Adjustment	14,550	0.0
Increase Cost: Motor Pool Rate Adjustment	1,690	0.0
Increase Cost: Help Desk - Desk Side Support	800	0.0
Decrease Cost: Outside Mail Services to the State Board of Elections - Ballot Mailing Expenses [Voter Registration Services]	-500	0.0
Decrease Cost: Operating Expenses Directly Related to Election Day and Canvasses [Administration]	-3,010	0.0
Decrease Cost: Short Term Furniture Rentals - Provides Tables and Chairs for Privately Owned Polling Places [Election Operations]	-5,000	0.0

Figure 1.11. Board of Elections: Budgeted versus Approved FY 10–12 Budget: Montgomery County (MD).

	Expenditures	WYs
Decrease Cost: Verizon Point to Point T1 Replacement	-5,450	0.0
Decrease Cost: Metropolitan Area Travel for Voter Outreach [Election Operations]	-9,880	0.0
Decrease Cost: Polling Place Supplies [Election Operations]	-22,670	0.0
Decrease Cost: Retirement Adjustment	-28,870	0.0
Decrease Cost: Building or Space Rental or Leases (Polling Place Rental) [Election Operations]	-33,000	0.0
Decrease Cost: Annualization of FY11 Operating Expenses [Administration]	-33,670	0.0
Decrease Cost: Group Insurance Adjustment	-35,360	0.0
Decrease Cost: Maintenance Cost - Statewide Election Management System (MDVoters) [Voter Registration Services]	-39,080	0.0
Decrease Cost: Election Cycle Changes - Legal Services and Advertising [Administration]	-47,000	0.0
Decrease Cost: Sample Ballot Printing Contract [Administration]	-52,500	0.0
Decrease Cost: Printing [Election Operations]	-74,200	0.0
Decrease Cost: Sample Ballot Postage [Administration]	-80,000	0.0
Decrease Cost: Early Voting Operations [Election Operations]	-122,220	0.0
Decrease Cost: Payments for the Touchscreen Voting Machines [Election Operations]	-262,710	0.0
Decrease Cost: Election Cycle Overtime [Election Operations]	-340,760	0.0
Decrease Cost: Election Judge Stipends Due to One FY12 County-wide Election [Election Operations]	-606,480	0.0
Decrease Cost: Temporary Clerical Services [Voter Registration Services]	-666,600	-5.4
FY12 RECOMMENDED:	**4,891,160**	**40.3**

PROGRAM SUMMARY

Program Name	FY11 Approved Expenditures	WYs	FY12 Recommended Expenditures	WYs
Voter Registration Services	1,786,880	17.5	1,156,140	14.5
Election Operations	4,811,440	19.4	2,743,750	18.8
Administration	1,373,360	7.0	991,270	7.0
Total	**7,971,680**	**43.9**	**4,891,160**	**40.3**

FUTURE FISCAL IMPACTS

Title	CE REC. FY12	FY13	FY14	(5000's) FY15	FY16	FY17
This table is intended to present significant future fiscal impacts of the department's programs.						
COUNTY GENERAL FUND						
Expenditures						
FY12 Recommended	4,891	4,891	4,891	4,891	4,891	4,891
No inflation or compensation change is included in outyear projections.						
Motor Pool Rate Adjustment	0	3	3	3	3	3
Subtotal Expenditures	4,891	4,894	4,894	4,894	4,894	4,894

Figure 1.11. Continued.

Combining Multiple Formats

The object of expenditure classification is used to display planned, approved, or actual expenditures for each type of fund. For example, in Figure 1.12 on page 30, Gaston County provides revenues and expenses for its solid waste proprietary fund for the two-year period 2012–14 for maximum transparency.

Similarly, in contrast with some state and local budget presentations, Gaston County spells out its annual debt service expenditures by providing it as one of its fourteen financial condition indicators. Figure 1.12 indicates the balance in its one proprietary fund for solid waste.

Budget Summary

	Actual FY 2012	Adopted FY 2013	Recommended FY 2014	Adopted FY 2014	$ Increase (Decrease)
Estimated Requirements					
Bond Proceeds-Local	-	-	-	-	-
Operating Expenses*	-	-	2,427,219	-	-
Capital Outlay	40,153,930	2,644,619	-	2,427,219	(217,400)
Operating Transfers Out	98,680	-	-	-	-
	$40,252,610	$2,644,619	$2,427,219	$2,427,219	($217,400)
SOLID WASTE FUND					
Means of Financing					
Other Taxes & Licenses	317,454	290,000	295,000	295,000	5,000
Restricted Intergovernmental	15,910	15,000	15,000	15,000	-
Fees, Licenses, & Permits	6,122,321	5,289,356	4,566,068	4,559,626	(729,730)
Sales & Services	1,705,659	1,916,558	1,866,000	1,872,442	(44,116)
Investment Earnings	4,240	-	-	-	-
Miscellaneous Revenues	552,953	618,000	18,500	18,500	(599,500)
Installment Purchases	(0)	-	-	-	-
Operating Transfers In	-	-	-	-	-
Fund Balance Appropriated	1,958,997	-	-	-	-
	$10,677,534	$8,128,914	$6,760,568	$6,760,568	($1,368,346)
Estimated Requirements					
Salaries & Benefits	1,550,059	1,541,640	1,582,400	1,582,400	40,760
Operating Expenses	4,782,205	4,857,274	4,888,474	4,888,474	31,200
Principal Retirement	-	-	-	-	-
Interest & Fees	-	-	-	-	-
Capital Outlay	174,228	1,730,000	289,694	289,694	(1,440,306)
Operating Transfers Out	-	-	-	-	-
	$6,506,492	$8,128,914	$6,760,568	$6,760,568	($1,368,346)
TOTAL ALL FUNDS					
Means of Financing	$382,060,241	$271,527,119	$280,490,182	$270,433,622	($1,093,497)
Estimated Requirements	$307,168,082	$271,527,119	$280,490,182	$270,433,622	($1,093,497)
TOTAL ALL FUNDS - NET OF TRANSFERS					
Means of Financing	$345,958,181	$237,665,052	$240,316,182	$234,404,566	($3,260,486)
Estimated Requirements	$269,224,990	$237,665,052	$240,316,182	$234,404,566	($3,260,486)

* Amounts listed as operating expenses in Debt Service Funds comprise building installment-purchases principal and interest, which are classified as operating expenses in the accounting system.

Figure 1.12. Gaston County Proprietary Fund Balance: Solid Waste 2012–14.

Gaston County provides multiyear debt service/net operating revenue data as a transparent measure of risk and burden, for example, 11.6 percent in 2012. The county also provides an annually updated summary of all financial condition indicators. Note that its fiscal policy on debt (#6) (2014, p. 55) requires that ratio of debt service/total expenditures not exceed 15 percent. This is a different indicator than that highlighted for financial condition in Figure 1.13 on pages 32–34. That figure is not clear from the functional breakdown of expenditures (2014:19), which includes only "non-education debt." Adding both education and non-education debt ($24.1m) and dividing by total adopted 2014 expenditures ($234.4m) gives a ratio of 10.3 percent (well under the 15 percent policy limit. It might have been simpler to provide this indicator in the budget so that readers would not have to calculate this or ponder the distinctions between different types of debt and debt service: there should be a consolidated figure.

In addition to the standard input or resource-oriented budget format, to maximize transparency and to provide information of use to service managers, governments develop budgets by *performance* and *program* formats. Medium and larger-sized jurisdictions (such as Milwaukee) typically spend more time doing this; smaller jurisdictions (such as Gaston County) often limit themselves to departmental activity statistics. These formats and systems rely on much of the same fiscal information used in the object format but attempt to provide a picture of what is being achieved for expenditures. To gauge efficiency, the performance budget provides unit costs or unit expenditures. This provides a solid basis for questions on service efficiency in comparison with similar jurisdictions. For example, the State Social Assistance Department (SSAD) and Salt Lake City Snow Removal performance budgets in Figure 3.2 on page 90 provide measures of: demand, workload, efficiency/productivity, and effectiveness that can be monitored easily.

Similarly, the budget for Montgomery County transit (Ride-On) presents physical and performance data. But it displays (Figure 1.14 on page 35) only physical data (e.g., riders, complaints, collisions) and no unit cost data. As part of the federal capital assistance program, the USDOT (FTA) has long required urban transit systems to provide activity statistics on such unit costs as operating cost/passenger mile.

Performance budgets may present confusing information. Some governments spread or disaggregate the expenditures for one activity or function across different departments. To get a comprehensive picture, analysts using only one format would have to add them up across categories and departments. For example, as indicated in Figure 1.15, the Montgomery County transit budget includes

32

Debt Service

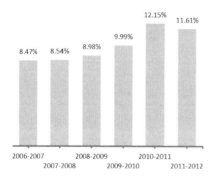

	12.15% 11.61%
	9.99%
8.47% 8.54% 8.98%	

2006-2007   2008-2009   2010-2011
　　　2007-2008   2009-2010   2011-2012

Description:

Net direct debt service as a percentage of net operating revenues

Calculation:

$$\frac{\text{Debt service}}{\text{Net operating revenues}}$$

Warning Trend:

Increasing net direct debt service as a percentage of net operating revenues

This indicator provides another perspective on Gaston County's debt. Rather than measuring the county's capacity to generate revenues to pay off its debt, this indicator shows the budget impact of debt payments.

This indicator divides annual debt service payments for the years indicated into revenues to determine debt service as a percentage of operating revenues. An increase in this indicator over time could indicate excessive debt. Excessive debt payments reduce a government's spending flexibility, causing fiscal strain.

The biggest increase in debt service payments over the indicated period has been principal and interest payments for school bonds. School debt service in FY 2007 was $9.1 million and increased to $24.4 million in FY 2012. For the adopted FY 2013 budget, $16.8 million was appropriated for school debt service; for the adopted FY 2014 budget, $16.2 million was appropriated for school debt service.

By contrast, the average amount of annual debt service payments for non-school debt from the actual FY 2007 budget to the adopted FY 2014 budget is $8 million.

Figure 1.13. Debt Service Indicator and Debt Policies: Gaston County 2006–12.

 **Financial Policies**

Capital Improvement Budget Policies

1. It is the responsibility of the Board of Commissioners to provide for the capital facilities necessary to deliver municipal services to the citizens of the county.
2. The county will consider all capital improvements in accordance with an adopted capital improvement program.
3. The county will develop a five-year capital improvement program (CIP) and review and update the plan annually. The Gaston County Schools and the Gaston College will submit their respective capital improvement requests annually and will provide a prioritization for the improvements within their request for the County Commissioner's review. Additional projects can be added to the CIP at any time, but funding for projects added in this manner are subject to normal operating budget constraints.
4. The county will enact an annual capital budget based on the five-year capital improvement plan.
5. The county, in consultation with the Gaston County Schools and Gaston College, will coordinate development of the capital improvement budget with development of the operating budget. Future operating costs associated with new capital improvements will be projected and included in operating budget forecasts.
6. The CIP will include the estimated costs for the county to maintain all county, Gaston County Schools, and Gaston College assets at a level adequate to protect the county's capital investment and to minimize future maintenance and replacement costs.
7. The CIP will include a projection of the equipment replacement and maintenance needs of the county, Gaston County Schools, and Gaston College for the next several years and will update this projection each year. From this projection a maintenance and replacement schedule will be developed and followed.
8. The county, in consultation with Gaston County Schools and Gaston College, will identify the estimated costs and potential funding sources for each capital project proposal before it is submitted for approval.
9. The county will attempt to determine the least costly and most flexible financing method for all new projects.

Debt Policies

1. The county will confine long-term borrowing to capital improvement projects.
2. The county will take a balanced approach to capital funding using debt financing, capital reserves, and pay-as-you go funding.
3. When the county finances capital improvements or other projects by issuing bonds or entering into capital leases, it will repay the debt within a period not to exceed the expected useful life of the project.
4. Target debt ratios will be annually calculated and included in the review of financial trends.
5. Net debt as a percentage of estimated market value of taxable property shall not exceed 2.5%. Net debt is defined as all debt that is tax-supported.

Figure 1.13. Continued.

Financial Policies

6. The ratio of debt service expenditures as a percent of total governmental fund expenditures shall not exceed 15.0%.
7. The county will retire tax anticipation debt, if any, annually and will retire bond anticipation debt within six months after completion of the project.
8. Payout of aggregate outstanding tax-supported debt principal shall be no less than 55% repaid in 10 years.

Reserve Policies

1. General
   The term *fund balance* describes the net assets of the county's governmental funds calculated in accordance with generally accepted accounting principles (GAAP). It is intended to serve as a measure of the financial resources available in a governmental fund. The county's policy on fund balance recognizes the importance of this measure in determining credit worthiness to bond rating agencies, investors and other interested in the economic condition of the county. This policy establishes a minimum acceptable level of available fund balance and describes the factors which were considered in order to establish it. This policy also establishes the action to be taken if fund balance falls below the minimum acceptable level.

2. Standards
   A. Governmental Finance Officers Association (GFOA)
   B. North Carolina General Statutes

3. Planning and Performances
   A. In order to establish an appropriate level of available fund balance in the General Fund, the following factors were considered:
      - Predictability of revenues and volatility of expenditures – The county's general revenues sources are somewhat stable and predictable, however because of the annual tax billing, cash flows are much greater in the late fall and winter than in the spring and summer. The level of the county's available general fund balance must be sufficient at June 30th of each year to cover this fluctuation in revenue collections. General Fund expenditures are generally stable and spread evenly over the course of the year. The county experiences unanticipated expenditures due to events such as equipment breakdowns, funding requests from other agencies, and natural disasters.
      - Liquidity – The county experiences liquidity issues due to the annual tax billing cycle. Other factors affecting liquidity are the financing of initial capital project expenses with general fund balance. These expenditures are reimbursed once the financing proceeds are available. The county frequently has grant-funded capital projects underway, which are funded on a reimbursement basis. Available fund balance should be sufficient to cover this liquidity issue.
      - Designations – Some portions of the available general fund balance may be designated for a specific purpose and may require higher levels as appropriate.
      - GFOA's recommendation – GFOA recommends that all general purpose governments maintain at a minimum unreserved (available) general fund balance of five (5) to

Figure 1.13. Continued.

PROGRAM DESCRIPTIONS

Medicaid and Senior Programs

Special Transportation Programs provide: transportation to and from Medicaid appointments for those eligible; a user-side subsidy program that provides travel options for low-income elderly and disabled; and information on all public transportation programs available to seniors and persons with disabilities.

FY12 Recommended Changes	Expenditures	WYs
FY11 Approved	7,571,330	7.9
Increase Cost: Increase in grant funded Medicaid transportation services	314,760	0.0
Increase Cost: Additional Call N Ride Book	136,490	0.0
Miscellaneous adjustments, including restoration of employee furloughs, employee benefit changes, changes due to staff turnover, reorganizations, and other budget changes affecting more than one program	63,610	0.0
FY12 CE Recommended	8,086,190	7.9

Ride On

Fixed-route bus service is provided by the Ride On system throughout the County. Ride On operates primarily in neighborhoods and provides a collector and distributor service to the major transfer points and transit centers in the County. Ride On supplements and coordinates with Metrobus and Metrorail service provided by the Washington Metropolitan Area Transit Authority. The Ride On transit program operates and manages more than 80 routes; maintains a strategic plan for replacement of the bus fleet; trains new bus operators and provides continuing safety instruction for existing operators; coordinates activities with the Advanced Transportation Management Center; and operates Ride On's centralized radio system.

Program Performance Measures	Actual FY09	Actual FY10	Estimated FY11	Target FY12	Target FY13
Passengers transported per capita (ratio of the number of passengers boarding a Ride On bus within the fiscal year and the County population)[1]	31.2	29.97	28.64	28.64	28.64
Percent of Ride-On customers who report a satisfactory customer service experience[2]					
Passengers per hour of service[3]	27.0	25.2	24.8	24.8	24.8
Hours of Service[4]	1,096,930	1,061,550	1,028,490	1,028,490	1,028,490
Scheduled Ride On roundtrip circuits missed, in whole or in part, per 1,000 roundtrip circuits[5]	5.02	7.8	7.02	5.9	5.9
Reported Ride-On complaints per 100,000 bus riders[6]	13.6	15.4	26.6	25	25
Passengers Transported (millions)[7]	29.6	27.9	26.2	26.2	26.2
Number of reported collisions between Ride On buses and a person or object, per 100,000 miles driven	3.95	4.06	4.0	4.0	4.0

[1] Population data changed for FY11 to 971,600 from 931,000
[2] New measure; data to be collected in the future.
[3] FY10 experienced a drop in ridership; service cuts were implemented in FY11
[4] FY11 Reduction in service, assumed straight line service level for FY12 and 13
[5] FY11 based on 2nd quarter assumptions, will be updated with additional information in FY11
[6] FY11 utilizes MC311 call data which captures a larger intake of calls and complaints
[7] Service reductions and fare increases in FY11 are assumed for the decrease in ridership

FY12 Recommended Changes	Expenditures	WYs
FY11 Approved	88,122,880	733.5
Increase Cost: Motor Pool Rate Adjustment	995,250	0.0
Increase Cost: Maintenance of Trapeze system licenses and system support ($65,000), Bus Radio maintenance contract ($89,890)	154,890	0.0
Technical Adj: Reduction of Program Transportation (HHS funded)	0	-1.0
Decrease Cost: Leased Tire Contract	-100,000	0.0
Decrease Cost: Use of Retreads on rear tires	-100,000	0.0
Decrease Cost: Redundant fleet inspections	-942,240	0.0
Decrease Cost: Master Lease payments	-1,225,220	0.0
Miscellaneous adjustments, including restoration of employee furloughs, employee benefit changes, changes due to staff turnover, reorganizations, and other budget changes affecting more than one program	-949,200	26.1
FY12 CE Recommended	85,956,360	758.6

Commuter Services

The Commuter Services program centralizes commuter services efforts and promotes transportation alternatives to the single occupant vehicle in Silver Spring, Bethesda, Wheaton, North Bethesda, Friendship Heights, and other areas of the County. The program provides efficient and coordinated administrative support for services to employers and employees or residents. It uses

Figure 1.14. Program Performance Measures: Public Transit.

all program operating and capital expenditures for direct and support costs, for example, administration, parking, Ride-On bus service, taxi regulation, and commuter services. But to calculate the combined operations and maintenance (O&M) costs of only the Ride-On bus mode, (which is a major service and an important issue for local residents) analysts or untutored citizens would have to consult the separate program activity under the motor pool internal service fund.

As indicated in Figure 1.15 in a budget for Fleet Management Services, the trouble with separating transit program operations and maintenance expenditures is that the amount within the fleet management/motor pool budget allocated to transit maintenance is unclear from its Program Summary. It could be 29 percent, but that would have to include a portion of the administrative expenses, 47.5 percent, which would raise the amount budgeted to transit services substantially.

One remedy for the problem of fragmenting objects of expenditure spread around different budgets is to use a *functional* budget classification. Functions are groups of activities aimed at accomplishing a major service or regulatory program (GFOA, 1994, p. 164). The nine functions and many sub-functions of the U.S. budget relate budget authority, outlays, and loan guarantees and tax expenditures to national needs. Congressional budget resolutions actually target these needs (Mikesell, 2011, p. 284) and via *cross-walking* (interformat reconciliation), every cent of functional expenditures can be translated into objects, programs, or organizations. Functions are independent of the government organizational structure (Schiavo-Campo, 1999, p. 70). Fourteen major ones are recognized as the U.N. Functional Classification of the Functions of Government (COFOG). There are also 61 groups and 127 subgroups (ibid.). For example, Social Service function includes the subgroup of Education and the subgroups of Primary, Secondary, and Tertiary Education. The format facilitates transparency and comprehensiveness through cross-walking expenditures by objects across organizational units into combined functions. The Gaston County budget presentation by functions is illustrated in Figure 1.16 on page 38.

For example, Gaston County will spend 28.3 percent of its total budgeted funds in 2014 for the education "function." The City of Milwaukee calls its "functions" "strategic objectives" and allocates accordingly. Note the similarity between functions and programs. *Programs* are also groups of related activities performed by one or more organization (like functions). But an important purpose of a program is to carry out the function (GFOA, 1994, p. 166). This gives the concept of a program budget an active meaning—the budget should allocate resources to a range of programs and not simply objects of expenditure. As noted above, since elected legislatures work from district constituent needs, it is more feasible for

PROGRAM CONTACTS

Contact Tammy Mulford of the Division of Fleet Management Services at 240.777.5733 or Bruce R. Meier of the Office of Management and Budget at 240.777.2785 for more information regarding this department's operating budget.

PROGRAM DESCRIPTIONS

Heavy Equipment and Automotive Services

This program is responsible for the maintenance and repair of the heavy equipment fleet which includes heavy dump trucks, construction equipment, snow plows, leafers, mowers, backhoes, gradalls, and other specialized pieces of heavy equipment. In addition, this program is responsible for the maintenance and repair of the automotive fleet which includes administrative vehicles, police vehicles, vans, and light trucks. The maintenance and repair service for the automotive and light truck fleet is provided through contractual service at the Seven Locks Maintenance facility.

Program Performance Measures	Actual FY09	Actual FY10	Estimated FY11	Target FY12	Target FY13
Heavy Equipment Fleet Availability	95.0	94.7	94.7	94.7	94.7
Percentage of Customer Satisfaction for Police Vehicle Maintenance	99.0	98.2	99.0	99.0	99.0
Percentage of Fleet Availability for Police Vehicle Maintenance	98.0	97.3	98.0	98.0	98.0
Mean Distance Between Failure: Heavy Equipment (in miles)[1]	1,559	5,100	5,610	5,610	5,610
Mean Distance Between Failure: Administrative Light Equipment (in miles)[2]	2,906	8,926	9,246	9,246	9,246
Mean Distance Between Failure: Public Safety Light Equipment (in miles)[3]	2,848	11,833	12,970	12,970	12,970
Turnaround Time - Average amount of time equipment is unavailable for operations during each shop visit: Heavy Equipment (in days)[4]	10.2	8.0	8.6	8.6	8.6
Turnaround Time - Average amount of time equipment is unavailable for operations during each shop visit: Administrative Vehicles (in days)	1.1	2.8	2.0	2.0	2.0
Turnaround Time - Average amount of time equipment is unavailable for operations during each shop visit: Public Safety light equipment (in days)	3.0	3.3	2.2	2.2	2.2

[1] Data regarding mean miles between service interruptions will be collected for all classes of vehicles. Fleet has refined measure to exclude small or incidental parts failures beginning November 2009.
[2] Fleet has refined measure to exclude small or incidental parts failures beginning November 2009.
[3] Fleet has refined measure to exclude small or incidental parts failures beginning November 2009.
[4] Turnaround data for all classes of vehicles will be collected.

FY12 Recommended Changes	Expenditures	WYs
FY11 Approved	8,787,810	38.5
Miscellaneous adjustments, including restoration of employee furloughs, employee benefit changes, changes due to staff turnover, reorganizations, and other budget changes affecting more than one program	198,920	0.0
FY12 CE Recommended	8,986,730	38.5

Transit Equipment Services

This program is responsible for the maintenance and repair of the transit equipment fleet which includes Ride On transit buses.

Program Performance Measures	Actual FY09	Actual FY10	Estimated FY11	Target FY12	Target FY13
Average Days Out of Service per Bus for Parts	4.0	3.9	3.9	3.9	3.9
Mean Distance Between Failure: Transit equipment (in miles)[1]	2,847	18,195	18,195	18,195	18,195
Turnaround Time - Average amount of time equipment is unavailable for operations during each shop visit: Transit equipment (in days)	6.5	5.0	4.8	4.8	4.8

[1] Fleet has refined measure to exclude small or incidental parts failures beginning November 2009.

FY12 Recommended Changes	Expenditures	WYs
FY11 Approved	19,389,210	112.4
Increase Cost: Transit Bus Service Lane Contract	219,680	0.0
Increase Cost: Transit Bus Enhanced Cleaning Contract	61,660	0.0
Decrease Cost: Leased Tire Contract	-100,000	0.0
Decrease Cost: Use retreads on rear bus tires	-100,000	0.0
Decrease Cost: Redundant transit fleet inspections	-942,240	0.0
Miscellaneous adjustments, including restoration of employee furloughs, employee benefit changes, changes due to staff turnover, reorganizations, and other budget changes affecting more than one program	-45,120	7.3
FY12 CE Recommended	18,483,190	119.7

Figure 1.15. Public Transit Operations and Maintenance Expenditures.

38

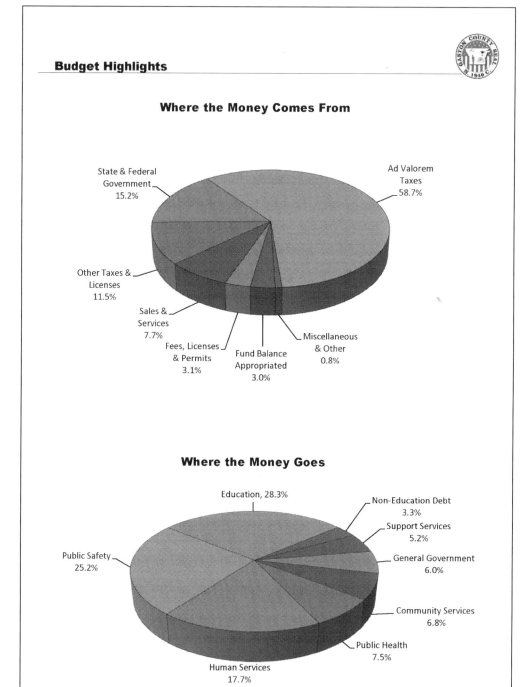

Figure 1.16. Functional Budget Format: Gaston County 2014.

them to use objects for allocation rather than programs. In fact, programs can hide as much as they reveal and need to be broken down into objects via cross-walks to provide political meaning and facilitate fiscal reporting. As indicated in Figure 1.17, the Salt Lake City Fire Department 2012–13 budget cross-walks to the operating and program budgets for the current and past fiscal years. Salt Lake City's relatively smaller population (186,000) masks the fact that like many cities in the United States and Canada, the metropolitan area (1,175,000) is much larger.

FY 2012-13 MAYOR'S RECOMMENDED BUDGET

FIRE DEPARTMENT

Fire Department
Kurt Cook, Fire Chief

	FY 2010-11 Actual	FY 2011-12 Adopted Budget	FY 2012-13 Recommended Budget	Explanation of Changes
Full Time Equivalent Positions	358.0	356.5	324.5	21 Positions transferred to 911 Dispatch Bureau, 11 Positions transferred to SAFER Grant
OPERATING BUDGET				
Personal Services	30,116,481	31,304,853	30,857,927	
Operations and Maintenance Supply	939,963	1,063,169	1,293,659	Funding to Equip new Fire Apparatus
Charges for Services	2,339,538	2,327,064	1,381,737	
Capital Outlay	72,793	125,000	125,000	
Total Fire Department	**33,468,775**	**34,820,086**	**33,658,323**	
PROGRAM BUDGET				
Office of the Chief	1,553,165	1,498,131	1,708,415	
Support Services Division	1,667,783	2,031,849	1,398,321	
Communications Division	2,059,788	2,363,860	834,253	
Training Division	1,004,348	888,560	927,499	
Operations	24,947,608	25,862,502	26,419,771	
EMS Division	858,977	839,476	886,993	
Fire Prevention	1,377,106	1,335,708	1,483,071	
Total Fire Department	**33,468,775**	**34,820,086**	**33,658,323**	
FUND SOURCE				
General Fund	33,468,775	34,820,086	33,658,323	
Total Fire Department	**33,468,775**	**34,820,086**	**33,658,323**	

Figure 1.17. Program Cross-Walked to Objects of Expenditure.

Despite the political constraint of district representation and the appeal of logrolling, some jurisdictions have used program performance information for approved budget allocations (not just for planning or formulation, which is much more common). Expenditures are measurable in *outputs* (workloads such as numbers of miles paved, patient days, student contact hours, response times, and passenger miles of bus or tram service). *Outcomes* measure whether programs achieve broader policy objectives for their intended clients, such as reduced congestion for transit; reduced fire safety deaths for residents. For instance, Milwaukee defines one Health Department program objective: promotion of child development by reducing the ratio of African American infant mortality to white infant mortality to less than 1.3 percent by 2010. As is evident from Figure 1.18, the ratio was reduced in Milwaukee from 4.13 percent to 2.50 percent but still short of the 1.3 percent objective.

Often, the link between object expenditures and program results is unclear. Decision makers inclined to use such information for allocates need to know how cost and spending should be changed to improve volume and results. Two examples are provided in Figure 3.2 on page 90. The first is a generic presentation of a program-performance budget for a hypothetical social services department (SSAD) and police patrol services for Long Beach, California. Note that these are normative examples and suggest how program-performance budgets should be presented. But even the generic examples do not suggest transparent narrative and statistical linkage of objects with results. The third example is of a recent Salt Lake City performance budget. Both presentations provide only limited connections between expenditures, costs or volumes. The Salt Lake City budget provides cost/unit information (i.e., productivity) but makes no effort to cross-walk objects of expenditure, functions, and results in activity statistics or effectiveness (outcomes). In chapter 3, we will try and bridge this link with cost and expenditure analysis. Reduction of reporting time through the use of IFMS systems and elimination of redundant requirements altogether can allow reprogramming of PFM staff to perform more analyses of the kinds that can link activity and program results to object of expenditures.

surveillance activities, and developed a community West Nile Virus Action Plan that includes emergency mosquito control and abatement measures in collaboration with other county and municipal agencies. The department has also worked to increase public awareness and to provide health risk information to citizens and healthcare providers by conducting news conferences and staffing a telephone information hotline.

Communicable Disease Reduction Initiative: In 2003, the department will start a new CDBG funded program designed to reduce communicable disease in a targeted neighborhood. The goal of this program is to provide a coordinated approach to combating sexually transmitted diseases, tuberculosis, and other communicable disease in the community. The STD Clinic will be moved into the Keenan Health Center

where it will be co-located with the Tuberculosis Clinic. The co-location will provide increased accessibility for clients in the highest morbidity area of the city. CDBG funding of $250,000 will enable the department to provide a more focused, neighborhood approach to communicable disease education, identification, and prevention.

Environmental Planning: Funding for the CDBG Environmental Planning Program is increased by $41,538 in 2003. This funding provides an Environmental Scientist position that coordinates federally mandated environmental impact reviews of all proposed rehab projects and new projects in CDBG areas. It also screens tax delinquent properties and coordinates inspections and historical land use research.

OBJECTIVE 2

To promote reproductive health, healthy child development, and school readiness in Milwaukee by reducing the ratio of African American infant mortality rate to White infant mortality rate to less than 1.3% by 2010.

OUTCOME HISTORY

Infant mortality serves as a measurement of the health of the city's children. The Health Department has been using the five year average infant mortality rate as an outcome indicator for many years. Although the rate has been declining, serious disparity remains between African American and Caucasian and Hispanic infants. In an effort to eliminate this disparity, the department will now monitor the ratio between the two rates as its primary maternal and child health indicator. As Figure 4 illustrates, although overall city infant mortality is on the decline, the disparity between white and non-white infants remains wide.

The Health Department's 2003 budget dedicates approximately $5.7 million to promote maternal and child health, which includes over $2.5 million in state and federal grants.

Outcome Indicators and Funding

	2001 Experience*	2002 Budget*	2003 Projection
Ratio of African American infant mortality rate to White infant mortality rate.	4.13	NA	2.50
Funding by Source:			
Operating Funds	$4,131,377	$4,047,715	$2,907,529
Grant and Reimbursable	5,731,789	5,353,184	2,549,937
Capital Budget	46,180	56,100	241,602
Total:	$9,909,346	$9,456,999	$5,699,068

*2001 experience and 2002 budget reflects a prior maternal and child health objective that has been revised.

Figure 4

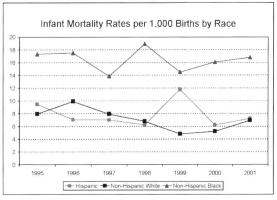

Figure 1.18. Linking Outcomes to Health Program Expenditures.

ACTIVITIES

- Prenatal and reproductive health
- Care coordination
- Infant and preschool health
- Pregnancy testing and counseling
- Assessment and monitoring of vulnerable and chronically ill children
- WIC Nutrition Program
- Newborn screening for heritable disorders
- Sudden unexpected infant death services
- Refugee child health
- Fetal infant mortality review
- Vital statistics/epidemiology
- HealthCheck Screening Clinics
- Immunizations

PROGRAM CHANGES

Early Child Care Grant: During 2002, the Health Department received a $565,000 grant from the U.S. Department of Health and Human Services to address the health, immunization, and environmental safety of children in child care centers. Since the onset of Wisconsin Works (W2 Welfare Reform), large populations of preschool children have been left in the care of childcare providers. Many of the providers are new to the field due to the influx of daycare needs. This grant improves the ability of the Health Department to monitor these providers.

Healthy Family/Healthy Infant Initiative: As part of its continued efforts to reduce the city's infant mortality rate, the Milwaukee Health Department's Maternal and Child Health Division launched a new collaborative effort to reduce the racial and ethnic disparity in infant mortality rates. In 2000, 79 of the 127 (62%) City of Milwaukee infant deaths occurred in the Neighborhood Strategic Planning Areas. As shown in Figure 4, the infant mortality rate amongst non-white residents is substantially higher than that of white residents. In 2003, the program will continue to proactively address the high proportion of births, infant deaths, and risk factors that occur in the CDBG target areas with $500,000 in CDBG funding.

OBJECTIVE 3

To reduce illness and injury related to the home environment in Milwaukee by reducing the percent of all children aged 0-5 years with blood lead levels exceeding 9 mcg/dL to 0% by 2010.

OUTCOME HISTORY

The Health Department has stepped up its focus on health issues related to the home environment, primarily lead poisoning, asthma, and unintentional injuries. Broadly recognized as one of the most successful lead poisoning control programs in the United States, the Health Department's Lead Program has significantly reduced the rate of lead poisoning amongst Milwaukee children. As Figure 5 shows, the percent of children tested aged 0-5 with high blood lead levels has declined from about 40% in 1995 to 16% in 2001. The program's success is derived in part from focusing on cost-effective abatement of contaminated homes before the children are poisoned.

The 2003 budget provides $3.2 million in funding for home environmental health activities. Approximately

Outcome Indicators and Funding			
	2001 Experience*	2002 Budget*	2003 Projection
Percent of children aged 0-5 tested with blood lead levels exceeding 9 mcg/dL.	16.0%	14.0%	14.0%
Funding by Source:			
Operating Funds	$729,744	$1,044,005	$1,121,489
Grant and Reimbursable	213,899	197,680	1,997,983
Capital Budget	46,179	0	82,856
Total:	$989,822	$1,241,685	$3,202,328

*2001 experience and 2002 budget reflects a prior environmental quality objective that is no longer tracked.

$2 million in funding comes from federal and state grant programs.

ACTIVITIES

- Lead poisoning prevention and treatment
- Asthma control
- Unintentional injury prevention
- Clinical and environmental lead laboratory

Figure 1.18. Continued.

Capital Plan and Budget

To measure the expenditure *baseline*, or costs of continuing existing levels of service in the current budget year, another major component must be included: the capital program composed of capital projects. In chapter 4, we review how projects are selected and ranked into a capital program (CIP) for funding. In this chapter, we examine only the measurement of expenditures and presentation of the expenditure budget. As indicated in Table 1.1 on page 44, the multi-year capital program is a ranking of approved projects and the capital budget is the first year of the capital program.

The budget cycle and calendar were noted above. In the calendar, capital budgets should be approved at the same time as the current or operating budgets. The calendar should integrate the processes of strategic, physical land use and the annual budget planning. The capital planning and budgeting process for the year should come together with one integrated or two separate budgets approved together consistent with the calendar. For example, a five-year Washington, D.C. Public Schools capital program was approved at $2.5b and the capital budget for the first year was set at $500m.

The core building block of the *capital program* (Capital Improvements Program or CIP) is the project. This is a major construction, acquisition, or renovation activity that adds value to the government's physical assets (Strachota, 1994, p. 162). Figure 1.20 on page 45 provides a good example of how projects should be presented from the Montgomery County CIP. Like the others in its 2010–14 CIP, the Animal Shelter project provides: a proposed cost schedule,

Figure 1.19. Capital Planning Problems. DILBERT © 2008 Scott Adams.

Table 1.1. Capital Budget in the Capital Plan

CIP	Capital Budget (Appropriation)		Capital Program			TOTAL
YEAR	2012	2013	2014	2015	2016	
Local Hospital	$500,000	$150,000		$3,000,000		$3,650,000
Local School		$100,000	$50,000	$1,000,000		$1,150,000
Local Clinic			$75,000		$2,000,000	$2,075,000
TOTAL	$500,000	$250,000	$125,000	$4,000,000	$2,000,000	$6,875,000

impact on the operating budget, especially maintenance and debt service, benefits justification, and sources of financing.

Questions

1. Referring to the Milwaukee Department of Administration chart above, it is said that organizations are frameworks for management—they cannot guarantee management. Recognizing that PFM staff work involves repetitive tasks such as filing purchase orders, recording invoices, and payroll data, what could a manager do to ensure that staff remains motivated? How can the budget director within the Milwaukee structure ensure that systemic integration of PFM functions occur where budgeting is only one function?

2. Several obstacles to fiscal transparency and the assessment of financial condition were noted above. Which of them can you identify in the Milwaukee FY 2005 and Montgomery County FY 2012 budgets? How could you improve their transparency?

3. The FY 2012 Montgomery County Transit Services budget is presented in a combined format. Which formats are used and how might the performance format be improved? What additional budget classifications might be used to increase fiscal transparency?

- The Training Division is responsible for the training and performance evaluation of police recruits, and for developing and providing in-service training for sworn officers and civilian employees, as well as supervisory and non-supervisory training.

FY09 Changes

	Expenditures	WYs
FY08 Approved	**52,946,570**	**348.1**
Increase Cost: Recruit Class Adjustments	165,080	-1.2
Shift: Telecommunication Specialist	108,300	1.0
Increase Cost: Executive Tow Regulation	19,140	0.0
Decrease Cost: Reduce 2nd Recruit Class (January 2009) to 20 Police Officer candidates	-706,840	-10.5
Miscellaneous adjustments, including negotiated compensation changes, employee benefit changes, changes due to staff turnover, reorganizations, and other budget changes affecting more than one program	4,481,700	-32.5
FY09 Approved	**57,013,950**	**304.9**

Notes: Miscellaneous adjustments for reduced workyears are due to reduction in overtime hours, and the reduction in the size of the two police officer candidate classes.

Security of County Facilities

The Security Services Division, which is located in the Management Services Bureau, provides security staffing at various County facilities in order to prevent or mitigate disorder and/or disruption. The division focuses on County facility and personnel security, vulnerability analysis, and target hardening initiatives. The Security Services Division is also responsible for providing executive protection duties for the County Executive.

As the result of reorganization, the Division of Security Services will be transferred to the Department of Police from the Office of Emergency Management and Homeland Security. This will result in the creation of a new division in the Police Department.

FY09 Changes

	Expenditures	WYs
FY08 Approved	**4,374,880**	**60.8**
Enhance: Update County Identification Badges	123,000	0.0
Add: Security Services Information Technology Systems Administrator	70,200	0.8
Miscellaneous adjustments, including negotiated compensation changes, employee benefit changes, changes due to staff turnover, reorganizations, and other budget changes affecting more than one program	424,530	1.1
FY09 Approved	**4,992,610**	**62.7**

Animal Services

The Animal Services Division, which is located in the Management Services Bureau, provides protection from communicable diseases (rabies, salmonella, and psittacosis), physical injury from vicious or dangerous animals, and animal nuisance problems. Citizens are protected from the hazards posed by deer carcasses on County roads. Domestic animals are protected from physical injuries, disease, and starvation by impoundment when at large, and by correcting or preventing inhumane conditions under which they may be kept.

The Division also provides shelter and services to animals and birds which come into the County Animal Shelter. Animals are received on a 24-hour basis. These animals include stray, trapped, and unwanted animals, or injured wildlife. Wildlife are sent to licensed rehabilitators or euthanized. The program also maintains kennels; answers calls from the public (24-hour emergency phone service provided); administers a low-cost altering program; provides information to the public about wildlife problems; provides traps to the public when rabies is suspected; and provides for the disposal of animal carcasses at the Shelter.

Administratively, the Division provides advice to citizens over the phone; issues pet licenses and animal business licenses; responds to citizen complaints made by mail, phone, or in person; performs clerical functions for the Animal Matters Hearing Board, including receiving filings, scheduling hearings, drafting responses to citizen letters for the Chairman, and preparing orders; performs other administrative actions related to animal bites, rabies issues, and citizen complaints; and administers the contract with the Montgomery County Humane Society.

FY09 Changes

Figure 1.20. Montgomery County 2010–14 CIP: Annual Shelter Project.

46

	Expenditures	WYs
FY08 Approved	3,212,990	17.6
Miscellaneous adjustments, including negotiated compensation changes, employee benefit changes, changes due to staff turnover, reorganizations, and other budget changes affecting more than one program	186,500	0.0
FY09 Approved	3,399,490	17.6

Grants

The Department of Police receives grant funding from a variety of Federal and State agencies. These grant funds augment or supplement many programs within the Department and across every Bureau. Examples of current Federal funding are: Justice Assistance Grant Program (BJA), DNA Enhancement Capacity and Backlog grants (NIJ), Homeland Security Equipment Program, Bulletproof Vest Partnership grants (BJA), and the High Intensity Drug Trafficking Area (HIDTA) grant. State grants such as Vehicle Theft Prevention Program, C-SAFE (GOCCP), Commercial Vehicle Inspection (SHA), and the School Bus Safety Program (SHA) are examples of on-going State-funded programs. The Management and Budget Office is responsible for the acquisition, implementation, monitoring, auditing, and closeout of all grants received by the Police Department.

FY09 Changes

	Expenditures	WYs
FY08 Approved	230,300	2.8
Add: Community Prosecutor - Collaborative Supervision and Focused Enforcement Initiative Grant (CSAFE)	78,970	1.0
Add: Crime Analyst - Collaborative Supervision and Focused Enforcement Initiative Grant (CSAFE)	69,660	1.0
Increase Cost: Auto Theft: (Maryland Vehicle Theft Enforcement & Prevention Grant)	28,630	0.0
Increase Cost: DNA Cold Case Investigator Grant to review cold case files	13,010	0.0
FY09 Approved	420,570	4.8

Figure 1.20. Continued.

4. The FY 2010–14 Capital Program for Montgomery County includes an animal shelter project (Figure 1.20). Do you think ample justification was provided? Without knowing any facts about this county, what other information might have been provided to increase transparency?

5. Review the presentation of an object of expenditure budget for Code Enforcement in Table 1.2. As a legislator or financial condition assessor, what information would you demand to see before making a decision to approve it?

Table 1.2. Budget for Code Enforcement

Code Enforcement	Current Year Estimate	Budget Year Request	% Change
Personnel Wages and Salaries	$98,430	$120,475	22.4
Supplies	$2,245	$2,750	22.5%
Other Services and Charges	$17,575	$470	(10.5%)
TOTAL	$118,350	$139,420	17.9%

2

Analysis of the Revenue Budget

Figure 2.1. The Consultant Forecasts Revenues. DILBERT © 2003 Scott Adams.

Challenges and Responses

The Great Recession of 2007–09 starkly revealed the weaknesses in federal, state, and local government finances. One indicator of the subnational problem was that state deficit gaps reached 0.7 percent of GDP and 6.2 percent of total state-local spending in 2012 (Ebel et al., 2012, p. 9). For the past decade, the federal government has pursued a policy of tax cuts and spending increases, which resulted in a large debt. Powerful antitax and antigovernment groups resist compromises that could allow reasonable revenue increases which could contribute to needed growth without adding significantly to the debt burden. The recent recession revealed serious problems with the viability of state and local taxes. States have persistently narrowed their sales tax bases or failed to keep up with economic changes that narrowed those bases, such as Internet sales. In many cases, states made permanent reductions in their income taxes and have foregone changes in major taxes. Instead, they continue to rely on various fees and charges that are sensitive to economic conditions. Interstate competition for jobs and tax-reducing incentives continue to erode state corporate and local property tax bases. As the role of real property in commercial and industrial use decreases as a component of value (being replaced by intangibles such as patents, databases, and intellectual property), the tax burden continues to shift toward residential property.

Here the effects of the Great Recession and financial meltdown enter the picture, weakening demand for housing and consumption spending. The deterioration of state and local finances has been exacerbated further by deterioration in state and local pension plans. States and localities face an almost structural problem of declining revenue yields and increased mandatory spending. Widespread stock market losses and diminished portfolio values require increased contributions in order to keep pension plans sound actuarially (Ebel et al., 2012, p. 5). But reliance on obsolete taxes and fees have made it impossible to provide advance funding for the very generous pension plans encouraged largely by public sector unions. Unsustainable pension liabilities in cities such as Detroit have forced them into bankruptcy. Effective policy responses require the political and legal will to stabilize state and local finances. Technical options abound, such as replacement of the corporate profits tax with gross receipts or value added taxes; basing corporate tax breaks on performance; widening the sales tax base by including Internet sales and reducing exemptions for medical necessities and nonprofits (e.g., Washington, D.C., exempts one-third of its property mainly for universities and hospital nonprofits); taxing state income (five states levy no income tax); and eliminating constitutional rules that limit the growth of taxable value of individual properties (e.g. Proposition 13 in California and Michigan constitutional provisions) (Fisher, 2007, p. 339). Tax relief rules based largely on equity concerns have eroded local property tax bases and weakened local fiscal autonomy by, for instance, increasing dependence on state financing for schools and other services. Since the rules are often contradictory, local officials are caught in a bind, for example, Michigan's Headlee Amendment of 1978, which prohibits state imposition of unfunded mandates (which is often circumvented by the legislature) and Article IX of the constitution which prohibits increases in property and other taxes without voter approval (Kincaid, 2012, p. 77). Again, the lack of effective policy responses to the deterioration of state and local revenue sources is explicable more by lack of political and legal will than by lack of viable technical options.

The Revenue Function

The operating budget for state and local governments presents the revenue and expenditure plan for the fiscal year. It contains two parts: revenues and expenditures. In this chapter, we discuss the development of the revenue budget. Consistent with the calendar noted in the first chapter, the finance department issues policy guidelines and instructions for departments to begin preparing their budget requests. The policy guidelines indicate the constraints faced by the jurisdiction due to both economic conditions and current and past expenditure commitments. In order to gauge needed revenues for financing, the finance department fixes an expenditure ceiling. In this chapter, we review the core revenue sources available to cities and states and methods of evaluating their buoyancy. We also cover important methods used for: tax assessment, pricing services, and forecasting revenues.

Revenue Policy

Analysts use data and information to forecast options and develop preferred recommendations to resolve social problems. Evaluators question the data and assumptions behind both the options and preferred recommendations (Guess & Farnham, 2011, p. 3). An important component of fiscal policy analysis is the evaluation of tax and user charge alternatives. Revenue policy consists of rules governing taxes, fees, and user charges imposed in order to fund the operations of government. Many state and local governments lack formal policies; their tax and revenue actions are made on a fragmentary basis (Allan, 1996, p. 159). Finance officers and the public need to know the empirical basis for using existing revenue sources and contemplating other alternatives. The formal political decision to use one revenue source over another is made by state legislators and city councils.

It is suggested here that the seven most important revenue policy goals are:

1. *Political Acceptability*: This criterion refers to the fairness of tax and fee burdens that reflect the local political culture—local values

and traditions. To gain acceptance, it helps if leaders compare local revenue generation capacity (e.g., in relation to personal income) and revenue effort (e.g., revenue per capita) with similar cities and states (Allan, 1996, p. 161).

2. *Revenue Adequacy and Stability*: This refers to how productive the yields of particular sources are. More *inelastic* (i.e., demand relatively insensitive to price) sources such as liquor and tobacco taxes provide stable revenues despite their *regressive* qualities (i.e., tax burdens are inversely related to incomes); while income taxes are more elastic to changes in the economy (Allan, 1996, p. 160). Where states or localities depend on income tax receipts, recessions can result in major revenue shortfalls, for instance, California's overreliance since Proposition 13 in 1978 on income and sales local taxes over property taxes has created major service instabilities. An advantage of using revenue policy to stabilize state-local finances is that rates and bases can be changed in the short run by legislative action. By contrast, most public expenditures are held in place by concentrated special interests of users or employees; and it is harder to change expenditure patterns once the fiscal year begins. For example, almost immediately refuse fees can be changed (per pickup), local income tax rates can be changed (different share of state income tax), and new sales tax rates on auto rentals can be imposed (e.g., 2%).

3. *Revenue Diversification*: City revenues, like small farmers with limited land area, need to diversify if they are to protect against revenue collapse when markets change. The optimal revenue structure balances out: user fees, sales, property and income taxes. Tax bases should be the widest possible to allow greater efficiency through lower rates. The property tax base, for example, should be diversified among different classes of property, that is to say, commercial and residential. It was noted above that state and local revenue systems have yet to adjust to the major changes in economic structure and demographics of the past several decades. Nevertheless, the composition of local revenue sources has changed dramatically over the past seventy years. The relative importance of property taxes has declined and local sales taxes, user charges, and fees

have increased. At least local revenue sources have become more diverse (Sjoquist & Stoycheva, 2012, p. 430).

4. *Equity:* the tax burden for service benefits should be distributed fairly to ensure *vertical equities* for persons of different abilities to pay and *horizontal equities* to ensure that people in equal circumstances (e.g., income) pay their fair share of taxes.

5. *Administrative Feasibility:* Taxes and fees should be simple enough for easy compliance and efficient collection. For example, a commercial rent tax could cost more to administer than total revenues generated. Being price elastic, it could stimulate changes in business location and further revenue losses in revenue (Allan, 1996, p. 160). Another example is the market stall or kiosk tax, which is costly to administer, considered a nuisance tax by much of the public, and rarely produces much revenues. At worst, such taxes can drive microbusinesses to ruin and prevent any chance for their evolution into larger, legitimate businesses that can pay regular fees and taxes.

6. *Self-Sufficiency:* Cities and states should be able to survive on own-source revenues. To the extent this is not possible in practice, jurisdictions are dependent on grants from higher-tier governments. This creates the real risk that service delivery and overall financial condition could suffer where federal grants are cut along with other nondefense discretionary expenses. The 2013 *sequester* (i.e., across-the-board cuts of approved federal budget authority) did precisely that!

7. *Political Accountability:* Revenue policy requires political action to redress structural features of particular taxes. For example, the property tax is elastic, responsive to changes in economic growth, and flexible. For instance, the Great Recession of 2007–09 and accompanying financial meltdown reduced assessment values dramatically, which lowered local revenues. To prevent fiscal and service crises, local councils have had to raise their rates to finance budgets. Conversely, assessment increases in growing property markets may increase property tax burdens excessively. To be accountable, in such cases councils may have to lower the rates.

Using these and other technical criteria, cities and states will (1) develop their own fiscal policies, (2) base forecasts on their own assumptions, and (3) assess the costs and benefits of different revenue options. For example, as indicated in Figure 2.2, Gaston County includes in its budget development policies provisions for aggressive revenue collection and to avoid using one-time or special revenues to cover continuing operations (2014, p. 53).

Sound budget offices also develop forecasts based on transparent assumptions. To avoid relying on high-priced consultants that suggest you need more cash (see Figure 2.1), in more advanced communities revenue estimates are subject to sensitivity analyses for changes in economic and demographic variables. Figure 2.3 on pages 56–57 suggests that Gaston County develops its four-year forecasts based on worst/best case scenarios. It specifies its assumptions on rates of change in revenue (e.g., property tax collections) and expenditures (e.g., higher group insurance, maintenance costs).

Using the policies as constraints and the results of its forecasts, the county can then focus on options to deal with its projected medium-term revenue shortfall in the general fund. Required rates of tax and fee increases are considered to meet budgetary balance requirements. It is important that states and cities regularly evaluate their revenue sources consistently with the above seven criteria noted by Allan (1996, p. 161). The matrix developed for Baltimore County (MD) (Allan, 1996, pp. 164–165) is presented in Table 2.1 on page 58.

Focusing on the adequacy and stability criteria above (#2), state and local governments need technical capacity to assess the revenue productivity of all their sources. At the minimum, they need skills in four areas: (1) evaluation of the productivity and efficiency of all tax and fee sources, (2) assessing property taxes, (3) pricing services, and (4) methods of revenue projection.

Evaluating Revenue Sources

Before selecting a revenue option, governments should examine the comparative experiences of similar jurisdictions (Allan, 1996, p. 162). Review of demographic and economic information can help identify other similar jurisdictions for valid revenue structure and performance comparisons. For example, large, diverse states contemplating raising their sales and income tax rates in a recession (where growth is starting to return) should be examining the recent decision by California to increase both its rates to close the budget deficit. California raised its income rates on the wealthiest residents to 13.3 percent (twice that of Maryland and Virginia), which will almost erase its budget deficit (Eckers-

Financial Policies

Fiscal Policy Guidelines – Objectives

This fiscal policy is a statement of the guidelines and goals that will influence and guide the financial management practice of Gaston County. A fiscal policy that is adopted, adhered to, and regularly reviewed is recognized as the cornerstone of sound financial management. Effective fiscal policy:

- Contributes significantly to the county's ability to insulate itself from fiscal crisis,

- Enhances short term and long term financial credit ability by helping to achieve the highest credit and bond ratings possible,

- Promotes long-term financial stability by establishing clear and consistent guidelines,

- Directs attention to the total financial picture of the county rather than single issue areas,

- Promotes the view of linking long-run financial planning with day to day operations, and

- Provides the county staff, the Board of Commissioners and the county citizens a framework for measuring the fiscal impact of government services against established fiscal parameters and guidelines.

To these ends, the following fiscal policy statements are presented.

Budget Development Policies

1. One-time or other special revenues will not be used to finance continuing county operations but instead will be used for funding special projects unless a permanent funding source is identified as being available when such one-time revenues are no longer available.
2. The county will pursue an aggressive policy seeking the collection of current and delinquent property taxes, utility, license, permit and other fees due to the county.
3. The county will develop its annual budgets in such a manner to incorporate historic trend analysis for revenues and expenditures with an adjustment for current financial trends and developments as appropriate.
4. County staff will generate and review reports that show actual revenue and expenditure performance compared to budgeted performance and will present this information to the Board of Commissioners at least quarterly or more frequently as deemed necessary by staff.
5. Budget amendments will be brought to the Board of Commissioners for consideration as needed.

Figure 2.2. Revenue Policies: Gaston County 2014.

Financial Condition & Outlook

Additional Scenarios Assumptions

The forecast model can also incorporate additional assumptions involving revenues and expenditures. For this analysis, projected General Fund transfers to the Public Assistance, Debt Service, Special Revenue, and Capital Improvements funds are the only additional assumptions included in the forecast model.

Results

Under the assumptions listed above, the General Fund will face a growing mismatch between revenues and expenditures. Projections for FY 2015, the first year of the forecast, show a revenue shortfall of over $14 million. By FY 2018, the revenue shortfall more than doubles to $28.7 million.

As the revenue shortfalls graph depicts, shortfalls decreased with the adopted FY 2014 budget due to increased revenues from the tax increase, as well as decreased spending. Revenue shortfalls increase at a linear rate, however, after FY 2014.

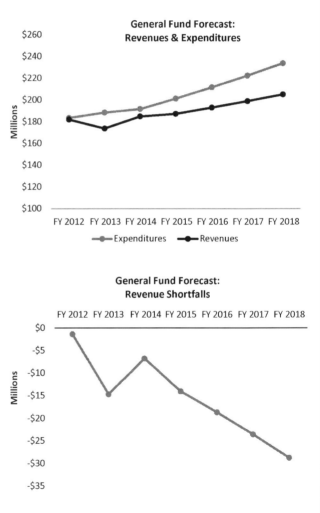

Figure 2.3. Forecasting Model and Assumptions: Gaston County 2012–18.

Financial Condition & Outlook

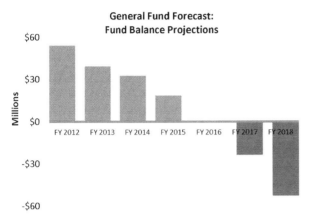

The projected disparity between revenues and expenditures results in a projected depletion of fund balance by FY 2016, with negative fund balances thereafter. This is because it is assumed fund balance would cover the revenue shortfalls, thereby contributing to fund balance depletion.

In reality, a local government couldn't have a negative fund balance for its general fund. Under the assumptions used in this forecast model, Gaston County would have to address its General Fund operating deficit during FY 2015, either by increasing revenues, cutting expenditures, or a combination of the two.

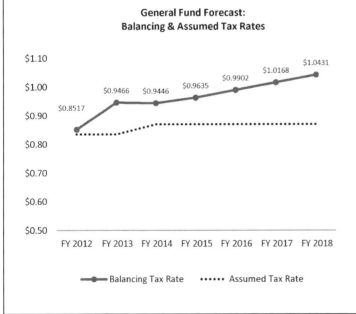

Finally, the graph to the left shows the tax rate Gaston County would have to adopt in order to balance its General Fund budget for each of the forecast years under the assumptions noted above. By FY 2018, Gaston County would need a tax rate of $1.0431 per $100 of valuation in order to balance its General Fund budget without using fund balance.

Figure 2.3. Continued.

Table 2.1. Alternative Revenue Options for Baltimore County, Maryland

OPTION	Proposed Revenue Change	Economic Efficiency	Equity Issues	Admin Effort	Political/ Legal Issue	Projected Yield (FY91)
Ambulance Service charge	Charge of $50/run	Demand is price inelastic	Benefits-based	Low: third-party collection	Narrowly-based	$700,000
Increase in Hotel/Motel Occupancy Tax	Increase rate 10%	Demand price inelastic-exportation possible	Benefits-based/ high income elasticity	Low	Narrowly-based	Additional $1,095,000
Expansion of Energy Tax	Natural gas: $.01/therm	Demand is price inelastic	Regressive	Low	Broadly-based	$2,360,000
	Electricity: 7.5% value			Low	Broadly-based	$13,407,000
	Fuel oil: $.02/gallon			Low-moderate	Narrowly-based	$1,471,000
	Coal: $1/ton			Low-moderate	Narrowly-based	$1,688,000
Transaction Tax on Automotive Rentals	$2/ transaction	Demand is price inelastic	High income inequality	Moderate-high	Narrowly-based	$370,000+
Boat Mooring Tax	$10/ foot of length	Demand possibly price inelastic	High income elasticity	Moderate	Narrowly-based	$566,000
Commercial Parking Tax	$10/ space	Price inelastic demand	Benefits-based	Low	Narrowly-based; potential legal problem	$428,000

ley, 2013). But that decision could choke off future investment and economic growth, which will threaten tax yields even further.

Conversely, Southern states and others such as Nebraska and Oklahoma rely on regressive sales taxes that hurt their poor by taxing them at a higher rate. Income and corporate taxes are almost nonexistent in these states. Other states with property tax limitations like California's Proposition 13 have moved in the direction of higher sales taxes and more fees and charges for service. While they raise revenues, they are regressive on the poor (Newman, 2013). Fees and charges are demand inelastic since the poor, in most cases, need the services. City transit authorities, for instance, are in constant contact with each other on the effects of raising fares on ridership and overall revenue yields. In some cases, transit charges are price elastic and result in revenue and ridership losses. In more complex markets, the charge may be more price inelastic and generate more revenue—but the effect is regressive. In short, to avoid comparing oranges and apples and relying on erroneous information, it is critical that jurisdictions and revenue sources be similar. To evaluate revenue sources properly, officials should apply common evaluative criteria to those currently in use and those used by similarly situated cities and states. GFOA and ICMA networks offer a rich source of comparative information for budget and finance officers; informal contacts across jurisdictional lines have been used for many years as well to learn about the wisdom of adopting particular sources. As indicated by Allan (1996, pp. 164–165), the most common criteria are:

1. *Economic efficiency* (i.e., demand and yield elasticity or sensitivity to changes in tax and fee prices),

2. *Equity* (i.e., targeted to beneficiaries such as road users; degree of regressivity, and administrative effort (i.e., cost of collection and possible harassment factor),

3. *Legal-political issues* (i.e., sources of opposition and need for higher level approvals), and

4. *Existing or potential yield.*

Review of sources provides a sound database and historical record of the strengths and weaknesses of existing sources and offers preliminary research into comparative city revenue performance, which can be updated annually. The budget department should examine this revenue sourcebook each year during the budget preparation phase.

Whether on the revenue or expenditure side, budgeting turns on: (1) *definitions* (e.g., Is this type of maintenance a current or capital expense?), (2) *assumptions* (e.g., Are the forecasted figures adjusted for inflation?), (3) *methods* (e.g., What methods were used to estimate demand or forecast revenues; Which numbers were used and why?), and (4) *tools* (e.g., Which statistical tools were used and why?). As noted in the previous chapter, both budget officials and overseers need to review definitional consistency to make certain they are using the same ones to assess individual expenses, revenues, and fiscal balances. In budget documents, memos, and reports, all of the above criteria need to be made explicit for defense of totals and for later verification by others who would want to replicate the numbers. One should remember that budgeting is a perennial clash between guardian and spender roles or between number controllers and program advocates. As discussed, expenditure budgets depend on the accuracy of revenue budget figures. Cities are in "resource-poor positions because balanced budgets are required and revenues are inelastic" (Wildavsky, 1986, p. 16). "Budgeting becomes a form of revenue behavior; income determines outgo" (ibid.).

Despite these real constraints and the fact that global forecasts depend on aggregation of sub-forecasts for each source, revenue budgets have been historically conservative and quite accurate. That changed in 2007, when it was clear that the baselines and forecasts did not include a recession (Francis, 2012, p. 501). Even in 2008, the recession was predicted to be narrow because it was restricted to housing markets. With hindsight it is clear that housing market exposure was not given proper weight (2012, p. 504). But even those data might not have changed revenue forecasting models since rating agencies had missed the extent of toxic mortgages that had been packaged, securitized, and sold as investment-grade debt. Since bond insurers relied on the same ratings that overlooked subprime mortgage debt, the subsequent collapse resulted in downgrades of municipal debt and higher borrowing costs for cities already strapped by loss of revenues from the recession (Petersen & Ciccarone, 2012, p. 691).

The revenue budget consists of estimates for tax, fee, and intergovernmental transfer or aid sources. In volatile economic times, the level of state or county aid will be affected by politics and institutional rules, which may throw off the total estimate of yields. The more a jurisdiction relies on a volatile income source, the greater its effect on the public finances. For example, since it has no income tax (which is usually more stable), the State of Texas relies heavily on sales tax receipts, which fluctuate widely with economic conditions. The state recently discovered that it had underestimated revenues in 2011 by about 28 percent. By law, the comptroller's revenue estimate ($72.4b forecast versus $101.4b actual) governs expenditure for the next two fiscal years. Texas is one of seven states to still have biennial legislative sessions and a two-year budget based on their decisions (*Economist*, 2013a). Such uncontrollable variables are a fact of life for budget practitioners, and perhaps the best way to deal with such uncertainty is to maintain open lines of communication with council and legislative liaisons. Such contacts can reduce surprise revenue fluctuations that diminish the accuracy of the planned budget, which leads to service and program disruptions during execution. To allow for course corrections in volatile economic times, revenues may have to be estimated on a rolling basis. It not unusual for cities to experience sudden losses from revenues that did not materialize from higher-tier grants or riders that did not patronize subsidized services such as transit.

Property Tax and Assessment

The property tax is still the most important revenue source for local governments. It provided 45 percent of local own-source revenues and 72 percent of local taxes in 2008 (down from 56 percent and 86 percent respectively in 1968) (Bell, 2012, p. 271). It is flexible and can be used to target growth. Despite weakening of this critical own-source of revenues by antitax legislation from property owners, for instance, California's Proposition 13, the tax still raised 73.9 percent of total local government revenue and 33.3percent of state and local revenue in 2009 (Mikesell, 2014, p. 488). Wisconsin state law, for instance, prevents localities from raising significant revenues from any other source but the property tax (*Milwaukee Plan and Budget*, 2003, p. 8). It is viewed as the most stable source of financing local needs and has been the bulwark of local fiscal autonomy. But the property tax is different, and rates are set outside the budget process.

Officials can juggle rates and bases to flexibly meet the fiscal demands and political limits of the approved budget. For example, commercial assessment values and rates are designed to induce local economic development. The purpose of taxing land value is to make hoarding expensive and force owners to sell to someone who can use the site. Once in use, the site value and tax rates rise, creating a virtuous circle, as the revenues pay for better local infrastructure, making the land more valuable. By contrast, in the British local tax system, owners do not pay taxes until offices and warehouses are built (*Economist*, 2013b).

Unlike other revenue sources, such as the sales tax, which are legislated and continue in place year after year without changes in rates or bases (Mikesell, 2011, p. 492), property tax rates are set annually to cover operating expenses that include debt service. The rate-setting process is an annual exercise that demonstrates among other things the flexibility of the property tax. It should be noted that to maintain fiscal discipline and comply with standards of internal control, functional separation (a form of check and balance) is needed for proper administration of property tax. The assessor is responsible for determining the taxable value of parcels in a jurisdiction; the local governing bodies determine the amounts to be raised for their budgets from the property tax; a clerk or auditor calculates the statutory property tax rate; and the treasurer collects the tax owed on each parcel and distributes the collections to the proper governments (Mikesell, 2011, p. 494).

There are six typical steps in developing the rate and actual tax bills:

1. Each year, a city decides how much property tax revenue it needs to finance its *operating budget*. Given legal and constitutional limits requiring balanced budgets, that means that at the subnational level, as noted, revenue needs effectively drive the budget process.

2. The city needs to develop its *assessment ratio*. "The heart of the property tax is assessment, the determination of property value for distributing total tax burden" (Mikesell, 2011, p. 505). The assessment ratio will always be a fraction of the total market value, for example, 30 percent of market value. Thus, the assessed value of a $100k home in this city would be $30k.

3. Then the city develops its *nominal property tax rate*. If the operating budget to be financed is $12m and the total assessed value is $300m, the rate will be 0.04 or 4 percent. Rates are expressed in dollars/$1000 of assessed value or mills/dollar. Mills are expressed as $0.01 or one-tenth of a cent. Thus, the *millage rate* of a 4 percent tax rate can be expressed as 40 mills/dollar or $40/$1000 assessed value. If the market value of a house is $100k and the assessed value is $30k, the tax bill would be 40 mills x $30k assessed value = 1.2m mills or $1200.

Tax Levy

Assessments = Tax Rate (x $1000 = mill rate)

4. Like many cities, Milwaukee includes a tax levy rate conversion table in its annual budget for added transparency.

5. The city then calculates and sends out *property tax bills*. This owner's bill would then be $1200/year or 0.04% x $30k.

6. Often market and assessed values will differ. Sales prices can push increasing market values over assessed values if reassessment has not yet occurred. The *effective tax rate* measures the difference between assessed and market values. In the example, the $100k home has an effective tax rate of 1.2 percent ($1200/$100k = 0.012) (Rabin et al., 1996, pp. 169–170), meaning that its assessed

TAX LEVY TO RATE CONVERSION TABLE

Assessed Value Used in Conversion Calculation: $19,410,468,634

Tax Rate Per $1,000 of Assessed Valuation	Levy Change	Levy Change	Tax Rate Per $1,000 of Assessed Valuation
$0.01	$194,105	$5,000	$0.00
$0.05	$970,523	$10,000	$0.00
$0.10	$1,941,047	$50,000	$0.00
$0.25	$4,852,617	$100,000	$0.01
$0.50	$9,705,234	$500,000	$0.03
$1.00	$19,410,469	$1,000,000	$0.05

Formula for deriving tax rate per $1,000 of assessed value from known assessed value and levy:

$$\text{TAX RATE} = \frac{\text{TAX LEVY}}{\text{ASSESSED VALUE}/1,000}$$

Formula for deriving levy from known rate and assessed value:

TAX LEVY = TAX RATE X (ASSESSED VALUE / 1,000)

Formula for deriving assessed value from known rate and levy:

ASSESSED VALUE = (TAX LEVY / TAX RATE) X 1,000

NOTE: Results are approximate due to rounding.

Figure 2.4. Milwaukee Tax Rate to Levy Conversion.

and market values are close to a perfect 1.0 percent score. If the market value increases to $125k, the effective tax rate (9.6 percent or $1200/$125k) suggests a wider gap. One interpretation is that higher value properties are underassessed relative to lower valued parcels. The *price related differential* (PRD) (PRD = Mean Assessment Ratio/(Sum of Assessed Values/Sum of Market Values) can be used here to indicate that the wide differential between 1.2 percent and 9.6 percent is a form of regressivity (Mikesell, 2011, p. 508).

The difference between assessed and market values may be due to intentional policy. California limits reassessments to keep homeowner tax bills down. Its jurisdictions also distinguish property classes by assessing them at different rates (e.g., commercial 16 percent versus residential 12 percent); local officials would want to know the effective tax rate for comparative analytic reasons. California cities have lost a lot of revenue because of underassessments when property has increased in market value. Under Proposition 13, cities could also not distinguish between residential and commercial property for assessment purposes. Since 1978, properties have been reassessed at transfer of ownership only, meaning that increased commercial property values were not taxed. Given revenue losses in California and other states, it is likely that a "split roll" annual assessment will be introduced (*Economist*, 2012a). This will increase the effective tax rate for commercial property tax and bring market and assessed value more into line.

In some states, the property rate-setting and assessment process is influenced by state-level activities. In Gallatin County, Montana, for example, the state department of revenue calculates the assessed value. The assessed value is then adjusted for residential factors. For a home of $100k assessed value, adjustments for home owner exemptions, tax abatements, senior exemptions, etc. are factored at 0.56. This produces the taxable market value of $56k. The state then provides a Tax Value Factor, which changes yearly. For FY 13, the amount of 0.0263 is multiplied by the taxable market value to produce a taxable value of $1473. The taxable value is then multiplied by the County Millage rate of 118.63 to produce a tax bill for $100k home of $174.74[1] (Blackman, 2013).

Pricing Services

Beyond taxes, such as the property tax, the major source of revenues for state-local governments is fees, charges, and fiscal monopolies. Governments charge *fees* for activities requiring licenses such as business, hunting, and driving; they impose service *charges* where there are enforceable charge barriers such as: student tuition, road tollgates, transit fare boxes, and water meters; and they generate funds from their utilities through the sale, for instance, of

---

1. The author again wishes to thank Ed Blackman, Finance Director of Gallatin County (Montana) and Earl Mathers, formerly Gallatin County Administrator for their assistance with this property tax assessment example.

liquor, operation of lotteries, and water supply (Mikesell, 2011, p. 553). Of total own-source revenues, states collect about 29 percent from charges, fees, and monopoly operations, and localities about 33 percent (Mikesell, 2014, p. 540). As indicated in Figure 2.5, in general, broad-based taxes yield more revenues than charges. Though the relationship is not precisely linear, broader-based taxes are less responsive to individual behavior and have lower incentive effects than charges. Tax burdens, for instance, may be shifted onto customers, while charges (e.g., transit fares) must be paid (i.e., changing commuting habits from buses to cars).

Officials need to know how and why to set prices for three types of services. With prices set, they are in a better position to estimate service volumes and to devise formulae for grants to cover services and programs to lower tiers of government, for example, state-city; county-city. First, there are *public goods* such as planning, zoning, and law enforcement, where it is difficult to identify consumers (Neels & Caggiano, 1996, pp. 173–174). These should be paid for out of the general fund, funded by taxation; no charges additional charges are usually levied.

Second, there are *private goods* where it is more feasible for public provision. Some services are naturally loss making and more efficiently delivered by single public monopoly organizations than multiple competing private firms.

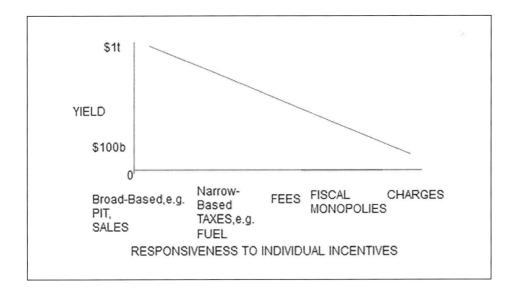

Figure 2.5. Yield and Efficiency Responsiveness of Revenue Options.

These are called *natural monopolies*, and the state or locality regulates them to provide optimal services and reasonable charges. Public transit, water and sewerage, and construction of public facilities are examples of natural monopoly service delivery. Technology has changed the status of this classification, allowing private firms to offer services at reasonable prices to customers in the public interest, for instance, road maintenance, sanitation services, animal control, public transit routes, and private concessions to build, operate, and maintain public capital facilities such as jails and highways. Localities also provide concessions to private firms to offer their services inside libraries, schools, and hospitals (e.g., food services and copying).

Finally, there are *merit goods* such as treatment of communicable diseases and social services that can be provided by nonprofit organizations (Neels & Caggiano, 1996, pp. 173–174). The city will contract with nonprofits to perform services that it can now regulate on the basis of performance and cost-effectiveness. While regulation and standards remain with the public sector, delivery is the responsibility of the nonprofit or private firm that bids successfully for the public service contract.

Prices for the second and third type of service vary by type and purpose. Officials set them to try and balance cost efficiency, revenue generation, and value to the consumer. Localities should attempt to recover the full cost of providing services to consumers (1996, p. 174). Failure to receive full cost recovery means that the jurisdiction is subsidizing the activity. For revenue analysis and fiscal transparency, it is critical to identify subsidy prices. Such leakages may be for a public purpose; but it is critical that the finance departments be able to measure them, ensure that they are targeted (e.g., often food and fuel subsidies are not), and to recommend sound pricing policies based on this information. There are four main types of pricing strategies:

1. Direct Cost Pricing

Localities set prices to yield revenues sufficient to costs and no more than that. The idea is that nonprofit entities such as governments should not profit off the public. What are costs? *Costs* are not *expenditures* or outlays that are measured by budget appropriations and which reflect political pressures (such as union labor rules) and procurement practices that may not purchase goods and services at market prices or least cost. *Costs* refer to the use and consumption of goods and services or to the market costs of production. For instance, the costs of health care are typically far less than public expenditures for them. Initially, they can be divided into direct and indirect. Direct costs include all the core costs associated with a particular service (1996, p. 178). For the city transit agency, the *direct costs* would include: salaries, travel, maintenance, and supplies. *Indirect costs* are for overhead support and include administration. Dividing the direct costs by the number of riders served produces the average direct costs per rider. This would allow efficiency comparisons with other services in similar cities.

2. Full Cost Pricing

Full costs reflect market-based costs or the sum of direct and indirect costs. As indicated, the latter are support costs, such as administration and overhead, charged to the activity. Indirect costs are often apportioned on the basis of a predetermined rate based on such factors as: time spent supporting the activity (e.g,. processing invoices, payment of staff, and common use of copier, fax, and phones). Income-generating activities such as local public utilities will often charge full costs to consumers plus a mark-up to provide returns to bondholders that pay for their capital improvements.

3. Cost-Volume Pricing

As the quantity of service increases, such as more passenger miles of bus service, costs will change in varying proportions. Costs behave unevenly with volume of service output. In the figure below, note that *fixed costs* such as salaries (in the short term), capital, rent, and maintenance will not change up to a volume point. As supervisors are added to cover additional volume and output, the costs become *semi-fixed*. *Variable costs*, such as fuel, numbers of trips, and salaries (to serve increased ridership in the long term) will vary by volume. But with greater output, some of the costs have a fixed component, for example, utility bills based partly on demand. These are *semi-variable* costs. Knowing cost-volume relationships allows more nuanced pricing to ensure that efficiencies are maintained. This type of pricing is especially useful for comparing service delivery costs with private contractors. Analysis of cost-volume relations may indicate that private contractors (e.g., private bus line operators) can charge the same price but be able to reduce their fixed or variable costs. By achieving the service level desired by the city, this can provide considerable budgetary savings.

Because of *economies of scale*, average costs per unit typically decrease with greater volume of output. As more productivity is squeezed out of existing fixed assets, natural monopoly organizations that deliver such services as transit

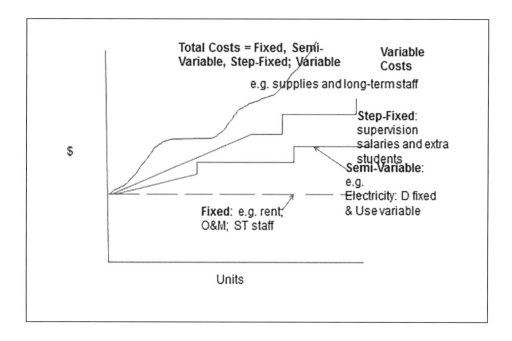

Figure 2.6. Cost Behavior in Relation to Volume.

services experience this as ridership and the number of rides increases. At higher outputs, however, the transit authority will also need to rehabilitate buses, replace them or add more rolling stock to accommodate more passengers. Note also that with increasing volume, the administrative workload also increases, meaning that indirect support costs will increase. Average total costs no longer can guide pricing since they are both increasing at different rates with volume. Full cost pricing to cover all costs would now be prohibitive to users. This is because demand for many services is sensitive to price. As indicated below in the example for local public transit, if the service is price sensitive, it is said to be *elastic*. Increasing the price too high will reduce ridership and encourage alternate means of mobility such as automobile use for middle-class riders, causing greater congestion and air pollution. But poorer, transit-dependent riders will suffer from the regressivity of a higher fare; they must pay the higher fares anyway to maintain access to jobs and other family needs.

Focusing on average or unit costs and their relationship to fixed-variable costs is not enough to set prices for some services. Marginal cost pricing is a better way to link cost-volume in the context of scarce resources and limited

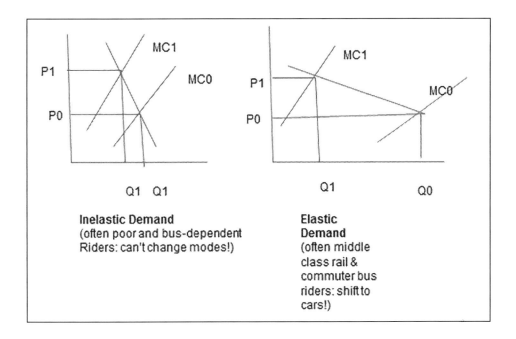

Figure 2.7. Price Elasticity of Demand.

possibilities to recover full costs. *Marginal cost* is the cost of the last unit of service provided. For comprehensive cost analysis, marginal costs should be compared with *average costs* (total costs/number of units) for such local decisions as *outsourcing*. Unit cost behavior does not capture the change in fixed and variable costs with greater output. Economies of scale at greater volumes should lower unit costs. Average costs, for example, might dictate outsourcing a service. But from a marginal cost perspective, it may save revenue to perform a task in house such as educating extra students.

Marginal costs are often the same as variable costs over a specific volume range. When volume increases, some variable costs become fixed, for example, salaries and wages, which were a short-term variable cost now become fixed in the longer term. Where school capacity exists and the question is whether to add extra students, the marginal cost of each of them would be equal to variable costs up to a point. When more fixed costs must be incurred to accommodate them (e.g., classrooms or teachers), the marginal cost of extra students will now be the sum of fixed and variable costs. Up to that point, no strains on capacity are required and the marginal costs are low, namely, only the variable costs (e.g., light, heat, desk space). If fixed costs change then, the marginal and variable costs will be different (Finkler, 2010, pp. 134–135).

Cost relationships vary by type of service. The marginal cost of additional riders, for example, is often below full or even direct costs. So, pricing to cover full or direct costs would be inefficient and likely reduce ridership. Given that public transit, like most *natural monopolies*, is a loss-making activitiy, the result would be an even higher subsidy requirement or reduction in service levels. The problems with using average or full cost pricing for natural monopolies is demonstrated in the figure below. Cost-based pricing, and particularly marginal cost pricing allows officials to recognize the maximum point at which all costs cannot meet demand. At this point, higher prices would reduce ridership, and some combination of alternative means such as greater subsidies, contracting out, negotiations with unions, and service reductions would be necessary. Continuously decreasing average costs imply that marginal cost pricing will result in more losses and a compensating operating subsidy will be needed (Hemming, 1991, pp. 79).

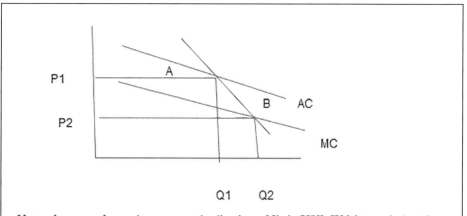

Natural monopoly used to prevent duplication of I's in UPT, W&S type industries. But increasing *returns to scale*, @P2/Q2 NM cannot generate enough $ to cover AC (TC/#units = AC). At P1/Q1 efficient but cost/unit > revenue/unit. Q1 too low to generate BE revenue. At P2, can generate normal ROR but Q required is inefficient. Context requires regulated monopoly + subsidy prices + other revenues.

Figure 2.8. Natural Monopoly Cost Behavior.

4. Income-Based Pricing

Here, officials consider both cost and revenue to set prices. For many services, marginal cost pricing, as noted, results in subsidy levels below both average and even direct costs. Low-cost housing is *subsidy priced* below both marginal and full cost for social policy reasons. *Penalty prices*, by contrast, to dissuade harmful activities such as pollution and smoking are charged above full and marginal cost levels. As indicated in Figure 2.9, below a break-even point, prices are subsidy and above that point they can generate surpluses.

The fact is that most public services do not cover operating costs even with sensible pricing. For instance, public transit fares typically cover no more than 35 to 50 percent of operating costs. On the other hand, cities do provide many services where certain patrons are willing to pay more and a reasonable attempt through pricing should be made to cover a greater percentage of total operating costs. Cities, of course, cannot simply gouge the public for use of parks where there are few alternatives. The goal would be to set a price to minimize

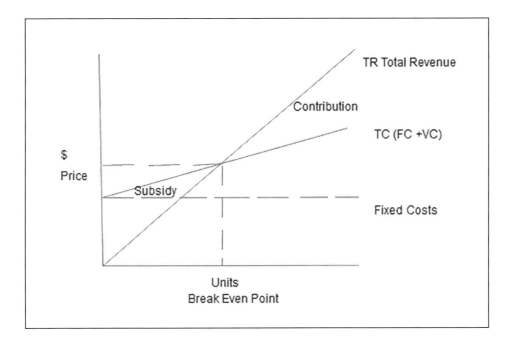

Figure 2.9. Income-Based Pricing.

losses (subsidies) rather than make a profit for these kinds of facilities. For other facilities and services such as: transit, parking garages, swimming pools, and libraries, officials recognize the availability of private alternatives, such as bookstores and automobiles. Nevertheless, the alternatives are not free, and in many cases cities can charge full costs and include markups to generate a profit. In other cases, such as rush-hour transit, cities can use discriminatory pricing to charge higher peak fares. This generates funding to pay for increased maintenance of operating more buses and encourages those who could take buses during off-peak hours to do so and reduce congestion.

Projecting Revenues

Local governments in the United States, Canada, Switzerland, and Germany are highly autonomous and rely on substantial own-source revenues to finance their budgets. The bad news is that maintenance of sound financial condition boils down to the accuracy of their revenue forecasts. Projected yields for budgeting purposes depend on accurate forecasts of: volume, bases, and rates. Rates are set according to transparent methods (as noted for the property tax). But if the price causes perverse incentives (e.g., excessive fares on elastic transit demand), forecasted demand could drop, reducing revenues. Bases might also vary (e.g., property values in the latest recession of 2007–09; and jurisdictional lines could change affecting the tax base). Projected yields also depend on collection rates or tax administration. In the latest recession, many homeowners could not pay their taxes or their mortgages. Despite these obstacles, state and local finance officers have applied compensatory methods and adjusted forecasts to probable reality. For example, forecasters often use group brainstorming techniques such as Delphi that include expert judgments to critique and adjust results obtained by statistical and computer models (Dunn, 2008, pp. 107). Overall, state and local finance officers have been largely successful at forecasting and reforecasting revenues accurately in order to minimize service disruptions caused by sudden revenue shortfalls during the year.

Some services such as urban public transit are absolutely dependent on accurate revenue forecasts. For example, in Atlanta, rail-bus transit is delivered by a public enterprise or proprietary fund operation. In contrast with many, it faces a real hard budget constraint. The Metropolitan Atlanta Rapid Transit Authority Act of 1965 (amended in 1984) provides for a 1 percent sales tax to be levied by the two member counties (Fulton and DeKalb). MARTA may

Figure 2.10. Revenue Assumptions. DILBERT © 2003 Scott Adams.
Used By permission of UNIVERSAL UCLICK. All rights reserved.

use no more than 50 percent of sales tax proceeds to cover operating costs. MARTA must also adjust fares, service, or staffing levels to ensure that operating revenues cover at least 35 percent of projected operating costs. MARTA relies on the sales tax for about 60 percent of its operating revenue. The problem is forecasting a single source of revenue that fluctuates with economic cycles and political action. Despite this problem, data going back almost thirty-five years reveals that year-on-year variation in total receipts is only 7.8 percent (Guess & Farnham, 2000, p. 190). This is serous revenue budgeting.

In this section, we discuss two commonly used forecasting methods: (1) *averaging* and (2) *linear regression*. We will not cover in depth more sophisticated methods such as multiple-equation regression modeling (see sources such as: Guess & Farnham, 2011, pp. 232–233). This is useful for predicting transit ridership, which translates into fare revenues. Ridership may depend on several independent variables such as unemployment rates, fare levels, and amount of service (USDOT, 1986, p. 56). Linear regression assumes that time is the independent variable (Finkler, 2010, p. 117) and that revenue trends vary over time allowing us to predict revenues for the next time period. But this is often insufficient, and including other variables into an equation can help predict fares more accurately than with single variable prediction. Curvilinear forecasting is used to deal with nonlinear patterns such as seasonal fluctuations (see sources such as Finkler, 2011, Appendix 3-B). Excel can be used to develop curvilinear trend lines. Once an Excel chart has been created from the data, the user can click on "add trendline" and choose among six types of trendlines that can be generated (Finkler, 2010, p. 121).

Proportionate Change or Averaging

Averaging techniques (aka moving average and proportionate change) are rudi-
mentary time-series analysis methods widely used because of their simplicity
and ease of calculation. In this case, simplicity and accuracy are not necessarily opposites. Moving averages are applied wherever it is necessary to make
an estimate of a variable value for a short-term forecast of one to three time
periods (e.g., months, years). "The concept of moving averages is based on the
assumption that past data observations reflect an underlying trend that can be
determined, and that the averaging of these data will eliminate the randomness
and seasonality in the data. The averaging of the data to develop a forecast
value provides a 'smoothing' effect on the data" (Toulmin & Wright, 1983, p.
226). Averaging depends on the assumptions that past patterns will continue
and that "turning points" (irregular components) will not take place in the
period to be forecast (Guess & Farnham, 2011, p. 219).

    The moving average technique is often used by municipal revenue forecast-
ers for annual budgeting. The accuracy of the revenue forecast will affect budget
management during the year as managers attempt to manage cash flow. It will
also determine the size of any budget deficit that needs to be financed (through
changes in tax rates, rates, or collection methods, as well as through arrears,
carryovers, or short-term financing). Local economic development policy financing could depend on the skillful use of the averaging technique. For example,
such cities as San Diego and Pittsburgh have based much of their economic
development strategies on new sports stadiums. Sustained bond repayments from
their budgets will depend largely upon earmarked revenue sources such as the
hotel tax (*Economist*, 1999a, p. 39). The question of whether revenues from
this tax will grow or decline needs to be included in the analysis of proposed
economic development policies. Hotel tax receipts are often successfully forecasted by using the moving average method. In the annual budget document,
assumptions underlying the revenue forecast will determine whether the city
attains its financial goals.

    Proportionate change trend analysis is an easy and reasonably accurate
statistical technique for predicting future revenues from revenue base or collection data over the past five to six years. This method allows determination
of the average rate of change from collections over a trend period of years and
application to the last year. Suppose we want to estimate anticipated revenue
from building permit receipts for FY 2015. The following five steps provide an
answer:

1. Needed are monthly receipts data for the building permits revenue source. Add this up for a yearly total, for examply, $1,000 for 2010.

2. To come up with the rate of change, calculate the difference in amount collected between each fiscal year. This can be done with a simple hand calculator. For six years, there will be five rates of change:

Current Year (CY)–Past Year (PY) = rate of change
Past Year

1. FY2011–FY 2010   =   1,200–1.000 = .2 or 20 percent
FY 2010   1,000

2. FY 2012–FY 2011   =   1,300–1.200 = .08 or 8 percent
FY 2011   1,200

3. FY 2013–FY 2012   =   1,500–1,300 = .15 or 15 percent
FY 2012   1,300

4. FY 2014–FY 2013   =   1,900–1,500 = .26 or 26 percent
FY 2013   1,500

5. FY 2105–FY 2014   =   2,100–1,900 = .10 or 10 percent
FY 2014   1,900

3. Add all rates of change and compute average rate of change for the period FY 2010–2015.

20 percent
 8
15
26
10
79 = 79/5 = 16 percent average rate of change

4. Multiply average rate of change by the current year collections: 2,100 x .16 = 336.

5. Add 336 to current year collections of 2,100 to obtain the estimated revenue from building permits for FY 2015: 2,100 + 336 = $2,436: estimated FY 2015 building permit revenue.

Using the $2,436 figure for FY 2015 in this case requires two assumptions that should be made explicit in the budget document. First, there has been no change in permit fees over the past year (or change in rates), and second, there will be not be a new local ordinance in the near future that would encourage or discourage people from building new structures or adding to existing ones. In addition, local tax offices should consider other factors affecting the accuracy of revenue estimates, such as inflation rates (price changes) and other regulatory ordinances.

From this example it is evident that the strength of the averaging technique is also its telling weakness. It is based on a straight-line projection of average past changes that assumes that average differences between years will be a guide to next year. Specifically, as in regression analysis (to be discussed next), the averaging technique gives each data point the same weight in the analysis, "whereas, in actuality, the latest data may be of more importance because they may indicate the beginning of a new trend" (Toulmin & Wright 1983, p. 234).

Linear Regression

This technique allows prediction of revenue trends over time derived from dependent variables such as: permits, riders, and sales. It is an improvement over averaging since it can plot a single line that can serve as a reasonably good trend predictor. Linear regression is useful for both causal (meaning only that a statistical technique can associate variables from which inferences can be made) and time-series analysis. For instance, it was noted previously that for pricing purposes, costs often depend on volume. If we know the cost and volume of previous levels of riders, students, patients, permits, etc., we can predict the future costs for given volumes. In Figure 2.11 below, Y is the dependent variable (e.g., future costs or revenues) to be predicted from X the independent variable, which consists of time (e.g., volume).

According to David Nachmias (1979, p. 113, cited in Guess & Farnham, 2011, p. 223), "The objective of regression analysis is to formulate a function by which the researcher can predict or estimate the scores on a target variable from scores on independent variables." From Figure 2.11, we note that each pair of X and Y values is a "coordinate" and where all coordinates fall on a straight line, the function relating X to Y is a linear function. The regression equation is $Y = a + (b)(X)$. This suggests that Y is a linear function of X. The slope of the regression function (b) indicates how many units in Y are obtained for each unit change in X. The more rigorously we can estimate a regression line, the better chance of predictive accuracy for the future. The symbol (a) represents the point where the regression line crosses the Y axis (where X = 0). The point at which the line crosses the vertical axis is called the y intercept

(Finkler, 2010, p. 119). Linear regression uses a set of paired x and y values to estimate the slope (b) and the intercept (a) (2010, p. 120).

The regression equation hypothesizes that observed coordinates will fall along a straight line. Needed is a means of averaging the distances to obtain the best fitting line. "Goodness of fit" tests such as the coefficient of determination (R2), discussed above, indicate the strength of the relationship between the dependent and independent variables. The most common form of regression analysis is "least-squares" regression, which focuses on the need to minimize errors (differences between observed and actual points due to randomness in behavior of other factors). By squaring errors, the possibility that distances above and below the line would cancel is eliminated. By not squaring errors, that is, by not using least-squares, we could use several lines to minimize the sum of non-squared errors (Schroeder, Sjoquist, & Stephan 1986, p. 20). "Thus, if we draw vertical lines from each of the points to the least-squares line, and if we square these distances and add, the resulting sum will be less than a comparable sum of squares from any other possible straight line" (Blalock 1972, p. 371). According to Nachmias, "The least-squares method is a way for finding the one straight line that provides the best fit for an observed bivariate distribution." Put more simply, the line will minimize the "residual" distance between the function line and any observed point on the scattergram (see Figure 2.11). Simply averaging, as we did before, ignores the possibility that several lines could "fit" if we ignore the need to minimize residual distances.

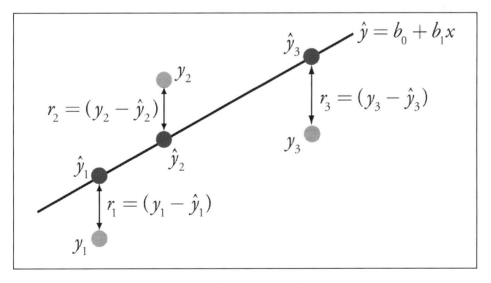

Figure 2.11. The Regression Equation.

The least-squares regression can now be used to extrapolate a trend from receipts data. Since the technique requires valid data, we can use whiskey excise tax receipts collected from Rockville City for five years to project collections for the following fiscal year. Based on the assumptions and formulas for least-squares regression, where a and b are calculated it is possible to estimate the Y variable (revenues) in the observed time-series or in any projected time period. While we are demonstrating how this and other forecasting techniques can be performed with little more than hand calculators, Excel or SPSS software can also be used that simply require data entry according to the programs. The calculations to project whiskey tax collected receipts for FY 2015 are illustrated in Table 2.2.

Calculating the trend values according to $Y = a + b(x)$, we now have enough data to calculate both a and b. Use the formula for a "level in the central year" in Tables 2.2 and 2.3 or

$$\frac{\Sigma Y}{N} \quad \text{or} \quad \frac{489.1}{5} \quad = 97.8 \quad \text{and for } b = \frac{\Sigma (xY)}{\Sigma (x^2)} \quad \text{or} \quad \frac{11.9}{10} \quad = 1.19$$

With a and b, one can now compute the values for the trend line for each fiscal year in the past series and project the trend line for FY 2014 and 2015 (Table 2.2).

Graphing the least-squares trend line (Figure 2.11) can be done by hand calculator or through the use of Microsoft Excel. Instructions can be found on the Web page for *Essentials of Cost Accounting for Health Care Organizations* at: http://www.musc.edu/hap/costaccounting/exercise/chapter7/Information/linear-regression.htm (Finkler, 2010, p. 119). Two questions arise on the utility of the least-squares method now that we have our forecasts. First, how confident can we be in the forecasted values? Second, how useful are linear methods such

Table 2.2. Least Squares Regression of Whiskey Tax Collected Receipts, FY 2010–14

Fiscal Year (X)	Collections (Y)	Coded Time (x)	Cross-Products (xY)	Squared (X2)
2010	$98,751	−2	−197.5	4
2011	$95,075	−1	−95.0	1
2012	$94,131	0	0	0
2013	$97,794	+1	+97.7	1
2014	$103,354	+2	+206.7	4
N=5	$\Sigma Y=\$489,105$	$\Sigma x=0$	$\Sigma(xY)=+11.9$	$\Sigma(x^2)=10$

Table 2.3. Whiskey Tax Receipts Forecast for FY 2015–16

(a)	+ (x)	(b)	=	Y
Fiscal Year	Level in Central Yr	# from Central Yr Slope	Slope	Trend Line
2010	97.8	−2	1.19	95.4
2011	97.8	−1	1.19	96.6
2012	97.8	0	1.19	97.8
2013	97.8	+1	1.19	98.9
2014	97.8	+2	1.19	100.2
2015	97.8	+3	1.19	101.4
2016	97.8	+4	1.19	102.6

as least-squares, when fiscal data is "often nonlinear, irregular, and discontinuous" (Dunn 2008, p. 144)? To increase confidence in the results, one can use a method known as "percentage calculation of trend." To deal with the nonlinear feature of many fiscal data, one may change the linear least-squares equation for secular trends to one suitable for nonlinear (often curvilinear) growth trends.

To measure confidence in the forecasts just obtained, we need to see how far past receipts data varied from the trend line. According to Charles Liner (1996, p. 185):

> Cyclical components will show up as high or low percentage of trend values during years of expansion and contraction. Major irregular components will show up as one-time deviations. . . . Confidence in the accuracy of the trend is gained if the percentage of trend values are close to 100% and the assumption can be made that the variation in actual collections is due to the underlying trend. In contrast, if the percentage of trend values varies significantly above or below 100%, many other factors might account for the collections.

The calculated percentages of trend values suggest that we should have a relatively high level of confidence in our forecasts since the past has been largely unsullied by cycles or irregular (nonlinear) events. However, where past observations reveal a nonlinear pattern—"the amounts of change increase or decrease from one time period to the next" (Dunn 2008:145)—other techniques must be used to forecast future time-series values.

It will be seen in the next chapter that public expenditure trends are typically less irregular than revenues. But problems still exist that make it difficult to fit a curve or line to revenue data. Trends or cycles within time-series data can confuse cumulative receipts from year to year, and this can weaken forecasts. Growth or decline curves (S-shaped patterns) can occur between years, decades, or longer periods. If one uses a linear regression equation for data in a scattergram with data points that appear to be increasing, the forecast will be off. For example, if the data suggest a growth curve, such as the increases for $1,000 gaining compound annual interest, a linear equation would produce a forecast appropriate only for constant increases, such as putting in $100 each year on a $1,000 account.

Summary

Generation of solid data and applications of modern forecasting methods are a prerequisite to good fiscal decision making, and more than rational organization of the city finance department can ensure good budgeting and financing. But sophisticated methods and databases cannot make good decisions happen. Policymakers often ignore or deny the obvious trends.

For example, Detroit's general fund has not been surplus since 2004; it has been relying on long-term debt to pay for short-term operations; the costs of services have not been reduced to match its declining population; and it continues to pay unaffordable pensions and salaries. With $18b in debt and a $1.3b general fund deficit, an emergency manager was appointed by the state of Michigan to assume control of contracts, assets, staff, pay, and benefits. The manager declared the city insolvent and issued a moratorium on debt payments. In late 2013, Detroit was finally declared bankrupt, making it the largest U.S city by population to file for bankruptcy in U.S. history. But the court held that federal bankruptcy law prevailed, meaning that pensions were contractual obligations that could be broken. This may allow the city to improve its financial condition. But it also implies that general obligation bonds could become unsecured debt, which could threaten the $3.7t municipal bond market (*Economist*, 2013d, p. 29; *Economist*, 2013c, pp. 29–30). Measures of poor financial conditions in Detroit were obvious for decades but few adjustments to revenue or expenditure trajectories were taken in response. The budget was not used properly as a tool for fiscal or program management.

In summary, to assess the condition of the revenue function for state or local governments, analysts need to focus on three questions: (1) How efficient and equitable is the design of the property tax and are the methods used to assess property sound? (2) Have prices been set to achieve their policy objectives and do they avoid creating any perverse incentives? And (3) How accurate and timely are the annual revenue forecasts?

Questions

1. Review the revenue options matrix for Baltimore County above. Suppose you are the finance director of a medium-sized, diverse, and complex city. Using the criteria listed, which revenue sources would you support or reject and why?

2. Multiple criteria should be applied to decide on revenue sources. But how should a finance director decide between them in a particular case? Suppose, for example, that a city wants to impose a tax or charge on mobile food businesses? These businesses in such cities as Washington, D.C., are very popular with employees, most of whom are also voters. The businesses and customers claim they are nuisance taxes and drive away legitimate business. The nearby restaurants claim they are paying taxes and demand that the mobiles be taxed as well or regulated to stay away from their potential lunchtime customers. Which criteria would you apply to application of a proposed 2.5 percent commercial rents tax on mobile food vendors? Could you suggest other equitable and efficient revenue sources to resolve the conflict?

3. Rockville City needs to finance a budget for FY 14 of $125m. Its total assessed value is $4.60b. What is its nominal property tax rate? How is this expressed in millage? Mr. Apple's residence is worth $400k and the assessment ratio in City X is 50 percent. What will be his tax bill for FY 14? What is his effective tax rate?

4. The following list contains government revenue sources (Mikesell, 2011:560). Which ones are: user charges, license taxes, franchise fees, or fiscal monopolies? What are the incentive impacts of each one of these revenue sources?

   a. A fee for the disposal of used tires

   b. A fee to reserve books at the library

   c. A charge for processing the arrest of a convicted drunk driver

   d. A charge for emergency services required when a driver causes an accident through negligence

e. A charge by the fire department to pump water from basements flooded by a downpour

f. A fee for the services of a probation officer

g. A fee for reviewing a developer's plans

h. A fee for police response to a malfunctioning alarm system

i. A charge for ball field use by the youth athletic league

j. Admission to the city zoo

k. A mandatory fee for municipal garbage collection

l. A charge for use of the city municipal garbage collection

m. A charge for yacht owners who dock at the city marina

n. Fees for summer day camp run by the city parks department

o. A higher peak usage fare for public transit users

p. No fees to park at downtown city garages on weekends after 6 p.m.

q. A congestion charge to enter the central city.

5. For pricing purposes, marginal costs are not equal to variable costs when (indicate all that apply) (Finkler, 2010, p. 159):

a. The time frame for a decision is more than a year

b. There is excess capacity

c. There is a change in fixed costs

d. Some costs are outside an organizational unit making the decision.

6. The Rockville Community Clinic had annual total costs of $2m/year at a volume of 10,000 patients. The fixed costs for the year were $1m.

a. What are the total variable costs for the year? A-$400K

b. What would the total costs be if the volume increased by 10 percent? A-$400K X 1.10 = 440K. Total costs = $2,040m. (Finkler, 2010, p. 161).

Table 2.4. Rockville City Property and Beer/Wine Receipts FY 2010–14

	FY 10	FY 11	FY 12	FY 13	FY 14
PROPERTY TAX					
Anticipated	$2,100,000	$2,200,000	$2,500,000	$2,800,000	$3,050,000
Collected	$1,884,063	$2,267,520	$3,591,164	$3,097,164	$2,717,573
BEER AND WINE TAX					
Anticipated	$780,000	$700,000	$860,000	$1,120,000	$1,280,000
Collected	$753,734	$892,864	$1,163,368	$1,297,038	$1,368,798

Here are some revenue collection figures compared with those anticipated or forecasted beforehand for Rockville City FY 2010–14. The top five sources are: property taxes, sales and use tax, special taxes and licenses, beer and wine excise tax, and gross earnings from the local power utility (based on full cost + markup pricing). Note the difference between collections and forecasts and ask what might have caused the variance. As noted, two large revenue sources for the general fund have been the property tax and beer and wine tax receipts. Receipts for the beer and wine tax exceeded forecasted amounts almost every year. Conversely, receipts for the property tax were about the same as forecasted during the period. What may be causing this? Use the averaging technique to forecast revenues for both sources for FY 15.

7. Below are ridership data for Washington Metropolitan Area Transit Authority (WMATA) for 1999–2008. Using the linear regression technique, forecast the number of unlinked trips for Metrorail for 2009–11. The unlinked trips measure counts multiple boardings and trips, which is a more accurate picture of ridership than linked trips, which assume that people take single origin-destination trips regardless of the number of intermediate boardings and departures.

8. In early 2013, the Virginia attorney general declared the governor's proposal to impose a special transportation tax on the two most congested regions, Northern Virginia and Hampton Roads, unconstitutional. It is estimated that the tax would generate $1.2b/year to cover state transportation needs. In his view, the constitution prohibits special taxes on regions, only on the basis of nongeographic criteria, such as population density. How could the General Assembly revise the formula to meet this constitutional hurdle?

Table 2.5. WMATA Ridership

Fiscal Year	Annual Vehicle Revenue Miles	Annual Vehicle Revenue Hours	Annual Unlinked Trips	Annual Passenger Trips
1999				
Metrobus	33,168,939	2,979,138	143,240,114	474,568,951
Metrorail	46,168,880	2,165,262	212,620,976	1,044,763,469
Metro Access	2,528,931	173,872	210,078	2,018,978
2000				
Metrobus	34,192,726	3,095,948	129,524,241	452,885,175
Metrorail	48,243,553	2,200,599	218,273,257	1,190,448,841
Metro Access	3,643,119	238,648	246,071	2,498,629
2001				
Metrobus	36,447,570	3,247,015	142,647,640	457,028,244
Metrorail	51,553,445	2,318,049	235,731,728	1,352,856,338
Metro Access	5,569,594	357,000	558,932	5,419,598
2002				
Metrobus	37,934,187	3,349,152	147,771,191	450,763,806
Metrorail	52,192,185	2,269,529	242,794,078	1,438,333,161
Metro Access	8,021,812	505,106	738,284	8,021,812
2003				
Metrobus	38,897,449	3,433,521	147,831,547	447,551,132
Metrorail	56,470,216	2,241,771	243,188,046	1,451,555,553
Metro Access	9,788,953	531,341	972,436	8,786,650
2004				
Metrobus	38,901,318	3,458,658	146,010,344	436,436,653
Metrorail	58,205,385	2,312,490	250,659,980	1,507,078,920
Metro Access	11,030,419	683,401	1,112,358	12,263,308
2005				
Metrobus	58,206,385	3,422,903	153,392,000	453,299,328
Metrorail	58,206,385	2,400,432	259,430,088	1,401,106,159
Metro Access	12,179,777	765,719	1,253,948	13,686,283
2006				
Metrobus	38,889,944	3,657,092	132,880,812	423,501,768
Metrorail	63,577,383	2,513,934	274,767,272	1,577,789,264
Metro Access	12,135,331	1,015,815	1,340,201	14,318,204
2007				
Metrobus	38,939,524	3,600,618	133,695,295	416,055,395
Metrorail	66,988,010	2,635,021	207,907,332	1,583,657,621
Metro Access	12,459,287	1,123,848	1,276,870	17,442,601
2008				
Metrobus	38,038,641	3,639,952	132,848,806	445,952,733
Metrorail	68,455,275	2,916,819	288,039,725	1,639,628,551
Metro Access	15,000,435	1,303,915	1,712,537	20,035,683

3

Budget Requests and Expenditure Analysis

Challenges and Responses

Unless the fiscal path of federal spending can be put on a more sustainable course, efforts will continue to push its deficit down to state and local levels through such devices as preemption of state revenues and unfunded mandates. Antitax and antigovernment forces at all levels of government continue to focus on spending cuts with the immediate result of fewer federal grants to finance state and local programs and projects. Nevertheless, with growing pension, infrastructure, education, and social safety net requirements, state and local governments are finding ways to improve their budget processes, modify the composition of their budgets to achieve more value for money, and find alternative sources of financing to make ends meet. Austerity focuses the mind.

The transport sector is critical for growth and employment at all levels of government. Highways, bridges, tunnels, railway, air, and seaport facilities in poor condition are bottlenecks to growth. Spending more on infrastructure is the classic way to stimulate the domestic economy. But, despite optimal conditions for investing in infrastructure to improve growth (i.e., low interest rates and high unemployment), the prospect looks bleak for more federal funding in the transport sector. Self-imposed austerity policies restrain spending and borrowing to try and balance the federal budget. This pushes responsibilities for infrastructure down to state and local levels in the federal system.

While federal capital grants for public transit declined in 1996–2006 from more than 50 percent to 43 percent, state and local governments must pay not only the other 57 percent for capital facilities and rolling stock but also 86 percent of the operating subsidies (Gifford, 2012, p. 605). The effects of the Great Recession on state and local capital stock have been severe. Part of the problem is that their capital budgeting processes have been pro-cyclical: cutting investments in recessions and increasing them during growth periods (Marlowe, 2012, p. 658). Subnational governments have redesigned their capital planning and budgeting processes to require more analysis and to ensure consistency with strategic objectives. Following the example of Europe and elsewhere, they have also experimented with private capital financing methods to build, operate, and maintain facilities. Pension liabilities continue to grow and wreak havoc on such cities as Detroit, as noted previously. More cities will face insolvency and bankruptcy unless budgets face the scarcities, fund effective services, and finance them equitably and efficiently. As is known, many pension systems are in trouble because their unfunded liabilities cannot be covered by investment earnings. It is difficult for state and local governments to contribute more to the funds to make up the losses since their operating budgets are in deficit and revenue sources have weakened.

In response, jurisdictions such as Michigan, Nebraska, and Alaska avoided much of the crisis by conservative pension fund governance and adding requirements that new employees receive defined contribution benefits rather than historically generous defined benefits (Listokin-Smith, 2012, p. 857). Other states, such a: Missouri and Utah, have followed suit with this and other reforms such as employee contribution increases, reduction of benefits, reduced cost of living adjustments, and increased retirement age requirements (2012, p. 860). These reformist jurisdictions used financial and budgetary analysis to make hard but effective pension management choices for long-term sustainability. They continue to use their budget processes to stay in solid fiscal condition.

Evaluating Expenditure Requests

As noted in the first chapter, the budget process is the singular opportunity to match program, service, and project needs with scarce resources. It is more than numbers crunching and requires realistic planning and performance analysis to be effective. It was also noted above that in addition to the object of expenditure format, which focuses on resources used or inputs, states and cities use formats that link inputs to outputs, such as performance budgets, and inputs to outcomes, such as program budgets. The latter two formats employ performance measures and cost accounting of the type discussed in chapter 2. It is critical that managers be able to estimate and track the costs and volumes of services in order to know what improvements might be made, and where cuts should be rationally focused if revenues collapse. The opposite is also true. With sudden surpluses, the state or locality needs to know how to sensibly allocate funds. In the above example of the sudden 2013 surplus in the state of Texas, partisan priorities immediately took over to govern allocations—GOP to infrastructure and Democrats to school operations (*Economist*, 2013d, p. 30). Useful methods to determine cost effectiveness can be employed by finance officers to at least recommend more objective criteria for spending than simple electoral or district level politics. For instance, use of such methods can point to services and programs that are not breaking even and might be outsourced to save funds. The budget formulation and request phase of the budget process affords this opportunity for analysis of needs and how they translate into programs and services.

This chapter focuses on two related parts of budget formulation: (1) the elements of a budget request, and (2) tools for estimating current or operating expenditures for the year.

Elements of the Budget Request

The annual request is built from departments to the whole budget in a bottom-up construction process. The top-down part occurs when fiscal and political constraints are applied from the top down by the finance department and later the city council or state legislature during the final approval process. As noted in chapter 1 using the example of the City of Milwaukee, the budget request is developed during the roughly five-month formulation phase of the budget cycle according to the budget calendar. This is the managerial or cost accounting phase during which information is generated for managers to improve service and fiscal results. The basic data needed to develop a persuasive request for funding are: expenditures or outlays, costs of resources needed, activity statistics or results measures, and revenues. These data should be developed and revised continuously throughout the fiscal year. The six key analytic steps in development of the budget request are: (1) identification of core performance results, demand, and workload measures; (2) identification of major issues and institutional constraints to cost and results performance; (3) analysis of cost-volume relations with results implications of reducing or increasing workloads;

(4) identifying alternatives to current methods of performing activities and their cost and service implications, including risks; (5) estimating expenditure needs for the year; and (6) developing the transmittal letter (Powdar, 1996, p. 63).

Identification of Core Performance Measures KPI

The first item on the agenda is for departments to develop performance measures for its activities. Fire Services can be used to illustrate the types of measures:

1. Inputs—salary and nonsalary resources such as supplies paid for from the budget. For urban transport, a useful measure is staff quality utilization, for example, labor hours/productive service hour (Glover, 1994, pp. B-5, B-6).

2. Demand—number and value of residences requiring fire protection. For urban transport this would be projected ridership for next year by mode, for example, para-transit, bus. and rail.

3. Workload—number of fires responded to. For urban transport, this could be number of buses, trains in service per day.

4. Efficiency—often called *productivity* an example would be the number of responses per crew. Beyond the physical ratios, such as pupil/teacher ratios or responses/crew/quarter, the measure typically relates costs or expenditures to results, for example, operating cost or expenditures per passenger mile or vehicle mile or number of revenue capacity miles for urban transport (Glover, 1994, p. B-5).

Figure 3.1. How to Meet Expenditure Targets. DILBERT © 2004 Scott Adams.

5. Effectiveness—outcomes or program impact—average response
time to emergency call (Powdar, 1996, pp. 61–62). For urban public transport, examples could be: percentage of population served;
route spacing; geographic coverage; percentage of late trips; fre-
quency of service (or average headway) (Glover, 1994, p. B-6),
and reduction of road congestion. Schools have moved beyond
amounts spent as a measure of effectiveness to what they actually
do—producing learning measured in test scores, graduation rates,
and retention rates. In some cities such as Milwaukee, accountability for outcomes is measured by linking resources spent with
the rate of household and commercial fire deaths. The departmental objective is to reduce the number of fire deaths as measured by
a three-year average (*Plan and Budget 2003*, pp. 121–122). While
linking resource inputs to outputs requires controlling for other
causal variables (the attribution problem), it allows for policy and
management questions to be asked in order to improve effectiveness. Analysis of input-outcomes data and possible causes for the
discrepancy in reduced response times and increased fire death
rates, found that lack of functioning fire alarms was the cause.
This enabled funds to be reprogrammed for greater effectiveness.
Ironically, the city then spent less on fire services and achieved
more outcomes! In Milwaukee's GFOA award-winning budget
presentation, the results measure then ties the objective to the
actual result. Figure 3.2 illustrates two examples of the above types
of measures, one for the City of Milwaukee Fire Department and
the other for a hypothetical social services assistance department
budget. Note how outcome objectives drive funding decisions in
the Milwaukee example.

The above chart provides the operating details, financing requirements,
and resources for a social services program that is in part the responsibility of
the social assistance department (SSAD). From the perspective of departmental program management, SSAD could then be viewed as an organizational
subunit or cost/responsibility center with three major subprograms, namely, (1)
administration, (2) social services, and (3) capital investment. Identification of
performance measures is by now a routine exercise and few budgets are available
to the public without such efforts. The more important issue is how to narrow
the vast number of performance indicators out there for all services to a core
list on which managers agree they should be monitored as well during budget

success in 2002, the 2003 budget provides $462,000 in CDBG funding to continue this expanded program.

"Fireflies" Child Care and Fire Education: Initiated in 2001, the Fireflies Summer Program provides fire education to children in the daycare setting. In 2002, approximately 150 children between the ages of 2 to 12 years spent two hours per week with Fire Fighters learning fire prevention and education techniques (e.g., Stop, Drop and Roll) and also participated in a basic exercise program. The Fire Department has found this program to be a valuable tool in teaching children the dangers of fire and other hazards. Due to its success, the department plans to expand this program to other daycare centers in 2003.

OBJECTIVE 2

Reduce effects of personal injury and property loss through timely provision of fire suppression, emergency medical, and other emergency services as measured by a response time of five minutes or less for 95.0% of calls received in 2003.

OUTCOME HISTORY

In 2001, the Fire Department responded to roughly 65,300 incidents. Response time to these incidents totaled five minutes or less in 92.7% of all cases. While slightly lower than the 95.0% goal, the 2001 response time data shows improvement in this area over past years. For example, for the years 1993, 1995, and 1996 only 90.5% of calls were responded to within five minutes.

Figure 2 illustrates that response times tend to lengthen during the winter months when weather conditions can adversely affect travel. The trend line indicates that the percentage of calls responded to in five minutes or less has remained relatively constant over 2000 and 2001. The Fire Department's goal is to improve this trend in 2003 by responding to 95.0% of calls received in less than five minutes.

In the 2003 budget, $66.7 million in operating resources will contribute to a total of $76.9 million allocated to this objective.

ACTIVITIES

- EMS operations
- Fire suppression
- Special teams emergency services
  - Haz-Mat
  - HURT
  - Dive Rescue

Outcome Indicators and Funding

	2001 Experience	2002 Budget	2003 Projection
Percentage of responses within five minutes of call.	92.7%	95.0%	95.0%
Funding by Source:			
Operating Funds	$72,853,924	$67,666,662	$66,728,916
Grant and Reimbursable	4,725,228	4,872,455	5,018,628
Capital Budget	412,800	2,730,000	5,105,000
Total:	$77,991,952	$75,269,117	$76,852,544

Figure 2

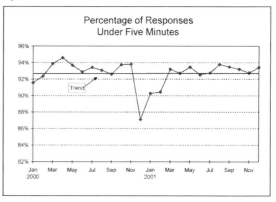

- Facility and equipment maintenance
- Inspections

PROGRAM CHANGES

Improve the Provision of Advanced Life Support Services Through Reassigning Paramedic Staff: The 2003 budget reduces staffing on the Fire Department's eight MED (ALS) units from three per-

Figure 3.2. Program Performance Budget Examples.

implementation. Very few states or cities fail to identify and use performance measures for programs and services. The days of simply using amounts spent as a proxy for results are long past.

This said, some jurisdictions do not go far enough and hide as much as they reveal by failure to focus on what is important; in other cases further progress depends on empirical research linking inputs to outcomes. More importantly, few governments have used performance budgeting to allocate resources by unit costs across programs or sectors. This refers to technical problems of comparing unit costs of diverse services rather than the disincentives to use performance information for allocations by practitioners (since it amounts to work on top of their usual reporting requirements) and legislators. The latter are elected by constituents in districts; they represent them best through line-item trading rather than rationally analyzed programs.

The problem of hiding issues within modern performance formats is illustrated by school and university budgets. For example, the FY 2009 budget for Anacostia High School in Washington, D.C., indicated that 76 percent of the resources were to be spent on *instruction* as opposed to *instructional support* or *leadership*. But computers and supplies were included in instruction (rather than as support), as well as administrators, such as principals and assistant principals (Guess & Farnham, 2011, p. 130). Washington, D.C., schools are famous for having the highest spending per pupil (about $13k/year compared to the $8k U.S. average [Fisher, 2007:504]), the highest spending per school administrator, and the lowest classroom results in the United States. By adding in unrelated categories of personnel to instruction, the problem is magically solved on the input side. But the results remain a problem! That is where more research is required linking expenditures to classroom results or outcomes. The black box of teaching is a well-known mix of art and science but also depends on other factors such as classroom disciplinary policies and exercise of fiscal accountability at the school level.

Similarly, the FY 2012 American University budget lumps faculty and staff together in the object of expenditure classification (2011, p. 6). This is false transparency in that one of the major issues causing rising tuition payments in the United States is the increase in administrative costs. According to Lane (2013, p. A15), in Minnesota, administrative and other nonteaching personnel costs have in the past decade increased three times as fast as the teaching payroll and twice as fast as student enrollment. This is a nationwide phenomenon that is a significant cause of the surge in tuition (Lane, 2013). Since 82 percent of the AU budget is financed by tuition and only 2 percent comes from gifts

AMERICAN UNIVERSITY FY2012 REVENUE AND EXPENDITURE BUDGET

REVENUE (S000's)	FY2011 Budget	Budget Changes	FY2012 Budget	% Change
Student Tuition and Fees	$390,960	$50,371	$441,331	12.9%
New Revenue Initiatives	0	500	500	n/a
Residence Halls	34,272	3,500	37,772	10.2%
Auxiliary Enterprises	28,418	9,279	37,697	32.7%
Investment Income	4,000	500	4,500	12.5%
Unrestricted Gifts	750	0	750	0.0%
Indirect Cost Recovery	2,200	(200)	2,000	(9.1%)
Endowment Income	3,200	0	3,200	0.0%
WAMU-FM Revenue	15,400	5,600	21,000	36.4%
Total Revenue	$479,200	$69,550	$548,750	14.5%

EXPENDITURES (S000's)	FY2011 Budget	Budget Changes	FY2012 Budget	% Change
Faculty and Staff Salaries	$162,204	$9,973	$172,178	6.1%
Adjunct Faculty Salaries	6,474	463	6,937	7.2%
Parttime Staff	15,906	768	16,674	4.8%
Employee Benefits	42,565	4,446	47,010	10.4%
Transfer to Fund Sept. 2011 Salary Increase	(3,800)	(100)	(3,900)	2.6%
Transfer to Pre-Fund Sept. 2012 Salary Increase	3,900	100	4,000	2.6%
Salaries and Benefits	$227,250	$15,650	$242,900	6.9%
Financial Aid	91,008	10,302	101,310	11.3%
Supplies and Expenses, etc.	92,048	19,572	111,619	21.3%
Instructional Revenue Centers (Institutes)	7,579	3,060	10,639	40.4%
Library Acquisitions	5,438	520	5,958	9.6%
Utilities	9,512	0	9,512	0.0%
Technology Capital Funding	5,650	2,925	8,575	51.8%
Deferred Maintenance Fund (including residence halls)	10,901	500	11,401	4.6%
Furnishings and Equipment Fund	1,900	0	1,900	0.0%
Facilities Modernization Fund	3,100	1,000	4,100	32.3%
Debt Service	17,294	3,000	20,294	17.3%
WCL Additional Expenditures	0	8,370	8,370	n/a
KSB Additional Expenditures	0	1,856	1,856	n/a
WAMU Additional Expenditures	0	4,321	4,321	n/a
Transfer to Quasi-Endowment Funds	9,600	1,110	10,710	11.6%
Enrollment Contingency Fund	900	2,207	3,107	245.2%
Transfer to Fund Strategic Plan Initiatives	(2,980)	(4,842)	(7,822)	162.5%
Total Expenditures	$479,200	$69,550	$548,750	14.5%

Net Surplus/(Deficit)	$0	$0	$0	

Figure 3.3. American University Budget FY 2012.

and investments, one would want this breakdown in order to identify possible efficiencies. But note that it is not there.

Four newer performance budgeting approaches are in use. First, formula funding systems present budgets based on an algebraic function of planned output activity and cost. This means budgeting based on unit costs, for example, cost/vaccination by number of expected vaccinations. So $20/units x 100k vaccinations planned = $2m budget request. The purpose of this system is to pressure departments to provide funding and improve their efficiency (Robinson, 2012, p. 241). Second, the purchaser-provider system applies the principle of payment by results, meaning that funding is determined by the quantity of output actually delivered times a price based broadly on unit cost. For example, if a hospital delivers fewer vaccinations than budgeted it loses money. If it delivers them for lower prices it makes a surplus. The most widely used system is the diagnostic-related group (DRG) hospital funding system developed in the United States and now used in twenty countries to fund public hospitals. DRG is one incentive mechanism used by the Affordable Health Care Act (ACA) to contain or lower health care costs and increase efficiencies.

Third, the bonus funding system pays institutions for performance. Agencies provide supplemental funding on top of core funding through grants or direct expenditures to institutions such as hospitals. This is also an incentive system to contain costs and achieve higher outputs or outcomes. For example, bonus funding would be provided for higher hospital customer satisfaction survey results, higher graduation rates (some U.S. states and Ontario province), and reduced operating costs/passenger mile (U.S. federal transit block grants to transit systems). Fourth, budget-linked target systems (unlike most performance budgeting systems) require linkage of government or departmental performance targets to budgets, that is, they are determined at the same time rather than in separate processes. The major example of this was the U.K. Performance Service Agreement (PSA) system 1997–2007 in which the finance ministry linked hundreds of service targets to multiyear budget allocations (Robinson, 2012, p. 243). Performance-program budgeting systems and their four improvements have been successful in improving sectoral performance, for instance, health, education, transport. As a government-wide system, they run into the problem of incomparable unit costs across services, such as cost/murder investigation versus cost/hospital emergency service provision. While each can be compared with norms and activity statistics in comparable jurisdictions, particular governments would be unable to use them exclusively to allocate funds between law enforcement and health care (2012:249). Governments should then use performance and value for money-based budgeting systems as one source of data for their global budgets but evaluate sectors on the basis of such data and information.

Major Issues and Institutional Constraints

Regardless of which formats are used, budget requests need to be persuasive; each department competes against all others for a limited amount of funds each year. This means that requests cannot simply beg for more money, perhaps on the theory that it needs to deal with the effects of increased inflation on the costs of its service activities. The departments must show that in spite of fiscal constraints, they face challenges from institutional and regulatory sources, as well as from problems unique to their program or service area. Each department represents an industry, such as health, education, urban transport, or social services, that is characterized by fiscal constraints and many reformist efforts by cities and states. Budget guardians in councils, legislatures, and central finance offices are often aware of these constraints and successful efforts elsewhere to deal with them. They know that such successes often did not require more funds and in some cases required less. It is wiser to preempt these arguments in the request and respond to them with illustrations of departmental efforts to be more efficient and effective. Each department needs to demonstrate this honesty and transparency and, as some have called it, "reveal their dirty laundry" in this section of the annual request.

For example, Medicare costs are rising rapidly and the political response has been fervor to cut entitlements. But many of these costs are due to outdated congressional rules that require inflated payments, for example $5000 for wheelchairs that cost the supplier $700 and sell retail for $2500. The institutional constraint to budget performance here is called durable medical equipment, prosthetics, orthotics and supplies, or DMEPOS (Lane, 2013b). These types of legal and regulatory constraints need to be detailed in the annual budget request.

Similarly, in the above Social Service budget example, note that the department indicates how it is constrained in monitoring social service homes by the absence of a performance monitoring system and the fact that the central government provides 100 percent of the capital financing but the local department must pay100 percent of operations. These are more structural or legal constraints to efficiency and effectiveness, that is, more funds will not necessarily improve things. The Milwaukee capital budget request for 2003–08 notes in compelling narrative that administrative challenges occurred in the past, such as budget overruns and contention regarding controlling decision-making authority for changes to the original plan. The split of authority and responsibility between the Public Works Department, the "customer departments" (service and program departments with projects), and the Budget and Management Department caused problems in accurate estimation of project expenditures and design/construction changes, as well as communications between units of government responsible for the capital budget (Milwaukee, 2003b, p. 5). The budget indicates how the city has responded to this challenge with greater authority exercised now by the BMD and tighter monitoring and reporting requirements for the Common Council. The request provides an honest appraisal of the problem, details its implications for spending results, and details what the city is doing to fix the problem (ibid.).

Cost-Volume Relationships

The amount of available funding may be clear before the request is even finished. The finance department issues a budget call often with a fixed ceiling and allowable inflation rates for particular items. The department finance officers will thus have some indication of whether more or less funding will be available. This knowledge is refined by indications of policy emphases according to the city or state strategic plan, for instance, more education, infrastructure, and environmental protection. In response, the departments should reveal their methodologies for either cutback or expansion of services. Beyond estimates of costs and consequences of service cutbacks (e.g., time and cost constraints imposed on commuters facing fewer buses and drivers) or additions (e.g., greater responsiveness, coverage, and social benefits), the departments should indicate cost-volume relationships. Finance departments have limited time and resources like all the other departments. In-house performance of basic cost-volume analyses should be possible without requiring "research" or calling in a consultant.

Referring back to the discussion of costs and service volumes in chapter 2, it is evident that: (1) costs are not expenditures because of distortionary factors and differences in timing; and (2) service cost-volume relations are not linear because fixed-variable cost behavior changes with volume for each type of service. *Expenditures* are budget outlays derived from legislative appropriations. They are affected by legal and institutional factors such as the rules noted above that inflate outlays. By contrast, *costs* are expenses related to use of goods and services, and reflect market prices. They may occur at different times than expenditures, such as purchases of supplies and depreciation on equipment for snow removal. *Marginal costs* are all costs that would vary from an extra unit of output or volume (e.g., serving one more student). The costs will be both fixed and variable but only some of them may vary or increase over certain ranges.

This needs to be known for each service. Thus, it is important to measure costs of services and unit costs for determining trend performance, comparison with an offer of a private contractor to perform the service, and determining how much is saved by cutting the program (Kory & Rosenberg, 1984, pp. 50–51).

One method is called *cost-finding* (1984:51) and involves piecing together source documents, such as invoices and purchase orders, to convert expenditures to expenses. Cost-finding is considered a less formal but easier to use system for converting expenditures to costs by assigning all costs (derived from examination of basic source documents such as invoices and purchase orders) and assigning them all to the period in which they occurred (Coe, 1989, p. 45). This allows more rigorous distinctions between fixed, variable, direct, and indirect costs for purposes of determining the cost of a unit of service. Once total and unit costs of service are determined, cost comparisons with private firms and impacts of service reductions and additions can be provided. For instance, even though payroll and purchasing transaction expenditures and expenses are about the same, expenditures can be distorted by such factors as: sicknesses, unfilled vacancies, random pay increases during the year, and overtime. These could inflate payroll expenditures (which may be up to 70% of some departmental budgets) and make comparison with a contract offering difficult.

Suppose that a refuse company offers Rockville City collection service at $30/household/year. Using cost finding, Rockville has determined that its cost/unit here is $40/household. But if fixed costs of $10/household continue after contracting out, the city should continue to perform the service in-house (Kory & Rosenberg, 1984, p. 58). Rockville will also need to project the point at which remaining fixed costs increase or decrease. Some step-function or semi-fixed/variable costs continue to run with the service. These need to be examined and explained in the request as the basis for indicating the costs and consequences of service increases or decreases. As indicated in Figure 2.6, step-function (semi-fixed; semi-variable) costs increase in tandem over a relevant range, then change based on fixed cost requirements. At that point, it may want to revisit the contracting decision.

In fact, full cost accounting or activity-based costing systems are rare in state and local governments. They are often costly themselves to install and maintain databases. In response, finance managers use a mixed form of negotiated systems that combine hard cost and expenditure data (using such techniques as cost-finding) with the realities of internal staff-line and strategic politics to make allocation choices (Guess, 1988, p. 60). Starting from the top, the reality is that most cuts and additions can be viewed according to the following technical-political matrix (Table 3.1).

Table 3.1. Political versus Technical Budget Cutting Strategies

Political Strategy	Technical-Economic Strategy
1. Capital Investment-infrastructure (i.e., ST invisibility) and maintenance use capital funds to balance operating budget (MC)	1. Discretionary-services like #37; positions/staff; reorganization; cut HC commitments (MD)
2. Fixed-cut fiscal transfers, social benefits, minor equipment	2. Fixed-move to cut rent; outsource to cut administrative costs; pensions 22% of MC budget
3. Discretionary-use reserve funds, maintain salaries, furloughs, and cut positions; no new programs; divert dedicated revenues to fund operations-salaries; arrears, delay	3. Capital-sacrifices growth and costs more O&M later

Based on political criteria, capital and other running costs are cut first in order to protect salaries and positions. This is why state and local governments often underinvest in capital during recessions. Technical-economic criteria produce the opposite order, with capital cut last and salaries and positions first. But that approach is simply unrealistic in most service areas. The sensible budget cutting method would be to use capital budgets as countercyclical tools to absorb unemployed labor, generate income and tax revenues, and generally stimulate demand.

A mixed system developed for MARTA (Guess, 1988, p. 61) was based on the familiar technique for allocating funds based on the estimated costs and consequences of increases or decreases from particular base percentages. Known as: *zero-based budgeting*, ZBB had a rough ride during implementation at all levels of government, to wit, it was never "zero" and usually required calculation of costs and consequences for less stringent effects such as 100 percent base, 75 percent base and 50 percent base. While it has been largely discredited in the academic literature, this ignores the importance of the technique in forcing a number of important reforms that still persist in many state and local governments often under other budget system names (!): (1) producing cost/unit calculations; (2) forcing departments to think in terms of cost centers as units of service delivery (e.g., schools and hospitals); (3) attempts at measuring costs/consequences of alternate funding levels; and (4) most importantly, the largely successful efforts to bring the legislature into the budget analysis process with executive finance departments. The fourth achievement meant that allocations would be based on political criteria using a good deal of technical cost information from the departments.

One sensible approach to budget cutting is for the county, city, or state to develop a cost-savings strategy that applies cooperatively across jurisdictions. Gallatin County (Montana) has implemented about thirty related efforts in this regard. Three of them should be emphasized for practitioners to share elsewhere. First, it consolidated functional services such as solid waste removal with the city and plans to focus on other functions. Second, it merged departments to reduce structural inefficiencies, for example, the procurement and facilities departments. Third, it employed deeper cost-effectiveness analysis in review of make-buy decisions. Gallatin County now uses skilled semiretired employees part-time to save costs below those offered even by private contractors (Mathers, 2009).

Finally, as discussed above, it is difficult for councils and legislatures to rationally allocate funds with dissimilar ends and results, for instance, cured patients versus educated students. While interpersonal utility preferences cannot be compared, rational criteria can narrow the range of debate on which programs should be given preference. To provide justification for more funding or to indicate the rationale for reallocation of resources within programs, it is possible to employ cost-effectiveness criteria using a marginal productivity or input-output curve. Cost-effectiveness presumes a benefit but does not compare it with costs. The method is focused only on primary benefits (i.e., time saved and fewer accidents versus lives saved by a railroad traffic crossing). The assumption is that the benefit must have monetary value; the value of the benefits themselves is not taken into account. It seeks the most effective high-quality alternative to achieve the most primary monetized benefits for the least monetary cost (Michel, 2001, p. 78).

The budget request, for instance, could answer the logical question likely to be posed by a council: How and why should the social services department invest (either in-house or through an NGO contractor) an additional $100k across its four subprograms to cure alcoholics for the next fiscal year? As illustrated in Tables 3.2, 3.3, and 3.4 and Figure 3.4 on page 100), the marginal productivity curve can combine performance measurement and basic costing to produce a rigorous justification (Lehan, 1984, pp. 41–55).

The unit cost and cumulative data (highest returns, lowest unit costs for lowest investment) for this program suggest that if additional funds are to be invested for alcoholic treatment, they should be invested in the mutual help

Table 3.2. Allocative Criteria: Unit Measures and Investment Returns Treatment of Alcoholics: Cost Data

Cost Centers	Clients	%	Hours	%	Fixed Costs	Variable Costs
Crisis Intervention	100	25%	600	10%	10,000	6,000
Mutual Self Help						
Groups	120	30%	1500	25%	12,000	15,000
Family Therapy	80	20%	2100	35%	8,000	21,000
Individual Counseling	100	25%	1800	30%	10,000	18,000
TOTAL	400		6000		40,000	60,000

Table 3.3. Treatment of Alcoholics: Data by Subprogram

Cost Centers	Fixed Costs	Variable Costs	Total Cost or Investment	Unit Measure, # of Clients	Unit Costs
Crisis Intervention	10,000	6,000	16,000	100	160
Mutual Self Help					
Groups	12,000	15,000	27,000	120	225
Family Therapy	8,000	21,000	29,000	80	362.50
Individual Counseling	10,000	18,000	28,000	100	280
TOTAL	40,000	60,000	100,000	400	

Table 3.4. Marginal Productivity Curve Schedule: Alcoholic Treatment Program

Cost Centers	Investment	Cumulative Investment	Estimated Cures	Cumulative Costs
Crisis Intervention	16,000	16,000	0	0
Mutual Self Help Groups	27,000	43,000	50	50
Family Therapy	29,000	72,000	25	75
Individual Counseling	28,000	100,000	15	90

groups where funding is yielding higher and increasing returns than in the other two subprograms, which are yielding fewer benefits and at a declining rate. The same kind of "Lazy S" curve (Lehan, 1984, p. 56) could be used to compare programs with dissimilar ends (V. O. Key's classic dilemma of how to justify

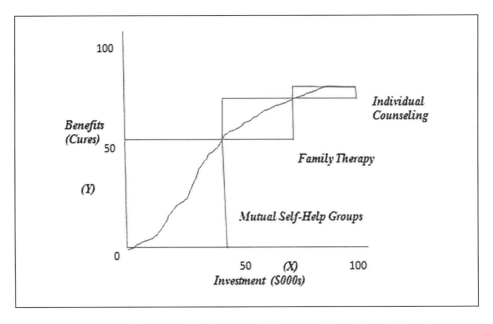

Figure 3.4. Marginal Program Productivity: Effects on Three Sets of Beneficiaries.

program A versus B?). To compare net returns, the benefits must be monetized, for example, changes in educational efficiency as measured by test score levels and trends versus cured alcoholic patients. Increasing or decreasing utility as measured by number of clients cured versus student test scores increased would justify a shift from one program to the other in the request. The value of educated students and cured patients cannot be compared morally or socially. But they can be compared if, as noted above, benefits are monetized using the cost-effectiveness method.

Alternative Service Delivery Options

Finance officers should include an "alternatives analysis" in the request, including the option of doing nothing (i.e., not investing in a project; not changing delivery systems). Based on its calculations of fixed, variable, marginal, and unit costs, projected service volumes, and core performance measures, the department should indicate in its request how it can deliver service more efficiently and effectively. As noted above, it may be able to work through a purchaser-provider system to obtain a fixed level of funding in exchange for results. Analytic aids to decision making are available and widely in use in state-local governments and should be considered as tools rather than sources of truth. Much of the problem of how to improve performance revolves around risks: risks that morale will suffer if programs are outsourced; risks that contractors will not provide service quality or coverage as expected; and risks that if the wrong choice is made hiring/firing decisions will raise institutional and political costs and delay plans for other activities. Decisions must balance potential savings with the risks that needed service quality and coverage will not occur, leaving finance departments and elected officials open to criticism. In short, just as budgets are more than mere accounting documents, service performance decisions cannot be made only on narrow financial criteria.

A recurring issue today for finance departments is how to decide whether it is cheaper to make or deliver services in-house versus buying or contracting for them. As noted, Gallatin County, Montana, even uses part-time skilled retirees to deliver services, which serves community employment needs, provides budgetary savings, and delivers quality services. There are three simple methods that are employed for make/buy decisions:

1. *Marginal Analysis*, or, out of pocket analysis for change in service volume. This method has been discussed and is largely useful for determining when fixed costs will increase to a point at which it is wiser to find a contractor that will perform the service (e.g., schools and more capital facilities for students; transit service and more rolling stock and rehabilitation costs to accommodate more riders). Since average or unit costs relate inversely and directly to volume (e.g., decreasing with more volume), cities and states will want to use marginal not average costs as the basis for pricing performance contracts where fixed and variable costs do not change in linear fashion with volume, that is, most services.

2. *Break-Even Analysis* is used to calculate subsidy (or losses) for activities with revenue potential, such as urban transport lines, public pools, conferences, community feeding programs, recreation services, and charter schools. For these, finance officers typically have the basic parameters: total costs (fixed and variable), total revenues, and they need the break-even volume. These figures are similar to those used for calculation of *operating ratios* (costs/dollar earned) in the private sector. This works for the many public sector fee–financed activities that generate profits or losses (review Figure 2.6 Income-Based Pricing for this section). Suppose the Rockville City Municipal Orchestra incurs $1m fixed costs/year. The variable costs for each person attending one of the orchestra's performances have been estimated at only $2. The average charge for a ticket to attend a performance is $60. How many tickets must it sell each year to break even?

The formula for break-even volume (BEV) is:

$$\text{BEV} = \frac{\text{Fixed Costs}}{\text{Price or Revenue} - \text{Variable Costs}}$$

The result indicates that the BEV is 17,241 tickets (Finkler, 2010:164).

Break-even analysis enables Rockville City to examine strategies on how services might be improved. Using the results of this tool, the first question is how to reduce the break-even volume in case it sales and patronage drop? It can do some or all of the following:

1. Reduce fixed costs by getting by fewer or less expensive ones (Finkler, 2010:142). This is usually not possible. In such cases, it may be cheaper to outsource the management of the opera to a firm.

2. Find internal variable cost efficiencies (e.g., consolidate schools; use part-time staff, consolidate personnel positions) to reduce the variable costs/unit.

3. Increase prices—which will raise revenue in the short term, but if the opera is price elastic (i.e., perhaps with watching opera on TV), this could reduce patronage and revenue.

4. Increase patronage or number of units of service by marketing.

3. *Flexible Budgeting*: provides budget figures for different levels of activity such as public transit and hospital health care. This tool provides two new sources of decision-making information: (a) fiscal managers can now see the

Table 3.5. Rockville Municipal Orchestra Break-Even Analysis

Fixed Costs:	$1,000,000
Variable Costs:	$2 per ticket
Price:	$60 per ticket
Q = FC/P-VC Therefore,	
$1,000,000/$60-$2	= 17,241 tickets

break-even point for an activity or service; and (b) it also reveals how fixed and variable costs are behaving because of changes in volume. For example, some variable costs vary proportionately with volume, such as fuel and supplies; others vary step-variably with volume, such as management and administration in the longer term. Similarly, fixed costs do not vary with volume over a particular range, for instance, fleet management and personnel in the short term. Eventually, some fixed costs will vary with volume. The key concept here is that the amount of resources consumed will vary with the level of workload actually attained (Finkler, 2010, p. 289). Flexible budgeting allows a different angle on break-even calculations for managers.

From Table 3.6, it is evident that the break-even point is about 42k delivered meals. The major contributor to results is the cost of supplies or meals. Using this tool allows managers to focus on that cost in the short term and seek more revenues from donations and the city.

Finally, states and cities in the twenty-first century are beginning to use a new option for service delivery and finance—one that had been typically used for long-term capital investment financing rather than current services: *social impact bonds* or SIBs. They are in use in such countries as the UK (where the tool originated in 2010), cities such as New York City, and states such as Massachusetts and New York (*Economist*, 2013e, p. 71), In New York City, SIBs are used to deliver and finance social services for problems such as drug abuse, inmate recidivism, and homelessness. Note the similarity with the purchaser-provider budgeting system discussed above. The difference is that programs

Table 3.6. Flexible Budget Example: Meals for Homeless

Meals Delivered	35,000	40,000	45,000
REVENUES			
Donations	$105,000	$105,000	$105,000
City	$52,500	$60,000	$67,500
TOTAL REVENUE	$157,500	$165,000	$172,500
EXPENSES			
Salaries	$46,000	$46,000	$46,000
Supplies	$87,500	$100,000	$112,500
Rent	$12,000	$12,000	$12,000
Other	$6,000	$6,000	$6,000
TOTAL EXPENSES:	$151,500	$164,000	$176,500
Surplus/(Deficit)	$6,000	$1,000	$(4,000)

are funded by individual and institutional investors rather than public budgets. SIB bonds are typically sold by the public entity to cover projects that have shorter performance impact expectations. NGOs bid on the service project and promise to meet carefully defined performance targets, for example, one SIB provides an annualized return of 13 percent if reoffending rates do not drop by at least 7.5 percent. The bond funds cover NGOs' (e.g., St. Mungo's, a London homeless charity) costs for periods longer than typical government contracts and this allows them the stability to perform more efficiently. Investors take equity risks in buying the SIB but exercise social responsibility. If the NGO meets the target, the investors that purchase the bonds win, such as individuals and firms like Goldman Sachs. If the NGO fails to meet the targets, investors lose. Investors can gain substantial returns on a typical SIB if the NGO achieves the targets in the time specified. The state or local government saves on service costs by selling SIBs to investors and having NGOs deliver them. Governmental resources consist of the performance measures and targets and monitoring and oversight of reporting of progress and results.

Estimation of Operating Expenditure Needs

This information should be persuasive and follow a sequence from: (1) measurement and (2) analysis to (3) an approval decision on the request from the department. Using some or all of the above tools and methods, the departmental annual service plan is now translated into a narrative with figures for the budget request. Much of what is presented for the request conforms to rather crude forms from the finance department that often seem to dissuade analysis and explanation. Such formality implies that the guardians may have already made up their minds and analysis and persuasion will not make a difference. But they do! Much of what is presented in this chapter may then have to be included in annexes—but they should be included! In this section, we cover several approaches to the first two steps.

1. Measurement

a. *Baseline*: This will be defined in the call for requests but remains an analytically slippery concept. At its simplest, the baseline or base budget is the point at which legislators and administrators measure cuts or increases in spending and taxes. For state-local governments it is often last year's appropriations. But it could also be the amount spent or actual outlays, which would include supplemental funds received during the year.

Each budget function or sector may have its own baseline definition. For instance, in Maryland, state "maintenance of effort" law requires that local schools receive the same minimum per pupil funding as in the past year. If counties spend more than the maintenance threshold, that amount is automatically part of next year's base. If the council fails to meet the legal minimum, the county income tax revenue is funneled directly to the school system! (Turque & Bui, 2013, p. B2). This mandated base can lead to loss of spending control and obligate the state beyond its fiscal means. At the federal level, the baseline is called the current services budget and is the cost of continuing existing programs and policies with no changes in policy and adjusted only for inflation and workload (Axelrod, 1995, p. 14).

b. *Shares*: For maximum transparency to persuade councils and legislatures and to impress rating agencies, budget composition in percentage shares should be indicated in a separate column. It is often frustrating for readers to translate large numbers into percentages so that more precise analytic questions can be asked about allocation and use of funds. Departments should demonstrate this in the proposal, for instance, personnel costs are 30 percent of the total Rockville City budget requested, a drop from past year levels of 32 percent. The request should also indicate the percent change, thus, –2.0 percent. The request should also note that the similar-sized city of Erehwon spent only 24 percent of its total budget for personnel; and the average for all cities of this size, using ICMA data, is 29 percent. In addition, percentages of total past year (two years if possible) and proposed expenditures for wage and nonwage components and capital should be included in the request.

c. *Trends*: Trend estimation is needed for proper forecasting (noted in chapter 2). This refers to the trajectory of spending at current rates or relative percentage changes. The formula is:

$$\frac{\text{FY2 (target)}-\text{FY1 (base)}}{\text{FY 1}= \%} = \% \text{ Change}$$

Examples of relative percentage trends include: (1) (from the U.S. government) the rate of change for current Medicare and Medicaid policies without policy changes will lead from 4.6 percent GDP in 2013 to 12 percent in 2050 and 19 percent GDP in 2082. If Social Security is included and all entitlements are included, the trend is from $1.2t and about 41 percent of total spending in 2013 to $3.0t and 60 percent by 2030; and (2) State of Maryland teacher pension benefit payments have been increasing10 percent/year in the last decade; but contributions to the fund have been only 8 percent/year; during the same years, the trend increase for general fund revenues is only 5 percent/year to 2015. This means that the overall state teacher employee pension gap (unfunded liability) will be $33b. Using the same relative change formula, the Illinois pension liability is now 17 percent of the operating budget; but only 51percent of it is funded (versus 101 percent in New York).

d. *Real Value*: the amounts purchased by departmental budgets depend on the *real* costs of goods and services. That means that the inflationary effects must be stripped away from price changes. Price inflation means that less will be purchased by the departments and that staff will ask for wage cost of living increases to compensate for loss of purchasing power (COLAs). Finance departments need real or constant dollar (as opposed to nominal, current, or cash) figures to demonstrate that (1) increases in spending are not driven mainly by bureaucracy, (2) programs are effective despite increasing costs (meaning fewer units produced unless budget reallocations are made internally), and to provide clear assumptions for budget policy. Often, the finance department will provide the rate of inflation to be used in preparing the annual request.

To measure and control for price changes, analysts need to convert nominal/current to constant/real dollars. To do this, analysts use price indices to measures the changes in the prices of a basket of goods and services purchased by similar buyers. The Implicit Price Deflator or IPD is an aggregate measure of price changes. It is based on updated U.S. Department of Commerce/Bureau of Economic Analysis data on goods and expenditures by level of government.

The formula to convert nominal to constant dollars is:

$$\frac{Current\ Year\$\ (\text{current = any other year than base}) \times Base\ (\text{or reference year})\ IPD}{CY\ IPD} = Constant\ \$$$

In other words, the index identifies how much spending is a reflection of more physical goods versus inflated price changes. For example, using the formula for police salaries/supplies from the base year of 1994 to the current year 2004: the CY nominal or current amount of $1.22m x base year IPD (0.8902 or 89.0 for 1994)/ (1.0917 or 109. 2 CY IPD for 2004) = Constant/real amount of only $997,567.28. That is, current year expenditures in base year dollars are 21 percent less.

e. *Ratios*: An important means of converting raw data into information for decision making is to develop ratios. Ratios do not answer analytic questions but can provide clues for further inquiry (Mikesell, 2011, p. 188). Use of physical and cost ratios can shift the terms of policy debate. For instance, California state government is often accused of bloat and for having too many bureaucrats. Using ratios to illuminate budget shares, it is evident that its 108 officials to 10k population is lower than the national average of 149/10k. Most measures noted for financial condition analysis in chapter 1 (Berne & Schramm, 1986) are ratios, for example, expenditures/capita; debt service as a percentage of total expenditures; operating costs/passenger mile for transit; cost/patient day for health; teaching-classroom expenditures as a percentage of total education expenditures; pupil/teacher ratios; and costs/unit of service. Ratios allow for useful interjurisdictional comparisons and permit analytic focus on the relationships between the numerator (costs) and the denominator (units of service).

2. Analysis

Analysis is the process of measuring, comparing costs (including opportunity costs), benefits, and the consequences of budget choices. Through the application of methods and tools, this process aims to develop reasonable options for mayors and councils, finance directors and legislators. It is not research and should be done in-house and rapidly—some might call it action research. Consulting firms should be used only after initial data and information analysis has taken place by state or local fiscal institutions charged with that purpose, for instance, by internal auditors, budget committees, budget analysts, drawing on existing databases from ICMA and GFOA and relying on NGOs that provide fiscal analysis as a public service.

Many budget format reforms, such as program, zero-based, and performance budgets, have shifted attention to the outputs and outcomes of public expenditures. The view here is that objects of expenditure can also be analyzed and produce similar performance information on which managers can make valid decisions to increase efficiency and effectiveness of programs and services. Use of object of expenditure budgets together with available performance information by program, service, or sector can save the costs in time and resources of changing the rules and repertoires to move toward new formats.

a. *Salary and Wages*: Given that most departments and activities are labor-intensive, it is necessary to develop the operating budget or work program for each segment of the organization (Axelrod, 1995, p. 48). This means estimating the demand, or activities, workloads and outputs. Performance measurement was discussed above and most budgets include results measures. Then the supply side must be estimated: the unit costs and unit times for each output, and the resources needed to produce the outputs. Consistent with performance budgeting, the department begins by estimating staffing requirements by work programming to develop the demand side. The department indicates: standards needing compliance, estimated caseloads, such as patient treatments, student contact hours, and inspections required. The workload then is a reflection of the demand requirements, for example the number of tax returns, the number miles to be maintained, bridges to be inspected, and the number of students enrolled. Multiplying the unit times by costs produces the staffing ratio, such as, the number of tax examiners per 100k returns (1995, p. 51). A sample work program with costs/position is show in Table 3.7.

For indirect and fixed costs such as administration, it is important to try and link positions with workload. That is often hard to do and some jurisdictions attempt to allocate administration costs to activities using predetermined formulae developed as industry rules of thumb, or more formally through such tools as activity-based costing This allows use of *cost drivers* to be used for support cost allocation to workload, for instance, square footage of the finance and administration offices devoted to that program (Michel, 2001, p. 26). Once workloads, labor hours required, and costs are determined, the department converts them into positions.

Many cities and states list positions. The Health Department in the FY2003 Milwaukee Plan and Budget (2003, p. 139), for instance, lists positions and explains changes in their status, such as eliminated, reclassified, combined with other positions, or tied to grants. The City of Ft. Collins (CO) describes the mix of staffing for its programs (Strachota, 1994, p. 48). It would be more useful if the personal services budget provided analysis including comparative staffing ratios with similar programs in other cities (e.g., the staff operating costs/passenger mile of Washington transit services [WMATA] are about double those of NYC Transit Administration but this is not in the budget of either system), and three-year trends (PY-CY-BY) in staffing costs/total program expenditures. Note that for salary analysis, the object of expenditure or line item is tied to simple outputs in ratios and analyzed for efficiency.

b. *Fringe Benefits Including Pensions*: State and local pension plans cover 19m public employees. Many of the roughly 2,000 public employee retirement systems (PERS) are tailored for specific workers, such as, teachers, judges, school janitors, and civil servants. The funds control $3.2m in assets and face up to $3t in unfunded liabilities (Listokin-Smith, 2012, p. 843). While there is wide-

Table 3.7. Analysis of the Salary and Wage Budget

Work program for program X in organizational unit Y to determine staffing requirements

ACTIVITY	Unit of Measure (Output)	Volume of workload	Staff-hours per unit	Staff-hours needed	Estimated staff-hours	Number of positions	Average cost per position	Estimated cost
Investigation	Invest. by type	10,000	2	5,000	3	3	$26,000	$78,000
Laboratory tests	Test by type	250,000	1	250,000	152	152	$30,100	$4.6 mil
Welfare clients	Client by type	100,000	85 per yr	8.5 mil	5,152	5,152	$30,000	$154 mil
Tax audits	Tax audit	175,000	5	875,000	530	530	$35,000	$18.6 mil

spread variation in the financial health of the plans in the United States, there is no question that many jurisdictions face serious funding problems in their retirement systems (2012, p. 844). The burden of fringe and pension benefits on future services is high in most states. It is estimated that about 60 percent of the revenues from the recent tax hike in California will simply ratify runaway health and pension costs and the massive unfunded promises in both areas. Fringe and pension burdens continue to crowd out all other state needs (e.g., education and infrastructure) for which financing is badly needed for future growth (Miller, 2013, p. A13).

There are two kinds of plan structures. Defined benefit (DB) plans specify retirement benefits to be collected in the future. Eighty-four percent of all state and local government employees have access to DB plans. Specified retirement benefits often include cost-of-living adjustments (COLAs). By contrast, defined contribution plans (DC) accumulate funds for employees and upon retirement the employee draws on the invested assets and bears the risk as to what their level will be (Listokin-Smith, 2012, p. 845; Finkler, 2010, p. 531). As noted above, only three states have mandatory DC plans. Public employee retirement systems also offer more than income, for instance, supplemental health coverage to Medicare, prescription drug coverage, dental and vision coverage, and life and disability insurance. Over the past twenty years, private sector firms have decreased access to DB plans from 32 percent to 21 percent (2012, p. 845).

In the United States, pension benefits are considered an accrued obligation to be paid out of current budgets, usually from fiduciary or trust funds. Benefits can be paid in one of two ways: (1) "Pay-as-you-go" from appropriations by the employer when benefits come due, or (2) "Reserve funding" from accumulated investment income used to defray a portion of required contributions. The second approach can be more financially secure and provide more equitable treatment of different generations of employees and taxpayers by assigning plan costs more closely to the years in which benefits were earned (Zorn, 1991, p. 377).

Pension funds (whether managed by government units or private financial investment firms hired by governments) invest their monies in government and corporate bonds, bank certificates of deposit, money market funds, and other investments. The intent is to make a reasonable return so that planned retirement benefits can be paid without incurring inordinate risk to the funds or, in the worst case, state or local budgets. Pension assets then represent government payables or liabilities. In at least twenty states, a portion of pension funds is earmarked for business investment. The pension fund either loans the money to the potential investor or exchanges it for an equity position in the firm (Fischer, 2007, p. 649). States and localities then have important economic incentives to ensure that pension funds maintain their value and grow. Referring back to the chapter 1 framework, two important indicators of financial condition in this area are: (1) the ratio of unfunded pension plan vested benefits to assessed valuation, and (2) pension plan assets to pension benefits paid (Valente & Valente, ICMA in Lewis & Walker, 1984, p. 309).

To increase the value of pension reserve funds, starting in the 1980s, investments shifted out of fixed-income securities and diversified into private equity, hedge funds, and alternative investments. Assets grew from $1.1t in 1995 to $3.2t in 2008. As investment policies shifted, assumed rates of return also increased. The alternative investments provided higher returns but also much higher risks. Losses in pension fund assets in 2007–08 amounted to $1t (Listokin-Smith, 2012, p. 851). Based on actuarial assumptions, the pension funding ratio was 80.9 percent in 2009 (others put it at 78%). It is believed that an actuarial funding ratio of 80 percent is an adequate amount for state and local pension budgeting. Specific pension funding ratios vary widely within these averages. Illinois, for instance, is only 51 percent funded, while Washington and North Carolina are funded at the 99 and 97 percent levels (*Economist*, 2011, p. 38).

Pension fund managers need to know the contribution rates required to cover future payments. This requires determination of the actuarial present value (APV) of total projected benefits, discounted to reflect the time value of money and the probability of payment. It is the amount that would have to be invested plus investment earnings that will be needed to pay total projected benefits (Zorn, 1991, p. 378). In developing actuarial assumptions, managers had to estimate: mortality rates, pay increases, withdrawals from employment, and investment returns (1991, p. 380). Considerable leeway was allowed on developing these assumptions, and managers became used to high returns in a growing national economy. GAAP does not specify an actuarial methodology or restrict those that are used. Government Accounting Standards Board (GASB) rules require only that discount rates be based on estimated long-term investment yields for the pension plan (Listokin-Smith, 2012, p. 853).

In response to this relative methodological vacuum, states and localities began to use higher discount rates for future returns, which lowered their contribution requirements. They adopted two approaches: (1) assumed investment returns, and (2) cost of borrowing or investment risk. Public pension plans over the past twenty-five years assumed an annual return of 9.3 percent, but in the past ten years actual returns have been only 3.9 percent. Most state and local plans still use between 7 and 8.5 percent discount rates. Many state and local officials had been using the first approach, tat is, assumed returns in the form of estimated long-term yield or expected growth. This assumed that risks to pension benefits were largely risk-free (2012, p. 853) and encouraged the types of risky strategies that led to the present funding crisis. In the "assumed return rule," returns are still mandated by many subnational governments. An assumed rate of return from investments (e.g., 8% below) meant a higher discount rate or lower present value of future liabilities. The higher ROR lowered pension liabilities ($2t as indicated in Figure 3.5 below). Based on assumptions that past economic performance would be like the future and laws that mandated returns would somehow achieve them, pension policy became based on wishful investment returns and artificially lowered pension liabilities. New GAAP standards require lower rates for pay-as-you-go financing but higher ones for trust funds to prefund obligations (2012, p. 852).

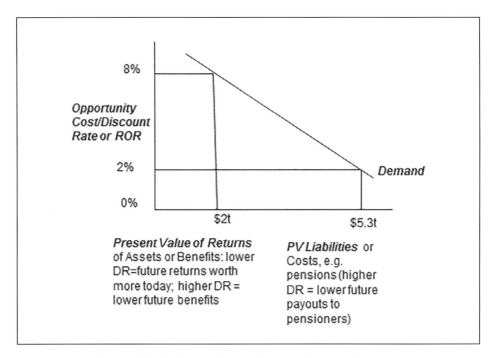

Figure 3.5. A Better Way to Estimate Pension Returns.

The second option was to use the *cost of borrowing* rule. Economists believe that contribution rates used should be based on the riskiness of liabilities (Listokin-Smith, 2012, p. 853). This is the more prudent approach as it is based on current yields on bonds (obviously lower in a low-inflation context). Using this rule, the present value of pension liabilities increased to $5.3t in Figure 3.5. That is, using the latter rule increased reported state-local pension liability by about 68 percent (*Economist*, 2012b, p. 23).

GAAP also allows considerable flexibility in reporting PERS liabilities and assets. Nevertheless, governments have had to report PERS on balance sheets and statements of revenues, expenses, and changes in fund balance (or activity/income statements). They have also had to include statements of changes in net assets available for benefits (Zorn, 1991, p. 386). But allowable use of lower discount rates, as noted, has exaggerated estimated investment yields and understated governmental contribution rates on these financial statements.

The weak economy continues into 2014, raising the important policy questions of sustainability and affordability of pension fund liabilities. Generally Accepted Accounting Principles (GAAP) do not require funding of pension liabilities (2012, p. 851) but those jurisdictions without prefunded postemployment benefit funds most likely have to contribute more from their budgets and therefore jeopardize their credit ratings (2013, p. 852). Colorado, Vermont, and Minnesota, for instance, have already enforced such requirements (2012, p. 860). But there may be democratic limits on how far pension burdens can be cut. The Santa Clara Superior Court ruled recently that the City of San Jose cannot require current employees to contribute more but may cut salaries to reduce pension costs (*Government Management Daily*, 12/24/13). If states and

Figure 3.6. How Not to Estimate Pension Returns. DILBERT © 2008 Scott Adams.

localities are blocked by courts from increasing pension fund contributions, they would have to reduce other current services or raise taxes. Voters and antitax groups limit actions here. If states continue to reduce benefits, as in Michigan and Missouri, they will have more conflicts with union members whose defined contribution benefits have been guaranteed by law (*Economist*, 2012b, p. 23).

In response to increasing liability disclosure requirements from GASB, rules for governing pensions and investment will have to be modernized. State and local government rules from GASB and GAAP will continue to move pension investment and management obligations more toward private sector practices, such as defined contribution systems and discounting on the basis of investment risk. In EU countries, by contrast, pension liabilities are considered "non-debt" or "implicit," but not "hard" debts of the government. In part, this is due to the view that governments that acquire unsustainable pension burdens can modify the social insurance or entitlement benefits as "contracts." Greece and Italy did this recently (Heller, 2013, p. 643).

Overestimation of returns (or underestimation of liabilities) is an issue of selection of the wrong investments (e.g., mortgage-backed securities, which turned out to be toxic mortgages that produced large losses in portfolio value) and discount rate selection. Discounting will be discussed in the next chapter under capital budgeting.

c. Operations and Maintenance (O&M) expenditures are recurrent outlays necessary to sustain a program or project at a sustained level (Heller, 1991, p. 52). *Operations* are the procedures and activities involved in actual service delivery. This is often a separate budget line called supplies, and includes expenses such as travel; it usually includes deprecation charges for the use of capital assets for the year. *Maintenance* refers to the activities that keep infrastructure in serviceable condition. Maintenance expenditures can be both recurrent (i.e., routine and periodic maintenance) and capital (i.e., rehabilitation). Maintenance is important in that for some services such as roads, drainage, bus and rail transit, and sewerage systems the condition of the capital infrastructure effectively determines the quality of services (ibid.). For other services such as health and education that require labor and other inputs, the role of associated capital maintenance is more variable.

The supply side for O&M consists of the totals spent for purchase of supplies, labor, and other intermediate inputs to maintain facilities. In the context of PFM, this requires that the purchasing system registers and reports commitments for budgetary discipline and control (invoices and purchase orders). An important issue here for most governments is the tendency to concentrate on new investments and fail to provide for the recurrent costs of O&M to maintain assets such as buses, road networks, and equipment (1991, p. 52). O&M spending is easily deferred to cover pension and salary obligations. Deferred maintenance can be hidden—equipment can always be patched up or fixed to run a few more miles. The average D.C. water pipe is seventy-seven years old, but many were laid in the nineteenth century; sewers are even older and should have been replaced decades ago (Halsey, 2012, p. A1).

The incentive to allow capital stock (e.g., buses) to deteriorate is that it can often be replaced prematurely as a capital item and financed by earmarked fees to special maintenance funds, long-term bonds, or capital grants from central government programs (e.g., USDOT). Since capital budgets are separate and financing registers only in the recurrent budget as greater debt service, the effect on the annual deficit should be minimal. But the costs are hidden. In 2005, the American Society of Civil Engineers estimated that $1.6t was needed over five years simply to bring U.S. infrastructure into good repair (*Economist*, 2008, p. 36). As the sewer and bridge examples illustrate, often both maintenance and replacement are deferred!

The demand for O&M is a function of technical maintenance schedules, available databases that provide norms and standards, and reports from regular inspections. O&M is labor intensive and requires significant monitoring and supervision (1991, p. 54). Since these data are often ignored in the context of more visible budgetary needs, there must be a means of forcing attention to the costs of deferred maintenance. One solution is to convert the O&M object into an input-output ratio and apply available industry norms (e.g., health equipment, transport facilities, educational equipment) and supplement with spending and results data from comparable jurisdictions. Transport departments regularly keep data on such ratios as: O&M as a percentage of total expenditures; and O&M expenditures per mile of highway maintained. This approach allows managers to focus on cost of service behavior and permits comparison with private firm contract offers. Many state-local governments now contract out the O&M activity at substantial cost savings without loss of quality results. WMATA, for example, recently compared fifteen years of using both private contractors and in-house services for escalator and elevator O&M. The results for cost and quality were inconclusive. Other explanations than private versus public delivery that still need to be examined are: escalator quality; design, manufacturer and age of equipment; and the quality of WMATA management oversight of O&M. For example, it was found that more than 75 percent of

Metro's escalators are more than twenty-five years old and most manufacturers that built them are out of business (Nourmohammadi, 2011:A-5). Needed is a baseline measure that fiscal managers can use to assess the degree of over or underspending for O&M. What are the O&M requirements for the state or city capital investment program (which includes existing stock)? A useful concept is the *r coefficient*.

For O&M expenditures this would be:

$$\frac{\text{net recurrent expenditures}}{\text{Total cost of program, project or service}} = \text{O\&M expenditures}$$

Average coefficients can be obtained by function, program, or sector. For example, from an average buildings coefficient of 0.01 provided by an industry source, it could be concluded that Rockville City should be spending at least $10k on buildings worth $1m for O&M (Heller, 1991, p. 56). Note that the coefficient is the product of using *average unit cost* for particular types of infra-structure. This assumes that maintenance costs are more or less constant in different contexts. But this may not be true.

As noted in the previous chapter, use of the *marginal* cost per unit may produce a different conclusion than average cost per unit because marginal costs assume that costs are not constant—they change in fixed and variable propor-tions over ranges of volume or output. If the city or state lacks managerial capability to monitor and oversee O&M, for example, the marginal costs rise, the price may be excessive and the volume of efficient O&M for infrastructure may be limited. In other words, spending on O&M may not produce desired results and might not be cost effective (Heller, 1991, p. 57). In a particular case, use of marginal cost measurement then may point to the need to outsource this function if it is to be efficient.

d. *Subsidies and Interfund Transfers*: As noted in chapter 1, state and local government fund structures include off-budget proprietary funds for enterprise activities (e.g., water-sewer, transit, ports, housing) and fiduciary-trust funds such as pension funds. Transactions between the government (i.e., governmental funds including general, special, capital, and debt service) take the forms of: subsi-dies, equity, and loans (Hemming, 1991:75). The major flow-of-funds to and from state-local budgets takes the form of subsidies. Subsidies to producers and consumers to cover excessive costs or prices can be explicit (showing up in the budget) or implicit (having no apparent budget impact, e.g., energy consumption) (Mackenzie, 191, p. 60). Budgeting and accounting for subsidies is more important at the U.S. government level for activities such as AMTRAK operations, stimulation of new energy sources, and public housing construction and operation. It is important that state-local subsidies and transfers be explicit and transparent. At the subnational level of government, they take two broad forms:

1. *Interfund transfers* as subsidies to cover revenue losses in particular funds, such as transport, golf courses; and to cover the cost of service provided by one fund to another, for example, legal, accounting, collections. The transfers must record the net cash flows: sometimes the general fund subsidizes water-sewer or transit services to keep rates down; in other cases, utilities and even water-sewer funds can subsidize the general fund to keep property tax rates lower (Coe, 1989, p. 23).

2. *Explicit Producer Subsidies* for such purposes as: lowering private investment risks of providing goods and services that can benefit the public while profiting the owners. It is important to register and monitor the performance of larger subsidies since they directly impact budgets. Given scarce funds for both capital investment and operations, major local development investments such as convention centers and stadiums are typically built with local subsidies to private firms. These create measurable costs and risks.

To provide producer subsidies, cities frequently set up a special fund for an investment project and agree to cover operations and maintenance and often provide associated infrastructure such as sidewalks, parking lots, and roads to the investors as part of an inducement. Local bonds are issued to cover the city share (e.g., 80 percent of the $600m Miami baseball stadium), which will increase debt service payments from the current budget. Cities may agree to guarantee loans to private investors, which are contingent liabilities that in the event of default governments must pay to creditors (Axelrod, 1995, p. 132). This increases direct expenditure obligations from the budget, which taxpayers must absorb by paying higher property taxes and/or suffer reduced services in other areas. These unfortunate results occurred with the Miami stadium project.

Cities often pay for private-public development projects by increasing tourist taxes (which discourages tourism!) and absorbing bonding authority needed for other projects. If the project fails, the impact on financial condition/creditworthiness will be serious. Some projects are successful, such as the Cincinnati

Bengals stadium and Washington Nationals stadium. These are offsetting payments from enterprise projects that contribute to government revenue and lower current expenditures. But these are not common, and such off-budget investment projects with private investors mean the fiscal health of the city depends on ability to pick winning teams as well as estimating ticket purchases by fans.

Cities also end up supporting activities that were intended to break even but did not, for instance, museums, operas, parking garages, city utilities, and subway lines (see Question 3 on the New City Subway below). Income-based pricing to cover subsidies was discussed above and described in Figure 2.7. Losses in special funds for these activities may be paid out of general funds. It is important to track such spending and losses to maintain sound financial condition. Operating costs, losses requiring subsidies, and gains contributing to annual revenues should be recorded in balance sheets, subsidiary journals, and ledgers depending on the activity and included in the Comprehensive Annual Financial Report (CAFR) of use to financial condition analysis. Figure 3.7 can be of use for subsidy analysis by activity.

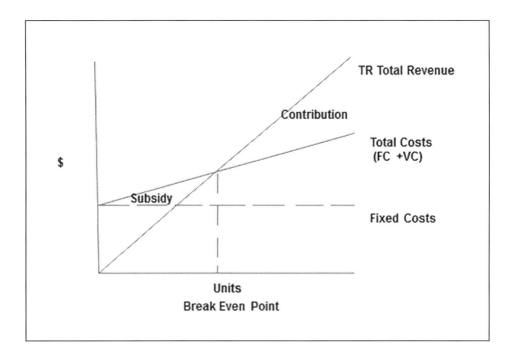

Figure 3.7. Subsidies and Contributions to Annual Budgets.

In short, state and local governments should record on budget or keep track in budget annexes, basic budgetary impact data from larger projects for:

1. *Interfund transfers*: to record flows between government, proprietary and fiduciary funds;

2. *Direct expenditures* made in support of the projects listed as: O&M, supplies, and minor capital investments such as sidewalks (below the capital asset value threshold);

3. *Project loan* as a percentage of bonding authority and available capital financing;

4. *Revenue losses* (or tax expenditures) are effectively public spending through the tax code. They take a variety of forms, such as: allowances, exemptions, and reduced rates to local investors for economic development projects; or blanket forgiveness. Tax subsidies can be substantial and mean that maintenance of other services must be financed by a narrower base and probably higher rates on local taxpayers. Their impact then is either on the expenditure side as higher outlays or revenue losses, or as the impact of a tax agreement that subtracts from estimated revenue collections. Fiscal transparency requires that these types of data be recorded in the budget where possible and feasible. It is also possible that the taxpayer can gain from explicit producer subsidies to local projects. Revenues and reduced operating expenditures should be recorded and attributed to each subsidy.

e. *Debt Service*: Questions during presentation of the budget request are likely to emerge on the debt burden, its composition, and the capacity of the government to repay obligations. It was noted above that growth of pension costs have created an enormous unfunded pension liability for state and local governments. Pension debt composition and payment obligations are reported in the fiduciary fund for pensions listed in the current budget under *fringe benefits* (#b) above. Long-term debt obligations for principal and interest are listed in the governmental fund for debt service. Long-term debt is used to finance capital expenditures such as land, buildings, facilities, and equipment. Revenue-producing activities such as convention centers, stadiums, and swimming pools are financed by fees and charges. These activities are largely self-financing but need to be tracked, as noted, to ensure that subsidies are not flowing from the general fund to cover losses. It is important for transparent financial condition reporting that all debt be reported, that is, not just the general purpose government but also school, special district, and portion of county debt. Debt reporting should go beyond *organizational* reporting to *overlapping debt* of all jurisdictions associated with the state or local government (Berne & Schramm, 1986, p. 239).

The important budgetary capacity measure is *debt burden*, an indicator of fiscal condition or capacity for timely repayment of principal and interest on loans. Late payments (e.g., after ninety days) should be reported as arrears; at some point of nonpayment determined by bond counsels the *arrear* converts into a *bad debt*. The debt burden can be measured three ways:

1. *Comparison with a reference group* by cross-section and over time. Using this measure, state-local government debt burdens are compared with other jurisdictional organizations and overlapping debt. This provides a good idea of how the state or city debt behavior is moving over time and with relevant reference groups (1986, p. 259).

2. *Use of established standards* that combine rules of thumb with rough standards. The standards are often the judgments of experts in the three main rating agencies, Moody's, Fitch, and Standard and Poor's. To determine creditworthiness and debt sustainability, they rely on ratios such as: net debt service/operating revenues; outstanding debt/full assessed value of taxable property; outstanding debt/population; and outstanding debt/personal income (which become more important the less property tax base is available and other sources such as income are important at state and local levels) (1986, p. 261).

3. *Debt as a percentage of the legal limit*: The limit may be constitutional or statutory and often relate to a percentage of property assessed value (1986:258). Using this standard, the budgetary guardians would focus on outstanding debt as a percentage of the legal limit. For instance, as indicated in the financial policies of its 2013–14 budget, the Salt Lake City statutory limit for general obligation debt is 4 percent of fair market value; annual revenues must be equal to or greater than 200 percent of maximum debt service (2013, p. C-2). Figure 3.8 provides an older but very professional example of analysis by Moody's rating agency of a

city debt burden. In its budget, Ft. Collins (CO) presents debt burden measures and places them in comparative perspective. The presentation indicates that the rating agency has serious concerns about its overlapping debt. While median debt burdens for cities of comparable size is 2.6 percent and no greater than 15 percent of operating expenses, its debt burden is 4.3 percent and 25.1 percent of operating expenses.

Debt Management Policies

In the 1991 Budget, the Council set the policy to monitor and manage its direct debt. The policy made general government annual debt service as a percent of general government operating expenses as the key debt indicator. The Council set a goal of 10 to 12 percent of annual operating expenses as the upper limit target for its debt policy. This level of debt service is a common measure of an issuer's ability to pay its obligations. In 1997, the Council revised the upper limit level to 15% of operating expenses and also simplified the calculation.

The following chart shows the City general government debt service percentage of operating expenses over past years and the five-year budget projection period.

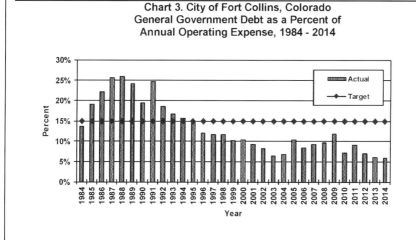

**Chart 3. City of Fort Collins, Colorado
General Government Debt as a Percent of
Annual Operating Expense, 1984 - 2014**

The chart shows that the debt service share of annual operating expense began to diminish in 1989. The general trend is downward since then with only three major increases. The 1991 increase was due to prepayment of debt service for special districts, the General Improvement District bonds and some general obligation park bonds. The 2005 increase is due to debt service on the 2004 Lease Certificates of Participation including principal payments for the first time. The 2009 increase is due to the new debt issue for the Wastewater treatment plant. The chart shows the City continues to have some unused debt capacity within its policy.

Figure 3.8. Ft. Collins (CO) Debt Service Burden.

The Policy Overview

Based on the above data and information sources, the policy overview may now be assembled. This consists of three parts: (1) transmittal letter, (2) budget message, and (3) departmental budget requests.

Transmittal Letter

Similar to a cover letter in a report, the chief executive (e.g., county administrator, mayor) conveys the budget document. Recognizing the time and capacity constraints on elected councilmembers, most executives use the cover letter as a vital communication opportunity. In about four to five pages, they (a) summarize budget changes in major program areas, (b) review changes to property tax bases, rates, and assessed valuation, and (c) present the next year of the multiyear capital program. An excerpt from the 2014 Gaston county manager's budget transmittal letter to the Board of Commissioners is provided in Figure 3.9 on pages 123 and 124. Note the structure: he provides clear revenue and expenditure summaries, followed by issues and challenges facing the county such as loss of state funding (e.g., lottery proceeds) and federal funding (e.g., Medicaid revenues and cuts due to the sequester in Build American Bond revenue). In the final section, the manager outlines the rationale for cuts in order to balance the budget.

Budget Message

This part emphasizes the goals, priorities, and assumptions behind the budget and demonstrates how it aligns with planned priorities (review the Dilbert cartoon in Figure 1.2 on how it should not be done). In practice, there may not be much difference between the transmittal letter and the message—elements of the latter are included in the former. For instance, Mayor Norquist of Milwaukee details his objectives of making budgeting more efficient and stimulating further economic growth in Figure 3.10 on page 125. He compares Milwaukee's efforts with similar-sized cities in the region such as Cincinnati, St. Louis, and Kansas City. He provides assumptions and rationale for the 4.9 percent tax increase and major cuts in response. He details internal efficiencies in such areas as licensing and permitting that will stimulate more investment and employment for city workers. In short, like many mayors, he combines the message and transmittal letters.

GASTON COUNTY

128 West Main Avenue
P.O. Box 1578
Gastonia, North Carolina 28053-1578

County Manager

Phone (704) 866-3101
Fax (704) 866-3147
e-mail: jwinters@co.gaston.nc.us

May 9, 2013

Honorable Chairman Price and Members of the Gaston County Board of Commissioners,

Budget Staff and I respectively submit for your review and consideration the FY 2014 Gaston County Recommended Budget. Each year we tell you how difficult this budget is going to be and after our collaborative efforts to review and revise the budget, the perception is that it doesn't seem so bad after all. The fact of the matter is that as we continue to run out of fund balance, we will have exhausted our options to balance the budget without seriously impacting services.

Revenues

The FY 2014 Recommended Budget includes an increase in General Fund revenues of just over $14.2 million, which includes a recommended tax increase of 5.4 cents to cover the voter-approved debt service for college and school bonds. This increase is projected to generate $7.56 million in additional revenue. We are also benefitting from a State-planned change in the way motor vehicle taxes are collected; in FY 2014 we are expecting an increase of $2.4 million from this change, but I caution that this is "one-time" revenue and will not be recurring in future years. The remaining increase in property taxes of $3.84 million is the result of a continued increase in our collection rate and of modest growth.

The proposed budget includes an increase of $700,000 in Sales Tax collections; we continue to lag behind other urban counties in sales tax, and our expected growth is below State estimates. All other revenues combine for a total decrease of $214,669 and are budgeted according to current year estimates. The decrease is primarily a result of a decrease in prior year tax collection; as we do a better job collecting current year taxes, prior year taxes naturally decrease.

To balance the Adopted FY 2013 Budget, the Board used $14.68 million in fund balance. The proposed budget appropriates $9.91 million to balance the budget. This is a decrease of just over $4.77 million in fund balance appropriated compared to FY 2013, which will move us in the direction of fiscal balance

Expenditures

The proposed budget includes increases to General Fund expenditures totaling more than $9.52 million over FY 2013. These are not increases we wanted to make. Unfortunately, these are largely beyond our control. They are the results of specific State actions, the need to replace

Note: The budget messages is as presented by the County Manager before budget adoption.
Changes made by the Board of Commissioners are not reflected in this letter.

Figure 3.9. Budget Transmittal Letter.

condition does not permit us to meet the request; the proposed budget includes $1,227,000 in capital funding for the School District next year, which is the same amount as FY 2013.

Gaston College

The proposed budget includes an additional $170,000 in operating funds for Gaston College next year. The College requested that the County return to funding a minimum of $697,259 in capital expenditures per year, but this budget keeps the funding level at $453,219 for FY 2014.

Our debt payments are not discretionary. Our capital funding for the School System is one of the lowest among urban counties, and our capital funding for Gaston College does not currently meet its needs. If we are to bridge the gap in our budget to cover the voter-approved debt service on college and school bonds without a tax increase, we will need to consider reducing the base operating budgets for Gaston County Schools and Gaston College.

Each reduction of 1% will save an estimated $484,860 towards our shortfall.

Additional Reductions

These additional reductions we have identified for consideration total just under $5 million (assuming a 1.5% reduction in schools and college),which means that if the Board chooses not to raise taxes and to take all of the above mentioned cuts, we are still looking for $2.6 million to bridge the gap. We have suggested previously that delaying action will require the correction to be even larger. Not only do we have less time to change the direction of our trend lines, but each year we are deferring capital that ultimately will have to be spent. The Commission may wish to schedule several budget work sessions between now and June 13, 2013 to review all facets of this difficult budget.

The Gaston County Board of County Commissioners will hold its regularly scheduled Work Session on June 13, 2013, at 6:00 pm, in the Harley B. Gaston Jr. Public Forum in the Gaston County Courthouse. Immediately following the Work Session, the Board has scheduled a Special Meeting to hold a public hearing on the proposed budget, and the BOC may consider adoption of the Budget Ordinance at that time.

The budget can be viewed at the Main Library located at 1555 East Garrison Blvd, Gastonia NC 28054, at the Office of the Clerk to the Board located in the County Administration Building, 128 West Main Avenue, Gastonia NC 28053 or online at http://www.gastongov.com/.

Public comment is appreciated.

Respectfully submitted,

Jan Winters
County Manager

Note: The budget messages is as presented by the County Manager before budget adoption.
Changes made by the Board of Commissioners are not reflected in this letter.

Figure 3.9. Continued.

John O. Norquist
Mayor
City of Milwaukee

September 24, 2002
Budget Transmittal Statement from Milwaukee
Mayor John O. Norquist

In public office, we have an obligation to properly manage our finances. When we make the right choices, we contribute to the growth and success of our community. When elected officials make the wrong choices, we weaken the community, and can make life harder for the people we serve.

In the City of Milwaukee we've approached budgeting with discipline. We work hard to make budgets more efficient. We direct funds to the services that people need most.

Applying these principles, we've reduced the size of city government by nearly 620 full-time positions over 12 years. In this budget, we reduced our workforce by 123 positions more.

In sharp contrast to the state and county, we've held the growth in our operating spending below the rate of inflation. Among the 59 largest Wisconsin municipalities, 56 have higher rates of spending growth than we have, according to the Wisconsin Taxpayers Alliance.

With a lot of hard work, this budget again holds operating spending below the inflation rate.

As for our pension system, the contrast with the county is "night and day". Here, the big fight a few years ago was between public employee representatives seeking bigger benefits for their members and elected officials taking the side of taxpayers.

Thanks to our commitment to sound budgeting, we're reaping rewards – not mopping up messes like those at the state and county. The health of the City of Milwaukee shows itself best in the citywide improvement of real estate values. All told, equalized property value grew by nearly $3 billion in the City of Milwaukee in the last three years. No city in the state has done more to build its tax base.

Our rate of value growth is way above average, ranking in the top four of Wisconsin's 20 largest cities – and top five among the 19 communities in Milwaukee County over the last three years.

We've seen values rise faster than Mequon, Brookfield, Whitefish Bay, River Hills and other wealthy suburbs. That's a striking turnaround from the lagging growth we saw during the 70s and 80s.

Driving this growth is an undisputed boom in downtown housing. While peer cities like Kansas City, Cincinnati, St. Louis, and Indianapolis struggle

Office of the Mayor
City Hall
200 East Wells Street
Milwaukee,
Wisconsin
53202
(414) 286-2200
fax (414) 286-3191

Figure 3.10. Budget Message.

Departmental Requests

The transmittal letter and message are summaries of basic data, statistics, and narratives on program, spending, and revenue priorities. Here, the issues raised, assumptions, and methods used in developing requests are described. The best requests include analyses of costs and consequences of different requested amounts for volumes, costs and service results. Refer back to Figure 1.18 for an example of the outcomes approach used by the Milwaukee Health Department. Additional departmental outcomes information is indicated below. Note the weaving of forceful, clear narrative and linkage of departmental program objectives to activity statistics.

Questions

1. Review the performance measures in Figure 3.11. Develop measures for service of your choice, Finkler (2010, Table 3-2, p. 91).

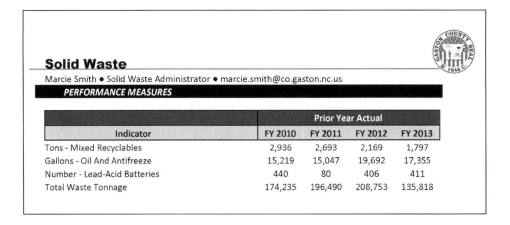

Solid Waste

Marcie Smith ● Solid Waste Administrator ● marcie.smith@co.gaston.nc.us

PERFORMANCE MEASURES

Indicator	Prior Year Actual			
	FY 2010	FY 2011	FY 2012	FY 2013
Tons - Mixed Recyclables	2,936	2,693	2,169	1,797
Gallons - Oil And Antifreeze	15,219	15,047	19,692	17,355
Number - Lead-Acid Batteries	440	80	406	411
Total Waste Tonnage	174,235	196,490	208,753	135,818

Figure 3.11. Performance Measures Exercise.

2. The New City Subway has 40,000 passengers every day. However, they are fairly price sensitive. If the current price of $2.00 were to increase to $2.50, it is likely that there would be only 30,000 passengers each day. On the other hand, if the price were to drop to $1.50, the ridership would increase to 50,000. The variable costs are only $0.08 per passenger. The fixed costs of operating the subway are $70,000/day. How many passengers are needed each day to break even at the current $2.00 price?

Using the template in Table 3.8, below, prepare a flexible budget for the subway system at prices of: $1.50, $2.00, and $2.50. Considering only the financial implications, what should be done and why? How can you reconcile the results of the flexible budget with the results of the break-even calculation (Finkler, 2010, pp. 164–165)?

Table 3.8. New City Subway Flexible Budget

Flexible budget			
Price	$1.50	$2.00	$2.50
Volume per day	50,000	40,000	30,000
Revenue per day			
Less fixed cost	70,000	70,000	70,000
Less variable cost $.08 volume			
Surplus			

3. Using the following Rockville City Parks and Recreation Departmental figures, calculate the rate of change from one year to the next (Rabin et al., 1996, p. 68):

Object	FY1 $	FY 2 $	% Change	FY 3 $	% Change	FY 4 $	% Change
Salaries	$306,562	$434,194		$774,780		$989,450	

4. Here are some current dollar expenditure figures for Rockville City. Using the implicit price deflators (IPDs) provided in this chapter, convert the figures to constant dollars (Rabin et al., 1996, p. 29):

	Current $	IPD	Constant $
Year 1	$5000	100	
Year 2	$6500	110	

What do your answers mean for Year II expenditure? They have translated into only X amount of Year I dollar terms.

5. Suppose Rockville City's capital asset value is $2.5b. Over the past three fiscal years, it has spent $20.0m, $19.5m, and $18.5m on O&M. What have been the average O&M expenditures of total asset value? What is the r coefficient of O&M Rockville's expenditures? If the norm for capital assets is 0.06 what can we say about the level and performance of O&M expenditures in Rockville? What has been the trend of O&M expenditures there? What does the norm and actual level of expenditures indicate about fixed cost behavior across sectors in Rockville?

4

Capital Planning, Budgeting, and Financing

Challenges and Responses

The recent Great Recession strained intergovernmental relations regarding capital budgeting and spending. Traditionally, subnational infrastructure had been funded through state and local taxes and user fees, intergovernmental transfers, and through borrowing from the tax-exempt municipal bond market. Capital transfers have been reduced, borrowing has reached the limit in many jurisdictions and state and local tax and fee increases continues to face enormous political resistance. The result is that state and local capital spending has slowed, available federal funds have diminished, and the effects of the recent recession on capital spending will continue for many more years. The negative effects on employment, investment, and incomes have continued beyond the 2007–09 period into 2014. Marlowe (2012, p. 659) argues that this latest recession will continue to cause unprecedented declines in capital spending and result in an erosion of the public capital stock. This is disastrous in that every activity requires capital facilities: education: classrooms; transportation: roads, runways, tracks, terminals, and rolling stock; residents and businesses need water and sewer plants and solid waste facilities to survive and to prosper (2012, p. 658).

One positive effect of the recession is that it has forced capital budgeting decisions to become more objective and less political. Capital improvement planning (CIP) processes are now taken more seriously in promoting the most efficient and productive capital projects. In addition, more innovative financing methods are being tried. Past efforts to leverage private financing to build, operate, and maintain road projects have now been extended to urban public transport projects in states such as Maryland. Other states are attempting to remedy the issue of stabilization clauses and revenue guarantee measures, which for financing projects such as the Indiana Toll Road protect investors but put the longer-term public interest at serious risk. In that case, weak and careless bargaining allowed the contractor to interfere with public road safety and to be reimbursed for its costly obstruction by taxpayers.

Smarter and harder bargaining by the public sector with contractors, such as requiring contractors to carry insurance, could save public monies and make privatization more effective (Dannin & Cokorinos, 2012, p. 734). The risks of private bankruptcy illustrated by the South Bay Expressway project in California resulted in costly and time-consuming claims and counterclaims by developers, operators, and other stakeholders (2012, p. 747). Despite the relatively successful examples from the UK, where infrastructure is treated as a regulated monopoly, and long-term capital leasing examples from Australia, Canada, and selected EU countries, it may be that for many subnational governments in the United States, the least expensive way to finance infrastructure in the future is through taxation rather than reliance on private investors (2012, p. 746). For instance, to finance the depleted Federal Highway Trust Fund, an increase in the tax rate of $0.15/gallon would raise $150b over ten years to finance deteriorating roads, bridges, and related infrastructure. Since many drive more efficient vehicles, another tax could be based on miles driven (*Washington Post*, 2013). Such efforts would reduce desperate moves to rely on private finance for public projects. If greater reliance on public capital financing is the future, additional efforts to improve and apply rigorous CIP methods to capital programs and projects at the state and local levels will be required by legislators as well as executive officials. Lack of a comprehensive capital process or budget for the federal government means that state and local reforms will occur from the bottom up (Marlowe, 2012:664) with continued variation in quality and standards across the country.

State and Local Capital Budgeting

Capital investments are made by state-local governments mainly for infrastructure and rehabilitation projects. Capital budgets are separate from the operating or current services budgets covered previously for three reasons: (1) the full cost of assets to be constructed will not be used up in one year; (2) operating budgets represent plans for long-term multiyear commitments, not just one fiscal year; and (3) since current revenues usually cannot pay full construction costs they are financed through debt over a period of years that try to match the useful life of the asset. From deferred maintenance and underinvestment, a significant infrastructure deficit of replacement or rehabilitation now exists for assets at all three levels of government in the United States. Roughly $3.6t is needed by 2020 to raise the condition of U.S. infrastructure, mainly rail, bus, roads, tunnels, bridges, and water-sewer facilities from a D to a B, according to the American Society for Civil Engineering (ASCE) (*Economist*, 2013h, p. 34).

There are at least three budgetary problems in responding to the current infrastructure deficit. First, in the current antigovernment, antitax context, cutting capital expenditures is politically easy and the results are almost invisible until future generations realize that bridges, tunnels, water pipes, rails, and roads are crumbling. Second, technical criteria for appraising projects and strategic policy frameworks for selecting portfolios of these projects are often compromised by local politics, so that that the allocation of resources to the most needed projects is not efficient. Third, legal, regulatory, administrative, and project management roadblocks delay implementation of projects. These vitiate many of the benefits to users and potential employees planned many years before.

In this chapter, we review (1) basic capital budgeting concepts, (2) common problems in planning and implementing capital projects, and (3) twelve important steps that require application of tools and methods for sound capital planning, financing, and implementation.

Basic Concepts

Capital Expenditures are for fixed assets that are considered factors of production for growth and contribution to service results (e.g., school buildings for education services and hospitals and major medical equipment for health care). Many cities and states use dual criteria for distinguishing capital from current expenditures: minimum cost and useful life. Some cities, such as Milwaukee, try to reduce their debt burden through "cash conversion policies," which increase tax levies to finance recurring infrastructure projects (2003–08, CIP, p. 6). Milwaukee makes an exception for durable equipment below $50,000, such as alleys, sidewalks, and communication systems, and finances them by cash or pay-as-you go from the recurrent budget.

Capital programs are portfolios of capital projects in rank-order. A *Capital Project* is for construction of *a* major nonrecurring, fixed asset with useful life of more than a year, for example, water/sewer systems, trams, buses, rehabilitation/ repairs at a specified cutoff figure. The asset itself is more critical that its length

Figure 4.1. Capital Purchasing Made Hard. DILBERT © 2007 Scott Adams.
Used By permission of UNIVERSAL UCLICK. All rights reserved.

or cost. For example, construction may take only a year. But the useful life of the asset might be thirty years, which means depreciation charges and O&M would be charged to future recurrent budgets for twenty-nine years. Depreciation simply allocates an amount of the original asset cost as an expense each year in the budget as part of operations (Finkler, 2010, p. 69). Sound life-cycle costing to cover future costs of depreciation and O&M is critical for good current services as well as capital budgeting.

The *Capital Improvements Program or CIP* consists of three components: (1) an integrated multiyear plan of projects across sectors from all departments and within departments in priority. (Priorities should clarify rank and urgency by distinguishing new or replacement capital v major rehabilitation, and providing a list of investments and justifications in support of projects such as utilities.); (2) estimated costs/benefits; and (3) available financing in preparation for matching the program of projects with capital funds from the budget or the capital budget. The budgetary links between the multiyear CIP and individual projects were illustrated previously in Figure 1.18. The CIP process should come together in one or two budgets approved simultaneously at the end of the approval phase. For instance, the capital program of Washington, D.C., schools for 2009–2013 was $2.5b, of which $500m was requested from the city budget in year one.

Common Problems

Eight recurring problems should be noted with capital planning and budgeting that impede the efficient construction and use of capital assets. These are mainly institutional problems and curable in the medium term by stronger management controls, wiser leadership, and improved institutional incentives.

Failure to Integrate Strategic and Land Use Plans into the CIP Process

Because of separate institutional responsibilities and funds available for commitment, the transportation and land use plan for Washington, D.C., that included light rail or tram lines was not integrated with the city procurement function. Thus, the cars were purchased first from a firm in Prague (Czech Republic), which received rent from D.C. for several years while the necessary road right-of-way, utility changes, exceptions to a 1790s law banning overhead electric wires (Rein, 2010, p. C1), rails, and signaling equipment were purchased in order for the cars to be shipped and placed in proper storage sheds in D.C. The three trains, consisting of three cars each, were purchased from Inekon in 2009 for $10m. Under an agreement, Inekon would store and maintain them until delivery for about $300,000/year. As they were only delivered in 2014, the extra charges amounted to about $1.5m. The trains are now being tested on the Anacostia Line in preparation for service in early 2015.

Failure to Learn Lessons from Comparable Jurisdictions/Projects

Public works and capital planning officials informally consult in all sectors with their counterparts in other comparable jurisdictions. ICMA and GFOA encourage these useful technical communications and exchanges via postings of lessons learned on their Web sites. But many officials ignore these databases and strike out on their own, with often wasteful results. For example, several cities along the Red River (which flows north) failed to consult on flood control and what options could be pursued in advance. Winnipeg, Canada, is farthest north and suffered damaging downtown floods for years. The public works department planned and constructed a series of canal diversions around the city in 1968, which continue to function well. San Antonio (TX) (nowhere near the Red River) had similar flooding problems and decided to construct a stronger set of canals combined with a tourist and economic development project in 1937, which evolved into the well-known and successful River Walk. Despite regular flooding and conversion of the problem into an opportunity by San Antonio, the cities of Fargo and Grand Forks to the south in North Dakota made no such public investments and suffered the consequences in 2009 and 2010 respec-tively. An important lesson is that capital design problems from similar cities can be converted to opportunities, here by combining flood control works and economic development objectives.

Politicizing Benefits with Low Discount Rates

The discount or hurdle rate is a charge that must be attached to funds com-pensating for the loss of principal and interest that could be invested today. It is a charge for the opportunity cost of using capital for one project option over not investing, something like buying a house when conditions would warrant renting and saving one's capital for a better project or investment. As indi-cated previously in Figure 3.5 (in the discussion of pension liabilities), use of lower discount rates increases the present value of project returns. By artificially lowering the opportunity cost of capital, the indication is that there would be greater benefits from the public investment than from current consumption or leaving the money to the private sector (Lee & Johnson, 1998:189). Overall project benefits can be inflated by this gimmick and as fiscal guardians, city-state officials need to know how this can occur. Discounting will be discussed further below under project appraisal.

Figure 3.5 illustrates the inverse relation between opportunity costs of capital and estimated benefits. Discounted borrowing costs need to be used for calculation of project benefits and costs as well as payments of debt service. As noted, debt service includes the cost of paying back principal and interest on loans to finance capital projects. Suppose the city health department proposes a five-year project with $10k projected benefits and $8k costs. Assume that only benefits need to be discounted, that is, the income to be generated. Using the discount table below for the present value of $1 (Finkler, 2010, p. 213), note how the lower discount rate (3% instead of 6%) decreases the present value needed to make the project feasible. The present value of $10k at 6 percent is only $7050 meaning the project should not be considered feasible.

Table 4.1. Present Value of $1

Discount Rate	Benefit	Cost
6%	$7050	$8000
3%	$8375	$8000

Lack of a Framework That Requires Combining Competing Economic Analyses of Project Option

Often, measurements of cost benefits and cost effectiveness vary. Needed is a mechanism to evaluate and combine best estimates into project proposals. For fiscal transparency, the variances between evaluation methods need to be included in a project's annexes. For example, assessments of options for the Purple Line corridor were widely different by mode, ridership, speed, and equipment, all of which affected costs and system effectiveness (Guess & Farnham, 2011, p. 190). In many cities and states, no such institutional framework exists with which to evaluate options.

Figure 4.2. Needed: Alternatives Framework and Analysis! TOLES © 2011 The Washington Post. Reprinted with permission of UNIVERSAL UCLICK. All rights reserved.

Failure to Integrate Current-Capital Costs into the Budgeting Process

Cities and states weaken their life-cycle budget planning efforts by failing to include such obvious downstream costs as maintenance in budgets. By failing to do this, they avoid making realistic hard budget constraints. For example, it was estimated that Washington, D.C., Metro system needed $244m over the 2008–10 period for worn equipment and rail car safety. But many have also noted that the Metro transit authority (Washington Metropolitan Area Transit Authority) has no CIP process to trade off or sequence projects for investments and rehabilitation (Sun, 2008). Multiyear budgeting systems that combine capital and current expenses will be discussed below.

Exaggeration of Developmental Benefits

This is often done not through discounting gimmickry but simple exaggeration of riders, users, investors without data and methodological justification, for example, subsidies and budget outlays for industrial parks; stadium revenues; airport cargo terminals and convention centers. Repeatedly in public project planning, fiscal guardians do not subject benefit estimations to rigorous technical analysis that are shared with the public.

Failure to Anticipate Implementation Costs during Design

Designers often ignore or downplay the institutional costs evident in the organizational machinery: decision and clearance points that produce delay (Pressman & Wildavsky, 1984, p. 143). Even under the best of circumstances, these factors, which drive up project costs, are hard to predict. But some are more obvious, such as the failure to cost out the Dulles airport station; the almost deliberate exclusion of maintenance facility sheds; and underestimation of new rail car price increases in the project design and costing stage for the Metro Silver Line (Rein, 2010b).

Weaknesses in Procurement and Internal Control Systems

Next to property tax refunds, the biggest opportunity for corruption is in government purchasing and contracting, largely for transportation projects. *Internal control* systems are rules for administrative and accounting transactions to minimize avoidable losses, such as purchasing cycle and inventory; personnel and issuance of paychecks. Separate and independent from finance departments are *Internal Audit* offices which review and analyze transactions to ensure that internal controls work as planned. Internal controls have to be checked repeatedly to ensure that: source documents produce clear audit trails; functions are separated (i.e., the one who approves payments should not be the same one who writes checks); formal authorization procedures are in place that require multiple officials to sign off on contract payments; and rotation of financial duties occurs regularly. Rotating personnel duties can prevent internal channels that facilitate corrupt practices such as fraud and embezzlement from solidifying (Finkler, 2010, pp. 303–306).

Twelve Needed CIP Steps

1. Determine Organizational Responsibility Structure

The planning and implementation authority structure is given in the short term, that is, few structural changes can be made immediately. But it is essential that there be a lead organization with sufficient authority to coordinate the twelve CIP steps (Guess & Todor, 2005). Lack of a lead organization allows some combination of political projects preferred by elected officials and their base of supporters to be placed unfairly in the queue. This weakens the capital program and often wastes scarce public monies. Thus, the lead organization should have authority to execute three functions:

Figure 4.3. Problems in Ordering Supplies. DILBERT © 2007 Scott Adams.

a. *Maintain control:* It should be able to ensure that only projects from operating departments that meet standards will be considered for the capital plan and budget; it must prevent systematic breaches, such as for political projects.

b. *Ensure Accountability:* The lead organization designs and enforces the vertical command structure for the CIP. It should provide clear feedback and access channels for line departments, citizens, and civil society groups. In this way, a wider range of community stakeholders are included in the CIP process.

c. *Permit Implementation Flexibility:* It should have the capability to monitor project progress directly as well as indirectly through departmental reporting requirements. It should provide rapid clearances for needed course corrections, changed strategic priorities, funding shortfalls, and required new investments.

For example, because of project cost overruns and excessive design changes in past CIP efforts, the City of Milwaukee centralized lead authority in its Department of Public Works for facility design and construction. In this new arrangement, the Budget and Management Division (BMD was charged with the function of ensuring project monitoring, reporting, and accountability. Concurrently, Milwaukee decentralized expenditure authority for each project to the line departments (Milwaukee, 2003b, p. 5). The reorganization tackled the common problem of a split between authority and responsibility in capital programs that drives up costs and often produces shoddy project construction.

2. Establish Capital Improvements Policies

These are advisory rules that establish parameters for local fiscal decisions at the *strategic* and *operations* levels. They should remedy real or anticipated problems. For example, Rockville City might be approaching its legal borrowing limit. Its formal policy response should be indicated in the budget, such as: Rockville City will convert its debt to cash via use of tax-levy financing. Borrowing will not be permitted for recurrent capital projects such as alleys, traffic control, street lighting, underground conduits, sidewalks. Such policies are important indicators of budgetary professionalism to rating agencies and bond buyers that assess financial condition before making decisions.

3. Develop a Realistic Capital Calendar and Budget Request Forms

State and local governments can improve their calendars and forms by:

a. *Improvements in Timing*: this ensures that capital programming will end before operating cycle begins; the lead organization must ensure that this happens;

b. *Increasing Citizen Inputs*: providing clear dates to enable critical feedback from citizen's groups on capital project plans; there should be channels for citizen groups to initiate their own projects;

c. *Reducing Departmental Reporting Burdens*: to increase incentives for better project management, forms should allow comprehensive justifications that include alternatives analyses with use of annexes and supplemental data if necessary. As an incentive, make-work reporting requirements should be periodically pruned and replaced with faster approvals for departmental transfer and reprogramming requests. Internal audit units should periodically review reporting requirement burdens—especially if budget reforms require additional burdens to generate activity statistics on such linkages as changes in budget composition and physical service and project results;

d. *Controlling Responsibilities*: maintain control of the calendar to prevent insertion of projects after specified dates; breaches may threaten CIP affordability and city debt sustainability; and

e. *Integration of Budget Planning*: the lead organization should ensure that the current and capital budgets are planned together.

4. Assess Capital Needs

The CIP should be based on an objective assessment of facilities condition. The state or city should have advance information on whether to repair, replace, or abandon facilities due to wear and tear or scheduled rehabilitation, and evidence that the asset is at the end of its useful life. Needed are three sources of information:

a. *Facilities Condition Database*: This is an updated technical inventory of age and condition of all facilities, for instance, a technical survey or engineering specifications indicating that bridge X should be replaced in five years; rail car Y in seven years. Milwaukee, for example, began in 2000 using a computerized Pavement Management Administration (PMA) Database. This was a data-driven computer model that measured the condition of the city street system through a Pavement Quality Index (PQI). Each street category was subject to a minimum PQI standard below which it had to be reconstructed for safety and efficiency. The model was also used to predict pavement quality and has been adapted to other kinds of infrastructure (e.g., alleys) for inclusion in the city's six-year paving program (Milwaukee, 2003, pp. 193–194). Similarly, using its facilities condition database, Washington, D.C., Metro (WMATA) now knows that 75 percent of its escalators are twenty-five or more years old. WMATA now uses performance measures for: preventive maintenance; and has instituted personnel shifts for priority evening inspections and added more hours for inspection purposes (Nourmohammadi, 2011).

b. *Citizen Survey Database*: This is an updated survey of citizen views based on complaints and instances of service interruption. The city often contracts with an NGO or firm to design and administer the survey and to report data to the city for review and decision making. For example, increasing user complaints might lead to replacement of bridge X in two years rather than five.

c. *Policy Foundation*: Based on state or local capital policies, the preferred option might be to preserve a facility rather than repair or replace. Reconstruction would then follow preservationist guidelines.

5. Analyze Financial Capacity

Every state and city finance department should regularly analyze the ability of its jurisdiction to generate taxes and other revenues from its own sources to carry out its functions (Johnson & Roswick, 1991, p. 177). As noted in chapter 2, evaluation of revenue sources should include yield (Allan, 1996). Measures should be examined to assess the financial condition (Berne & Schramm, 1986) and the risk of nonpayment of borrowed funds. The measures and indicators are similar to those used by the major rating agencies. Cities such as Milwaukee, for instance, specify capital financing objectives to meet rating agency borrowing standards, for example, to maintain the city's AA+ general obligation bond rating (S&P and Fitch Investor's Service) (Milwaukee, 2003b, p. 7). In 2003, Milwaukee received AA+ and Aa2 from the two agencies respectively and was told its debt levels were "moderately high" but "affordable." The main variables and sample measures that should be examined by finance departments are:

a. *Demographics*: The percentage of working population and its median age; personal income immigration and outmigration rates; poverty or public assistance households/1000 households;

b. *Economics*: Unemployment rate; plant closings, vacancy rates; retail sales; valuation of business property; business acres developed; property value; and residential development;

c. *Finances*: Debt/capita, revenue/capita, intergovernmental revenues/gross operating revenues; revenue shortfalls/net operating revenues; fringe benefit expenditures/total salaries and wages; general fund operating deficit/net operating revenues; long-term debt/assessed valuation; overlapping long-term debt/assessed valuation; and unfunded pension plan vested benefits/assessed valuation.

d. *Management*: this refers to the quality of the city's management and can be measured by such indicators as: uncollected property taxes; personnel turnover rates; overall tax collection rates; budgets presented and approved according to the calendar; and successful management of debt-financed projects.

6. Prepare the Project Request

This step is part of an iterative process during the budget formulation phase that requires careful coordination between the departments and the public works and finance departments. The first phase focuses on *project analysis*: problem definition; alternatives analyses, measurement of benefits and costs. The second phase applies *formal evaluation* and appraisal techniques to the project proposals.

PROJECT ANALYSIS

Problem Definition: The project must respond directly to an actionable problem. Problems should have an empirical basis, for instance, rate of rat complaints/capita in New York City. In some cases such as dog bites, fragmented databases and regulatory structures may prevent accurate recording of strays and rabies infections. Problems cannot be diagnosed unless they are based on valid and reliable information (Guess & Farnham, 2011, p. 29). Failure to define the problem properly often results in spending for the wrong solution, say, a capital project (e.g. dog pound) when a proper response might have been better regulation (a current services expense).

It is important that internal control and audit systems penetrate capital planning to ensure that conflicts of interest are avoided in problem definition, for example, a consulting engineer defining a city flooding problem as absence of the floodgates, which it also builds. Institutional weaknesses can allow problem definition to meet preconceived solutions, For example, the cost estimate of a proposed light rail line in Arlington (Virginia) increased from $120m to $250m in four years. Since this would have rendered the project ineligible for federal capital grant funding from FTA, the county did three things. It reduced costs by shifting them to other projects; and it had an updated "alternatives analysis" prepared by a planning and engineering firm with whom it did regular business. The firm examined return on investment but limited the options to light rail only despite evidence that bus rapid transit would cost 80 percent less to build and operate. Finally, the county board declared in advance that the light rail (LRT) project would move forward regardless of the update's conclusions (Vincent, 2013).

Alternatives Analysis: A formal alternatives analysis compares the impacts and benefits of proposed alternatives, including no action at all—it should lead to a preferred alternative. As noted previously, the analysis should be performed either in-house or by a consultant at arm's length. In the case of animal control, for example, alternatives could include: a new pound, a licensing drive, an animal census, a tighter leash law, steeper fines, and more sterilization services (Lehan, 1984, p. 27). The budget request should include data and information on rejected alternatives, for example, light rail option reduces travel time by 5 percent and generates 10 percent more ridership and 15 percent more revenue than better traffic management, more buses on existing routes, or a new bus rapid transit (BRT) system for corridor X. Since many state and city functions are contracted out and others might be, make-buy and break-even analysis, discussed in previously in chapter 3, should also be used for options analysis. "Buy" analysis, as noted, should also include legal-financial advice on how to negotiate smarter contracts with bidders on public projects that use private financing.

Estimate Financial Benefits: These are primary monetary benefits, such as lives saved, trashcans collected, and vehicles serviced, that can be compared to costs to determine the most cost-effective solution or project (Michel, 2001, p. 78). Monetized benefits are not official facts, like costs. They are measured on the basis of often elastic definitions and estimated by using different forecasting techniques of varying validity and reliability (Francis, 2012, p. 512). Such benefits as time saved from transit options are measured by surveys. Parking garage asset values are measurable by market values; other assets such as swimming pools or parks are measurable by consumer surpluses. That is, the benefits themselves are easily measurable; but their trajectories may not be.

Such benefits as jobs and investments attributable to projects must be forecast from models using comparative data. Demand must be formally estimated to produce an estimate of total benefits. To obtain monetary benefits, for instance, the number of users is multiplied by the fees. The users and the fees to be charged are estimated by explicit modes, for example, trip generation, gravity; or controlled experiment. In such cases as local economic development projects, this is not easy since the project is an intervening variable between other policies, public and private investments, and benefits expected, that is, more jobs, incomes, and private investments.

It is important for the finance department and other guardian institutions to identify and control the tendency for *creeping benefits*. Benefits are often elastic and can easily be inflatable by facile assumptions, faulty methods, and/ or exaggerated multipliers. For example, the estimated number of jobs from a pipeline (e.g., Keystone XL for shale gas and oil) should be broken down into: person years of temporary versus permanent employment, and direct versus indirect benefits (i.e., more health workers and teachers). These should be compared later to the fiscal cost impact of the project on local services. The same critical perspective on elastic benefits should be applied to projects such as: convention centers, bookings and attendance; rail projects and their expected ridership; stadium attendance; and the developmental impact of flood control canals. If fiscal guardians are not vigilant, benefits may be double-counted to increase the project benefit-cost ratio and its ranking in the funding queue. For instance, counting the *primary benefit*, trucker time saved by a new highway project along with *secondary benefits* such as increased trucker firm profits, and more gas sales illustrates the problem—the level of expected profits are really a function of time saved, and gas sales may occur beyond state limits (Mikesell, 2011, p. 329).

Estimate Project Costs: Resource costs include construction and operations for the useful life of the asset. In addition to the fixed and variable costs noted previously, capital projects also require estimation of opportunity costs. In most cases, resources used for a public project could also be used for a private project that would generate tax revenues, such as land for a public park or parking garage. The opportunity cost here would be the market value. An opportunity cost would have to be added to project costs for this value and compared with benefits. For public projects that would generate few alternative benefits or revenues, such as in an area with high unemployment, the social cost of an incinerator or highway project might be zero (Mikesell, 2011, p. 315).

While less measurable, an amount should be included for both unintended costs and benefits of proposed projects, for instance, congestion around transit rail stations that also generate tax and fee revenues. It is important also to include real and nominal costs as well as maintenance as part of life-cycle budgeting, such as escalator and track maintenance for rail systems; high increases in construction and running costs due to inflation. By failing to include inflation and maintenance estimates, for instance, construction costs for the New Jersey rail tunnel increased from $5b to $10b in five years of project approvals and negotiations. Excluding these amounts in the request for funds can reduce discounted cost totals, allowing contractors to lowball their bids. This leads to expensive change orders and overruns during implementation.

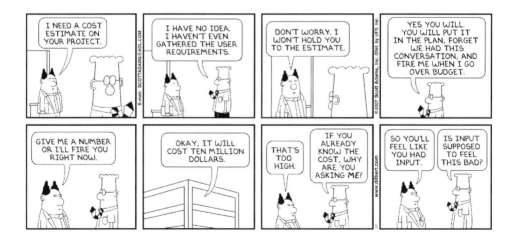

Figure 4.4. How Not to Estimate Project Costs. DILBERT © 2007 Scott Adams.

FORMAL EVALUATION

Following identification and measurement of costs and benefits, they must be compared formally in the second phase of request preparation. This is critical for individual project appraisal as well as for ranking it against others in different sectors for possible funding by the capital budget. It is useful to recognize (Figure 4.5 below) that for formal evaluation capital projects have a similar cost and benefit profile—with heavy capital costs early on followed by tapering off to operating costs. Returns are nonexistent or minimal the first few years and then increase rapidly (Lee & Johnson, 1998, p. 188). The differences in timing between costs and benefits over time require *discounting* to compare them for each year and over the life of the project. If total discounted benefits exceed total discounted costs, there is a positive net present value, and the capital expenditure is likely to be efficient (1998, p. 189).

There are four formal economic rules that can be used for project evaluation. The first one is considered more informal while the last three are formal:

a. *Undiscounted Payback*: projects net results for smaller projects, aka the eyeball technique. This simply compares annual net benefits over a payback period. Canadian local governments use this method, which assumes implicit benefits! But the opportunity cost of present cash use foregone is ignored. The undiscounted values can be seen in the last column of Table 4.2 on page 146 for three water and sewer projects.

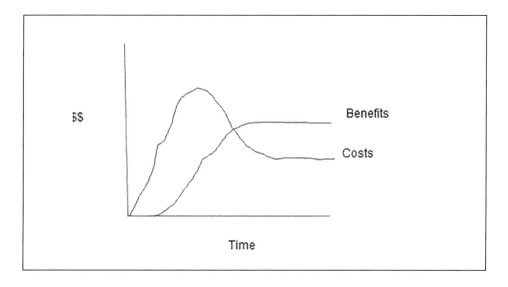

Figure 4.5. Profile of Project Cost and Benefit Timing.

Table 4.2. Undiscounted Payback Method of Project Appraisal

8.8 Project	Year	Capital Costs (A)	O&M Costs (B)	Total Costs © (A+B)	General Benefits (D)	Net Benefits (E) (D-B)	Payback Years	Net Benefits/Capital Outlay (E/A)	Undiscounted (B/C) (D/C)	Undiscounted Value of General Benefits Cost (D-C)
1	1	10000	4000	14000	9000	5000				
	2		4000	4000	9000	5000				
	3									
	T	10000	8000	18000	18000	10000	2	1	1.0	0
2	1	3000	4000	7000	9000	5000				
	2	7000	4000	11000	7000	3000				
	3		3000	3000	10000	7000				
	T	10000	11000	21000	28000	15000	2.28	1.5	1.23	+5000
3	1	15000	6000	21000	11000	5000				
	2		4000	4000	10000	6000				
	3		4000	4000	16000	12000				
	T	15000	14000	29000	37000	23000	2.33	1.53	1.27	+8000

As discussed, the discount rate compensates for the opportunity cost of present cash use foregone (review Figure 3.5 above). It is a weight attached to estimated costs and benefits for differences in their timing and the time value of money (TMV) in actual returns. Using the discount table, note how much more money is worth today than in the future. (For example, a promise of $100 in 5yr = $78.35 @ 5%). For a rational choice, we need to know the present *discounted* value of funds that someone plans to give us in X years—effectively reverse interest compounding (Finkler, 2011, 176). Discounting converts future value to present value (PV) which decreases over time.

$$PV = \frac{FV\,(n)}{(1 + r)\,(n)}$$

PV for 1st year @ 10% = 0.909
PV for 2 years @ 10% = 0.826

b. *Discounted Total B/C Ratio (PV or BCR)*: Table 4.3 on page 148 indicates the present value of net benefits for three projects using a 10 percent rate. To obtain the ratio for each project, one must discount each year and add them up.

c. *Net Present $ Value (NPV)*: Often the purpose of the investment is to generate more revenue or additional financial support. Since many public projects are expected to generate revenue, one needs to know the present value of their cash inflows and outflows (Finkler, 2010, p. 193). The NPV is obtained by subtracting total discounted cash benefits from total discounted costs as indicated in the last column of Table 4.3. Investment efficiency using NPV would be where NPV is greater than $0 and the benefit-cost ratio is also greater than one:

NPV efficiency = NPV > 0 and BCR > 1

d. *Internal Rate of Return (IRR or ROR)*: Use of the IRR o ROR method combines break-even analysis, the ratio from B/C and the cash behavior from NPV. It provides a more comprehensive perspective on projects than the other three tests. The NPV docs not indicate the project's ROR; nor does it allow ranking of projects of different sizes. This is important for development of a CIP

Table 4.3 Discounted Benefit-Cost and Net Present Value Methods of Project Appraisal

9.10 Project	Year	Total Costs (A) (Capital/ OM)	(X) DR 10% (B)	= Total Costs © (AxB) = C	Total Benefits (D) Const + Life	(X) DR 10% (E)	+ General Benefit (F) (D/E) = F	BCR-Discounted Total B/C (F/C) (Present Value of Net Benefits)	NPV (F-C)
1	1	14000	.909	12726	9000	.909	8181		
	2	4000	.826	3304	9000	.826	7434		
	3		.751			.751			
	T	18000		16030	18000		15615	15615/16030 = 97	-415
2	1	7000	.909	6363	9000	.909	8185		
	2	11000	.826	9086	7000	.826	5782		
	3	3000	.751	2253	10000	.751	7510		
	T	21000		17702	26000		21477	21473/17702 = 1.213	+3771
3	1	21000	.909	19089	11000	.909	9999		
	2	4000	.826	3304	10000	.826	8260		
	3	4000	.751	3004	16000	.751	12016		
	T	29000		25397	37000		30375	30375/25397 = 1.197	+4978
				Discounted Costs			Discounted Benefits		

in that often a smaller project may be more profitable than larger ones with large NPVs.

Thus, the IRR is the rate at which B/C = 1 and NPV = 0. It is a method to incrementally arrive at the break-even point for a project. A rule of thumb for analysis of IRR is that is should at least exceed the DR and break even. As noted, the discount rate selected is either on the basis of (1) the *opportunity cost of capital,* a market rate to compensate for bidding away capital from private sector, for example, a city convention center versus a private redevelopment project, or (2) the *social rate of time preference.* This is a planner preference that considers future welfare, for instance, water purification systems may or may not break even but they are essential to welfare. Use of this test allows for a lower discount rate, which would underestimate the value of current private consumption and favor large, long-term public projects by making later benefits more attractive. There is powerful pressure to use lower discount rates for public projects, for example, the Miami Metrorail project used the UMTA (now FTA) required 7 percent rate for urban rail projects when the inflation rate or market cost of capital was more than 15 percent in the 1980s. This inflated benefits and diminished costs on paper and served as a justification for later approval and implementation (Guess, 1985, p. 580).

Table 4.4 indicates the effect of discount rates on benefit and cost calculation for a ten-year health investment project. Where is IRR? Note that it would be at a 7 percent discount rate (BCR = 1), and $1.6m (where NPV = 0). What happens to the NPV of this local health care project as the discount rate? Why?

7. Review the Project Request

Prior to ranking the projects into a full CIP, the state or city must rely on a qualified institution to review four elements of each project proposal. This is the lead organization referred to in step one. In Milwaukee, for instance, there was no one organization with CIP request review responsibility. Formal authority for preparation and approval of the capital budget was shared between line departments and two staff organizations, beyond which the council and mayor provided approval decisions. That review process was strengthened. In Montgomery County (MD), there is still no formal unit with singular review

Table 4.4. Effect of Alternative Discount Rates on Project Efficiency

9.8 The Effects of Discount Rates on Project Efficiency Discount Rates

	0%	3%	5%	10%
Benefits (B) expenditures necessary to provide increased quality measured in minimally-treated patients (available drugs, proper tests, and functioning equipment)	15,000,000	10,448,000	8,456,000	5,442,000
Costs (C) construction site preparation and equipment	7,500,000	6,741,000	6,409,000	5,906,000
B/C	2.00	1.55	1.32	0.92
B-C (NPV)	7,500,000	3,707,000	2,047,000	-464,000

authority for capital requests at the staff level. Most states and cities rely on informal or semiformal structures for the project review function. For example, Gallatin County (Montana) relies on a review of annual departmental project requests from a citizen committee (CIPC). The county administrator and grants and projects coordinator advise this committee. These officials, along with the finance director and the facilities and procurement manager prescreen project applications for the committee. The same group of individuals and offices also manages the "Facilities Condition Inventory" as well as other, smaller capital improvements. According to the county administrator: "This system seems to be working" (Mathers, 2013).

Overall, there needs to be a strategic responsibility center charged with coordinating the review process which focuses on the four elements:

a. *Administrative Process*: Were requests backed by citizen needs surveys? Was there compliance with environmental impact statement requirements?

b. *Planning*: Were studies of fiscal service impacts and demographics used to determine the impact of this project on service cost requirements? Is the project consistent with physical land use and strategic plans? Would the project negatively affect other services, such as a parking garage afftecting bus-rail revenues?

c. *Financial:* Does the proposal include all costs (direct and indirect), noninvestment project alternatives, proper benefit and cost measures and data, impacts on tax rates, and downstream estimates of O&M costs?

d. *Engineering/Architectural:* Were other alternatives such as continued repairs or rehabilitation considered? Is the construction schedule realistic? Is the level of probable change orders included? Are there clearance points and potential legal bottlenecks that could clearly affect the implementation schedule? If so, what are the costs and liabilities for the city or state as well as the contractors?

8. Rank Project Proposals

Effective CIPs require a method that can organize project information and generate an approved rank-order of projects to be funded by the capital budget consistent with CIP strategic objectives. Unfortunately, this is the most contentious part of CIP process! Tools, methods, models, and systems are needed to narrow the range of disagreement over technical issues; and many technical disagreements often turn on fundamental value differences. As one might expect, there is disagreement over both which tools are appropriate and which criteria should be used to assess policies and programs. One remedy for this

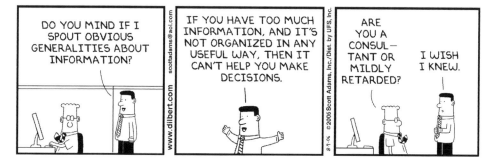

Figure 4.6. Project Information Should Be Organized for Decision Making. DILBERT © 2006 Scott Adams Used By permission of UNIVERSAL UCLICK. All rights reserved.

problem is the *weighted score table* or *weighting-and-scoring model* illustrated by Table 4.5. Weighting and scoring models serve the overt purpose of structuring choices where stakeholders have multiple values and argue about multiple criteria (Lehan, 1984). Such models or tables are useful because criteria in most decisions are not of equal importance, which makes it difficult if not impossible to evaluate alternatives (Michel, 2001, p. 14).

It should be noted that the decision models that are derived from methods used to select capital projects can also be applied to current programs and policies. Investment programs include not only physical assets such as buildings but human capital (health and education), as well as research and development. For example, health care requires medical personnel, testing and operating equipment as well as hospital and clinical facilities. This makes it difficult to distinguish relative rates of return for subcomponents of particular policies. Beyond the methodological problem, many policymakers do not have access to quantitative economic studies on relative rates of return before allocating funds to programs (Posner, Lewis, & Laufe, 1998, p. 17). For this practical reason, providing more criteria for decision making can increase the chances that a project will be transparent, acceptable, and ultimately effective. The weighting-and-scoring model uses multiple criteria that allow the ranking and trading of policy options based on stakeholder values. It can serve as a summary framework to structure choice once problems have been defined and analytic tools utilized to isolate potentially beneficial programs and policies.

Whatever method of project selection is used, it should incorporate elements of *soft* and intangible values (e.g., user occupancy as a proxy of need; health-safety effects; social benefits, health risk if deferred) as well as *hard*, quantitative criteria (e.g., ROR, BCR, economic worth, fiscal-economic impact, availability of grants, and cost sharing). There are many possibilities here and analysts should develop a framework and system that utilizes the values from assessments (e.g., health clinic facility conditions) to produce a separate and overall summary score for decision making. The goal of such systems should not be to replace judgment or exclude political considerations. Rather, a ranking system is needed to make issues and tradeoffs explicit.

For example, as indicated in Table 4.5 using a combination of existing and recommended criteria, health project planners could assign scores of 0, 1, or 2 for each category (Guess & Farnham, 2011, p. 359). The weighting-and-scoring model would produce rankings based on the combined scores.

To distinguish importance or intensity of need, the scores can be added and projects classified according to six categories of urgency (e.g., 14–16 = urgent).

Table 4.5. Weighting and Scoring Matrix for Three Health Investment Projects

CAPITAL REPAIR PROJECT	Cost Sharing	Benefits	Condition	Needs	Location	Investment	Score
	2- High 1- Some 0- Low	2- High 1- Some 0- Low	2- Bad 1- Fair 0- Good	2- Minimal 1- Increased 0- Higher	2- Rural 1- Semi 0- Urban	2- Repair 1- Replace 0- Complete	
A							
B							
C							

For example, the World Bank uses an ascending scale of project rehabilitation (1–3) to program needed renovations: (1) minimal level, (2) increased level of services, and (3) higher level of services. These criteria are in the fourth column under "Needs" in Table 4.5. Since the interest is typically to bring health and education facilities up to minimal levels of service, a "2" might be assigned for "minimal" existing levels of service; a "1" for "increased levels"; and a "0" for "higher levels" of service. The Table 4.5 matrix can be used for ranking health, education, and similar projects.

There are four major steps to developing a weighting and scoring model:

1. *Develop Strategic Decision Criteria (hard-soft)*—participants must develop a range of criteria based on probable impacts of capital project investments. The criteria will be hard fiscal and economic as well as soft social and environmental.

2. *Establish the Scoring Range* (e.g., 1–10): including preference ranges for criteria to be applied to each project. This score will reflect the consistency with strategic decision criteria and the preference range;

3. *Calculate the Weighted Score* (e.g., 1–10): The score reflects the extent to which stakeholders believe the project meets the strategic decision criteria; and

4. *Rank the Projects*: on basis of the total weighted score. This provides the cutoff point for funding in annual capital budget (which is for a multiyear period). Note that the total project score and rank-order provide a transparent cutback or add-on point for that allows later adjustments for changes in revenue availability and needs. Table 4.6 provides an example of how to calculate a weighted-score for three fire engine purchase options using three decision criteria.

9. Evaluate Financing Options and Conduct Affordability Analysis

In budgeting with scarce resources, necessity is the mother of invention. Deadlock at the federal level has generated extreme fiscal uncertainty on both tax rates as well as grant availability to states and cities. While it varies by program, states on average rely for about 30 percent of their revenue from U.S.

Table 4.6. Weighted Scores for Three Fire Engines

Decision Criteria	Fire Engine A			B	C
	Weight (Of Strategic Criteria: Cost, Reliability Speed)	Score (Project Consistency with Hard/Soft Decision Criteria)	Weighted Score		
Cost	0.60	5	3.0	4.8	3.0
Reliability	0.80	6	4.8	1.6	1.6
Speed	0.30	5	1.5	1.2	2.4
Total Weighted Score			9.3	7.6	7.0
Ranking			1 (A)	2 (B)	3 (C)

government grants; and cities and counties rely for about 36 percent of their revenue on state sources and about 4 percent from the federal government. The effect of the blanket sequester (i.e., hard budget constraint) applied in the Budget Control Act of 2011 required innovation and reform from increasingly cash-strapped states and cities. For example, Indiana turned to privatization to raise roadbuilding funds; and Chicago created a special trust fund to refurbish city facilities (*Economist*, 2013f, p. 13).

The three components of financial options analysis are:

a. *Affordability Analysis*: The purpose of affordability analysis is to determine if the project poses unreasonable risks to the state or city public finances. The proposed project should be analyzed in relation to the debt structure. Two financial condition measures are useful here to determine debt sustainability with the project: (1) *debt service/operating revenues* and (2) *project debt/total debt*. This review should be conducted as part of prudent budgeting and financial management. Many cities have approved and implemented capital projects without doing so, with disastrous results for their financial condition. For example, in 2003, Harrisburg (PA) borrowed $125m on the capital markets to rebuild an incinerator that was expected to generate revenues from burning garbage in the city and surrounding counties.

The failure of the project to meet expectations for a variety of reasons put the city $288m in debt. It has been unable to meet its total debt service payments (including one for $68m for the incinerator alone), was downgraded by the ratings agencies, may be forced into bankruptcy (Cooper, 2010), and users now pay the highest trash fees in the United States! The city's mistake was to inadequately assess the risk of failure for a project whose debt was disproportionately high in relation to total debt. It absorbed so much funding that little was left for other projects, and now Harrisburg must pay the price for a weak CIP process.

b. *Review of Capital Financing Policies*: These are straightforward and should be consulted to ensure that debt is sustainable and that the state or city credit rating is not jeopardized by one or more new projects. Examples include: (1) the legal debt limit (e.g., 30% of past year operating revenues or operating budget expenditures) and the project proportion of that limit (e.g., 25%); (2) borrow only for assets that meet capital definition, for example, minimum two-years' life; $50,000 durable equipment; exceeds $25,000 for construction; (3) borrow only to finance capital assets, (i.e., the "golden rule"); (4) ensure that current services are financed only with current revenues over a multiyear period; (5) balance current budgets; and finance the capital budget (this prevents future periods from bearing the costs of both current and past operating expenditures (Mikesell, 2011, p. 300); and (6) no debt should be issued beyond the useful life of the asset, such as equipment (2 years), financial management information systems (FMIS) (5 years), and hospitals (15 years).

c. *Review of Financing Options*: most projects will be funded by multiple sources. For transparency, cities such as Milwaukee present their CIPs by function and funding source (see Figure 4.7).

For further transparency, CIPs should be disaggregated into projects and linked to revenue sources. As noted, however, projects should be selected for the CIP on the basis of multiple criteria, only one of which should be funding availability. This prevents lower local priority projects with available funding from driving the CIP rather than needs and efficiency concerns.

SUMMARY OF DEPARTMENTAL APPROPRIATIONS
OVERVIEW OF 2003 CAPITAL BUDGET
GENERAL CITY PURPOSES

	2002 ADOPTED BUDGET	2003 ADOPTED BUDGET	CHANGE 2003 ADOPTED VERSUS 2002 ADOPTED
Special Projects	$14,880,000	$11,325,000	$-3,555,000
Administration	324,945	811,500	486,555
City Attorney	352,000	0	-352,000
City Development	17,850,000	16,850,000	-1,000,000
Fire Department	2,730,000	5,105,000	2,375,000
Health Department	130,900	1,129,700	998,800
Library	3,415,000	990,000	-2,425,000
Municipal Court	1,833,900	0	-1,833,900
Neighborhood Services	2,949,990	260,000	-2,689,990
Police Department	9,862,914	4,571,793	-5,291,121
Port of Milwaukee	785,000	400,000	-385,000
Public Works	47,727,664	65,685,390	17,957,726
SUBTOTAL CITY FUNDED	$102,842,313	$107,128,383	$4,286,070
GRANT AND AID FUNDING			
Port of Milwaukee	$1,980,000	$1,600,000	$-380,000
Police Department	0	3,000,000	3,000,000
Public Works	23,139,373	36,094,950	12,955,577
SUBTOTAL GRANT AND AID	$25,119,373	$40,694,950	$15,575,577
ENTERPRISE FUNDS			
Parking	$822,000	$1,661,000	$839,000
Water	15,050,000	14,900,000	-150,000
Sewer Maintenance	17,400,000	19,700,000	2,300,000
SUBTOTAL ENTERPRISE	$33,272,000	$36,261,000	$2,989,000
TOTAL CAPITAL PLAN	$161,233,686	$184,084,333	$22,850,647

Figure 4.7. Milwaukee Capital Improvements Plan by Function 2003–08. (*Continued on next page*)

| Table 3 — 2003-2008 Capital Improvements Plan by Department | | | | | | | |
DEPARTMENT	2003 ADOPTED BUDGET	2004 BUDGET PLAN	2005 BUDGET PLAN	2006 BUDGET PLAN	2007 BUDGET PLAN	2008 BUDGET PLAN	TOTAL SIX-YEAR PLAN
CITY FUNDED CAPITAL PROJECTS							
Special Projects	$11,325,000	$12,325,000	$18,490,000	$19,625,000	$22,825,000	$22,825,000	$107,415,000
Department of Administration	811,500	390,000	0	0	0	0	1,201,500
City Attorney	0	0	0	0	0	0	0
City Treasurer	0	0	0	0	0	0	0
Common Council City Clerk	0	0	0	0	0	0	0
Department of City Development	16,850,000	16,850,000	17,350,000	17,550,000	17,550,000	17,550,000	103,700,000
Comptroller	0	0	0	0	0	0	0
Fire Department	5,105,000	5,395,000	6,415,000	4,525,000	4,915,000	3,375,000	29,730,000
Health Department	1,129,700	1,128,900	1,038,500	1,077,200	1,020,600	1,032,000	6,426,900
Library	990,000	3,815,000	5,740,000	4,635,000	1,245,000	675,000	17,100,000
Municipal Court	0	0	0	0	0	0	0
Neighborhood Services	260,000	0	0	0	0	0	260,000
Police Department	4,571,793	10,290,293	8,745,679	4,913,072	4,675,000	4,735,000	37,930,837
Grant and Aid	3,000,000	0	0	0	0	0	3,000,000
Port of Milwaukee	400,000	2,275,000	1,100,000	950,000	800,000	3,425,000	8,950,000
Grant and Aid	1,600,000	900,000	1,600,000	2,500,000	1,600,000	2,850,000	11,050,000
DPW-Administrative Services	626,000	1,795,000	664,000	684,000	704,000	725,000	5,198,000
DPW-Operations	29,526,205	36,596,080	25,223,300	29,613,300	25,975,600	26,484,700	173,419,185
DPW-Infrastructure	35,533,185	31,035,084	31,274,681	28,972,891	31,348,598	30,233,781	188,398,220
Grant and Aid	36,094,950	17,220,645	14,624,900	14,352,245	15,434,750	20,387,245	118,114,735
TOTAL CITY FUNDED CAPITAL PROJECTS	$107,128,383	$121,895,357	$116,041,160	$112,545,463	$111,058,798	$111,060,481	$679,729,642
TOTAL GRANT AND AID.	$40,694,950	$18,120,645	$16,224,900	$16,852,245	$17,034,750	$23,237,245	$132,168,735
NON-CITY FUNDED CAPITAL PROJECTS							
Parking	$1,661,000	$1,395,000	$1,240,000	$1,565,000	$1,625,000	$850,000	$8,326,000
Milwaukee Water Works	14,900,000	15,070,000	15,496,400	15,482,388	16,078,247	16,309,271	93,336,306
Sewer Maintenance Fund	19,700,000	21,500,000	21,500,000	23,500,000	23,500,000	25,900,000	135,200,000
TOTAL NON-CITY-FUNDED CAPITAL PROJECTS	$36,261,000	$37,965,000	$38,236,400	$40,557,388	$41,203,247	$42,659,271	$236,882,306
GRAND TOTAL CAPITAL INVESTMENT	$184,084,333	$177,981,002	$170,502,460	$169,955,096	$169,296,795	$176,956,997	$1,048,766,683

Figure 4.7. Continued.

The two broad sets of capital financing options are: (1) pay-as-you-go from the recurrent budget, and (2) pay-as-you-use from debt term financing.

Pay-As-You-Go: Recurrent Budget: Depending on the type of project, such sources as:

a. *Earmarked taxes* can be used to link a capital needs (road maintenance, and rehabilitation) to a logical funding source, such as fuel tax;

b. *Capital grants* from higher level governments can serve as effectively a source of operating revenue for particular projects. These should be performance-based where possible, for instance, expenditures/ mile; usage/facility;

c. *Own-source revenues* from sources such as: utility charges and transit fares, which partially cover subsidies and debt service payments;

d. *Reserves*: special funds, replacement funds, and retained earnings from utilities;

e. *Private finance*: Options include: lease-purchase (often a form of transferring investment tax credits/depreciation to a supplier/lessor for lower "rent" payments); concessions; build-operate-transfer (BOTs), private public partnerships (PPPs); and tolls from which to repay road debt. The State of Florida, for example, is using PPP financing for a tunnel; Colorado is using this method for commuter rail system; Texas and Virginia are using it for roads (*Economist*, 2013g, p. 14). For example, Denver has financed seventy of 122 miles of its light rail/commuter rail system by PPP. The city pays an annual fee to the private partner. The partner pools all sources of funds (e.g., fees, federal grants, state grants, its own funds) to build and operate the urban rail system. The fee paid by the state investor (e.g., Denver) is higher than annual operating subsidy; but the project is built more quickly and at lower cost than if the public sector planned and built it in-house. The state of Maryland is planning to use PPP for the "purple line" light rail system between two counties of Maryland near Washington, D.C.

In addition to the problem of public financial risk to private contractors noted by Dannin and Cokorinos (2012, p. 733) above, another problem with PPP financing (and any form of capital financing) is that if governments do not maintain the assets they deteriorate and require premature replacement, repeating the costly cycle all over again. One solution is for the government to let maintenance contracts simultaneously with the PPP for capital. The problem with that solution is that the contracts would have to renewed each year during current budget negotiations, that is to say, multiyear current services contracts are considered tax-financed and might not qualify for long-term financing methods. If they can pass muster with ratings agencies and local bond attorneys, the solution would be to build in maintenance to the PPP agreement, effectively a build-operate and maintain contract.

Long-term leases are used by state-local governments as an alternative to buying or procuring capital assets in order to: overcome legal limitations on debt; provide financial flexibility in that no initial down payment may be required; and compensate for equipment becoming obsolete (Finkler, 2010, p.

237). It is thus important to determine whether it is more efficient to lease or to buy. Capital leases resemble installment purchasing where the lessee (government) buys property from the lessor through installment payments over time. Interest payments on the capital lease are treated as debt and an asset on the government books. But from the legal perspective it is exempt from debt ceilings through nonappropriation clauses, which means that lease payments have to be appropriated annually (Mikesell, 2011, p. 661).

Capital lease payments are treated similarly to principal and interest on mortgage payments. To determine financial obligation, it is necessary to find the present value (PV) of the payments to be made (Finkler, 2010, p. 235). Since lease payments are equal payments over different periods, the amount needed is the present value of an annuity (2010, p. 236). As in pension and project cost and benefit calculations described above, the question is, How much is the payment worth today? Once this is determined, the financial benefits of leasing or buying (similar also for make versus buy problems) can be determined.

Pay-As-You-Use: Debt Financing: As one indicator of the vehemence of the antidebt movement that constrains both current and capital spending, in 2010 Colorado Amendment 61 would have prohibited all new borrowing unless paid by fees or current funds. If it had passed, the referendum would have prohibited all: long and short-term debt; capital leasing; and public enterprise borrowing. The implication is that all such assets should be acquired only by pay-as-you go financing. This would shrink capital budgets even further and contribute more to the ongoing deterioration of state and local capital facilities.

a. *Guaranteed Debt*: This type has an unlimited claim on taxes and other revenues (Mikesell, 2011, p. 637) and is used for general tax-levy supported projects, mainly by school districts. The main forms are bank loans or general obligation bonds (GO) (tradable securities of 1+ year maturity with regular coupon interest), often supported by property taxes. Full faith and credit (FFC) or guaranteed debt amounts to about 20 percent of all state and local bonds.

b. *Short Term Debt (1 year or less)*: Smaller projects often use commercial paper and treasury bills that have claims on tax, bond, and even grant revenues (TANs, BANs, or RANs); these mechanisms are also used for cash flow management problems to finance within-year shortfalls. As noted, some cities such as Milwaukee interested in reducing their debt burdens use current revenues to finance a separate category of minor or "associated capital maintenance" such as alleys and sidewalks. But most short-term borrowing is for "bridge financing" to make up for cash flow shortages during the fiscal year (Axelrod, 1995, p. 243).

c. *Nonguaranteed Debt*: About 80 percent of state debt is this kind, which requires a higher interest rate than full faith and credit or FFC debt. Used for self-supporting projects that generate their own revenues, such as transit lines, water-sewer systems; revenue bonds are also issued by public authorities and enterprises to pay off bonds with operating fees from bridges, power projects, and highways (Mikesell, 2011, p. 637).

d. *Municipal Development Banks (MDBs)*: These are used in some states to provide low-interest loans to more creditworthy local and county governments. A national version of this was recently proposed called the American Infrastructure Fund. The U.S. government would establish the legal framework and capitalization would be driven initially by investor purchases of fifty-year, 1 percent interest bonds. Their investment incentive would be tax-free repatriation of a proportion of overseas earnings (about $2t is overseas). Private investment in the fund would allow it to leverage initial capitalization through sale of nonguaranteed revenue bonds. Leveraging this initial amount by 15:1 through these means would produce $750b financing capability from the private sector. Each infrastructure project would be bid out and priced on the basis of the exchange ratio between investment and repatriated earnings to ensure a fair deal for the government. In that it is estimated that every $1 of infrastructure investment produces $1.92 in income and employment benefits, the AIF would help stimulate growth without adding to either fiscal deficits or debts (Delaney, 2013).

e. *Beneficiary Assessments*: Tax Increment Financing (TIFs), Betterment Districts for economic development, business improvements, and industrial parks. TIFs/BIDs are self-sustaining development districts to finance facilities with repayments from increases in property tax increments. Roughly 9 percent of the Milwaukee CIP is financed through TIDs or TIFs. They are considered self-sustaining and are funded through issuance of GO bonds. The issuer (Milwaukee) sets aside increments in property tax increases to retire the debt contracted by the city or special authority (Milwaukee, 2003b:10).

f. *Infrastructure Trusts*: Cities such as Chicago (CIT) have established these as conduits for multiple sources of funding for local infrastructure needs. Similar to MDBs described above, CIT in this case provides bond financing collateral and capital grants. CITs enable the city to raise funds even from foreign investors, charities, and pension funds not interested in municipal bonds because they have little tax liability in the first place. It means that projects with lower CIP rankings but clear benefits can go ahead sooner. The assets remain in city hands and under city management, which is to say, this is not pure privatization. Chicago is involved so far in $200m of the $7b infrastructure investments planned for 2013–16 (*Economist*, 2013g, p. 14).

g. *Supplier/Vendor Credit*: This option is used by cities with no or low credit ratings to obtain financing from such sources as bus manufacturers, or equipment and construction companies. The disadvantage is that borrower (i.e., the city or county) must pay higher than market interest rates.

10–11. Draft and Approve CIP and Budget Documents.

In these steps, the executive has the responsibility of drafting the CIP and matching it with the capital budget for the first year of the plan. The council, board of commissioners, or legislature then approves them. As indicated, the advantage of this system is that it is based on transparent criteria and weighted scores and matched against a budget that will only cover a small proportion of proposed projects. The legislature or council must provide a clear cutoff point. Should this not prove acceptable to either the legislative or executive sides, the opportunity exists to revise rankings based on revised criteria and scores. This allows stakeholders to be part of the process of matching capital needs to scarce resources in the most optimal way.

12. Implementing the CIP and Capital Budget

There are a number of systems that have been in use for many years to monitor and evaluate capital project implementation:

a. *M&E Systems*: State and local governments need to control physical and financial progress of capital projects in the CIP during implementation. Most governments have systems in place to perform these tasks.

b. *Current Expenses*: Governments must also ensure that once the construction phase is completed or rehabilitation finished, the O&M continues only as a current (not capital) expense.

c. *Internal Control and Audit*: Efficient implementation is important to ensure that "ghost projects" are not being financed, for instance, by the treasury for nonexistent works. The best safeguards against this are the internal control and audit systems noted above.

d. *Inventory Controls*: It is also essential that the state or local purchasing system is capable of monitoring the linkage between: invoices, purchase orders, deliveries or actual activities inspections of inventory or works completed, and actual payments (Coe, 1989, pp. 104–105). While the extensive use of FMIS of IFMS systems has strengthened this linkage, execution depends on the will and capacities of local institutions.

    For example, the $112m train and bus hub in Silver Spring (MD) is two years behind schedule (as of 2013) and $80m over budget. The project is "finished" but unusable. It is unusable because of problems in: (1) poorly designed structures (i.e., beams, girders, and slabs wound too tightly and contributing to cracks) and (2) failed inspections (i.e., poured concrete that failed compressive strength tests), which all slipped through the process because, as it turned out, Montgomery County inspectors were not properly accredited and certified (Turque, 2013).

e. *Contracts Bidding System:* The remaining control leakage is that of procurement and competitive bidding process where there is substantial potential for corruption at state and local levels. Again, the best safeguard against this problem is a functioning set of internal control and auditing systems.

Questions

1. What are some alternatives for Dilbert to obtain his bar code scanner more quickly?

2. The Rockville Department of Education requests a new middle school facility. Finding no space on the budget request form, Mr. X adds a section called "alternatives analysis." What data and information should he present to demonstrate the consequences with and without this project? What questions and responses from the city finance department should he expect?

3. Suppose Rockville City must decide whether to continue contacting out its animal control function or operate it in-house and build a new shelter? Using the budgetary and physical performance data for the two options in Table 4.7 (LaClair and Machado, 2011), on what basis would you select one option and reject the other?

4. Table 4.8 on page 166 contains economic data for *two sewage treatment plants* (A&B) each with a ten-year life. Assume that: (a) Construction and useful life are the same; (b) O&M costs are a proxy for depreciation expenses which are a portion of the total value amortized over the life of the asset; (c) 10 percent (0.386) is the discount rate and develop B/C ratios as well as data on NPV (use the methodology provided by Table 4.3); and (d) Formal economic BCR & NPV criteria are being used.
    Answer these 3 questions:

   a. Which project would you select and why?

   b. What components of the cost and benefit streams contributed to the kinds of BCRs each project had?

   c. Analyzing the same two projects using a 3 percent (0.744) DR, would you still make the same choice? Why?

Table 4.7. Rockville City Make-Buy Options Analysis: Animal Control

ABC KENNEL CONTRACT

Performance Area	Type of Activity	Output Measure	Budgeted Output	Expense Allocation	Total Cost	Average Cost (Unit)
Improve dog ownership tracking	Issue ownership licenses	Number of licenses issued	3,500	10% of salary and 40% of supply costs	37,000	10.57 ($/license issued)
Control transportation cost/stray dog complaint	Reduce transportation costs	Transportation cost/complaint	121,280 miles	25% of salary, 30% of supply, 100% of transportation costs	166,390	1.37 ($/mile)
Control impoundment costs	Impoundment of stray dogs	Number of dogs impounded	1,540	65% of salary, 30% of supply, 100% of impoundment costs	227,550	147.76 ($/impoundment)

NEW BUILDING

Performance Area	Type of Activity	Output Measure	Budgeted Output	Expense Allocation	Total Cost	Average Cost (Unit)
Improve dog ownership tracking	Issue ownership licenses	Number of licenses issued	3,500	10% of salary and 40% of supply costs	42,000	12 ($/license issued)
Control transportation cost/stray dog complaint	Reduce transportation costs	Transportation cost/complaint ($/mile)	72,000 miles	25% of salary, 30% of supply, 100% of transportation costs	139,250	1.93 ($/mile)
Control impoundment costs*	Impoundment of stray dogs	Number of dogs impounded	1,540	65% of salary, 30% of supply, 100% of impoundment costs	193,810	125.85 ($/impoundment)

Table 4.8. Budget Data for Two Sewerage Treatment Plants

9_11 Project	Year	Capital Costs	O&M Costs	Total Costs	Total Benefits
A	1	1000000		1000000	
	2	600000	50000	650000	200000
	3	400000	80000	480000	250000
	4		100000	100000	300000
	5		100000	100000	350000
	6		100000	100000	400000
	7		100000	100000	500000
	8		100000	100000	500000
	9		100000	100000	500000
	10		100000	100000	500000
Total		2000000	2500000	2830000	3500000
B	1	1500000		1500000	
	2	1000000	100000	1100000	500000
	3		1200000	120000	600000
	4		120000	120000	700000
	5		110000	110000	700000
	6		110000	110000	800000
	7		110000	110000	800000
	8		110000	110000	500000
	9		110000	110000	400000
	10		110000	110000	400000
Total		2500000	1000000	3500000	5000000

5. Using the weighted-score framework below in Table 4.9 for three decision criteria, develop a rank-order for the three rail car alternatives.

6. The Rockville City Recreation Department operates a summer camp. It is trying to determine whether it should lease a new handicapped transport van or buy one. The lease would be for four years and calls for the $7700 annual payment including maintenance and insurance that are shown in the column "lease" below. As an accommodation to the city, the leasing company has agreed to accept all payments except the $2500 cost of preparing the van for delivery, at the end of each year of the lease. At the end of the lease, the van would be the property of the leasing company.

Table 4.9. Weighted Score for Purchase of Three Rail Cars

Alternatives		Rail Car A		Rail Car B		Rail Car C	
Criteria	Weights	Score	Weighted Score	Score	Weighted Score	Score	Weighted Score
Cost	.60 (x)	5	=3.0	8 x .6	=4.8	5	3.0
Reliability	.80	6		2		2	
Speed	.30	5		4		8	
Total Weighted Score							

If the city buys the van, the camp plans to use it for six years. They will pay $31,000 to buy the van, $2500 each year for maintenance and insurance, and will be able to sell the van for $10,000 at the end of the sixth year. The cash flows associated with owning the van and using it for six years are in the column labeled "own" in Table 4.10 on page 168.

The camp was not able to negotiate a six-year lease for the van. If the cost of funds for the camp is 8 percent, which option should the city take? (Finkler, 2010, pp. 180–183, Problem 5-29).

The problem may also be solved by calculating the present value of the two annuities rather than the individual cash flows as shown in Table 4.11 on page 168.

Using the PMT (payment) and PV (present value) functions, on Excel, replicate the above numbers, and explain how you got them. Then recommend whether the city should lease or purchase the van and on what basis.

7. Arlington County (VA) is paying about $1m for twentyfour tram or streetcar shelters, called "super stops" for its new Columbia Pike corridor economic development and transportation project. The first one entered service and it was noted by riders that the shelter, though sleek in design, does not protect from the wind or

Table 4.10. Summer Camp Van Lease versus
Purchase Decision

Period	Lease	Own
0	($2500)	($31,000)
1	($7700)	($2250)
2	($7700)	($2250)
3	($7700)	($2250)
4	($7700)	($2250)
5		($2250)
6		$7750
Total	($33,300)	($34,500)

snow, and is not heated. The county is paying $575k for construction and $440k for construction management and inspections for each shelter. The State of Virginia is paying 80 percent of the cost of the shelters via capital grants; the federal government (FTA) is expected to pay 30 percent of the costs of the complete $250m tram system. Ridership is now16k/day and expected to grow along the corridor (Sullivan, 2013b). As a representative from a fiscal transparency NGO, what questions would you ask

Table 4.11. Solution to Lease-Purchase Using Present Value of Annuities

Period	Lease	PV Lease	Buy	PV Buy
0	($2,500.00)	($2,500.00)	($31,000.00)	($31,000.00)
1	(7,700.00)	(7,129.63)	(2,250.00)	(2,083.33)
2	(7,700.00)	(6,601.51)	(2,250.00)	(1,929.01)
3	(7,700.00)	(6,112.51)	(2,250.00)	(1,786.12)
4	(7,700.00)	(5,659.73)	(2,250.00)	(1,653.82)
5			(2,250.00)	(1,531.31)
6			7,750.00	4,883.81
Total	($33,300.00)	($28,003.38)	($34,500.00)	($35,099.78)
Annualized Cost		$8,454.80		$7,592.62

about the CIP process? What questions might you ask about the procurement function and its integration in the PFM system in this County? What questions would you have about the state and U.S. grants design program? What questions might you ask about making versus buying these stops? As a demonstration that public comment and participatory budgeting through the implementation phase works, County Manager Barbara Donnellan received hundreds of angry comments about cost and design of the stop and ordered bids for additional stops to be pulled (Sullivan, 2013).

8. Based on the following twelve assumptions and using the data provided, answer the three questions below:

Rockville City Medium-Term Expenditure Framework

Background

Rockville is a large Midwestern city of 2.6m that combines services and light industry with farming of wheat/grains, beets and corn. The unemployment rate is 15 percent; the foreclosure rate from the financial sector crisis was 25 percent and many homes are still abandoned in the city. Last year, its budget deficit was 10 percent of total expenditures and its long-term debt, from pensions and GO bonds, is unsustainable at about 95 percent of total assessed valuation. Vacancy rates are high at about 30 percent and retail sales have been dropping over the past three years. Most importantly, the ratio of public assistance households/1000 households is about 30 percent. The city population has been declining, suggesting that this is a relatively poor city with a shrinking tax base.

Assumptions

a. The Rockville economy is the same as its social services sector. The local budget provides 90 percent of the resources for social services, which are the responsibility of the Department of Social Assistance. Public expenditures from this department consist mainly of (1) cash benefits to eligible beneficiaries (social assistance payments) and (2) social services investments, mainly in elderly, handicapped, and children's homes, which include salaries and maintenance. Both kinds of social service expenditures are driven by available revenues (largely from the farming sector—which itself is subsidized) and credits (mostly from the state and federal grants). Social services capital investments are also financed by a matching grant or transfer from the state or federal governments. The state department of finance pays 50 percent of the approved amount for social services and the local governments match this amount at 50 percent.

b. Poor or delayed maintenance results in premature need for rehabilitation and reduces economic value of the homes to social services users. This is caused by: poor fiscal planning at the national level, poorly designed grant formulae, and lack of local contributions to finance social services investments. Capital financing grants contain perverse incentives which discourage use of recurrent funds for O&M while encouraging premature replacement of facilities. At the same time, the department does not budget for or advocate funding for maintenance resulting in continued repair of facilities that should have been replaced. (There is some evidence of this here).

c. Cancellation of projects after signed contracts results in a 10 percent penalty for the city. Project delays or cancellations after appraisal but before contract signature cause economic health losses to clients of existing facilities.

d. Each year, projects are being started, nearing completion, and being maintained and rehabilitated after completion. Rehabilitation takes place every four years (which explains the big jump in rehabilitation in year P + 3). Rehabilitation costs 50 percent of facility replacement.

e. Federal government subsidies support employment in agriculture, soft loans to small and medium-sized enterprises, health care, and water sector industries. Subsidy cuts lead to short-term increases in unemployment that require increased social assistance transfers from the city.

f. Recurrent implications of new starts have not been calculated, resulting in exceeded deficit targets by year P + 2.

g. Despite projections of declining revenues, and eventual cuts in both subsidies and new starts, the fiscal plan calls for overall increases in recurrent and capital spending. This could affect the stability of actual Rockville allocations for social services and assistance payments.

h. The wages and O&M proportions of the budget in year P will approximate those of the Rockville City Fiscal Plan. The plan quite accurately assumes that in the face of declining revenues, recurrent expenditures will remain roughly constant while capital expenditures will decline. The multiyear plan increases both recurrent and capital expenditures and this evolves into a serious fiscal crisis by year P + 4.

i. Wages are frozen for three years. Assuming inflation increases at 2 percent/year, wages are not meeting cost of living increases. This pressure leads to a planned wage increase in the fifth year. The multiyear fiscal plan ignores the revenue constraint in the interest of generating a crisis.

j. Because of increasing new starts up to year 5, debt service to external lenders (i.e., banks and bondholders) increases.

k. Rockville will seek a $10m loan guarantee to finance infrastructure in the social assistance sector.

l. The Rockville budget is consolidated or unified (current and capital combined). The deficit target of 5 percent is as a proportion of total consolidated expenditures.

Define the problem(s)? What are the dimensions of the evolving Rockville fiscal crisis?

1. *Calculate* Total Recurrent Deficits, Total Capital expenditures, the Budget Deficit, and its percentage of total expenditures.

2. *Decide* the proportion of expenditure-revenue causation for growing deficits. Focus on particular expenditure items that should be increased, decreased, or modified; and do the same with revenue sources.

Fiscal management requires adjustments in expenditures and revenues that anticipate future year needs in the current budget year

Using the data from Table 4.12 recommend changes to revenue sources and any expenditure item that will change the forecasted trends; and justify their feasibility, for example, expenditure fiscal and user needs implications; revenue yields, regressivity, etc. Consistent with the notion of a "hard budget constraint," these changes should ensure that Rockville fiscal performance meets a 5 percent deficit target for the CY.

Propose any reasonable options that you think are necessary given the dimensions of the crisis. The options should lead to policy decisions that ensure current and medium-term fiscal sustainability and stability.

Design a rolling medium-term expenditure framework for Rockville that could avoid future fiscal crises at the levels of (1) fiscal discipline and policy level, (2) functional allocation, and (3) operational efficiency and effectiveness. What data and information are missing to perform this task fully? What proxies or "action research" could produce sufficient information to justify decisions at all three levels?

Table 4.12. Rockville City Medium-Term Expenditure Plan

Year	P	$P + 1$	$P + 2$	$P + 3$	$P + 4$
REVENUES Billion $	150	180	170	160	140
Property Tax	106.5	127.8	120.7	113.6	99.4
Sales Tax	24.0	28.8	27.2	25.6	22.4
Transfers	12.0	14.4	13.6	12.8	11.2
Fees	7.5	9.0	8.5	8.0	7.0
Recurrent Expenditures					
Salaries & Fringe Benefits	80	85	85	85	90
Transfers (social services/benefits)	15	15	20	25	25
Subsidies (functional or sectoral)	15	20	15	10	10
Debt Service	5	10	15	25	25
Operations-Maintenance	10	15	15	25	30
TOTAL RECURRENT					
Capital Expenditures					
New Starts	10	10	10	10	5
Near Completions	15	20	35	10	5
Rehabilitations	5	10	5	40	55
TOTAL CAPITAL					
CONSOLIDATED TOTAL					
Deficit					
Deficit Target (%Total Expenditure)	5	5	5	5	5
Deficit (%Total Expenditure)					

5

Budget Implementation and Control

Challenges and Responses

For effective budget implementation, a smooth flow of funds to line departments and reporting based on clear accounting standards are required. Appropriated funds must be released and controlled rapidly to ensure efficient management of programs and services. Recipient departments must provide timely and accurate reports for expenditure control decisions. The regular exchange of information allows fiscal guardians to modify budgets during the year. In the shorter term, the flow of information and reports also allow fiscal managers to engage in effective cash management. The effects of the Great Recession of 2007–09 have not been markedly different on budget implementation and reporting than previous fiscal and economic crises. Budget offices have had to balance efficiency and control issues during the year for centuries, sometimes with drastic budget modifications and cutbacks through the allotments process. Cities and states have also experienced debt and creditworthiness problems for decades (e.g., New York City's and Cleveland's near bankruptcies in the 1970s) (Spiotto, 2012, p. 760). The Detroit bankruptcy of 2013 (largely from pension obligations and decades of a declining tax base) is unique only because it is the largest city to file for Chapter 9 protection. Since the 1970s, state and local governments have shifted to accrual accounting rules from cash to improve financial reporting. But as noted by Chan and Zhang (2013, p. 761), state and local governments still need to know both their cash positions and accrued liabilities. In that computerized general ledger systems (i.e., FMIS or GFMIS) allow real-time reporting on the basis of both rules, they contribute to improved control of government finances and better fiscal decision making.

Control of Public Expenditures

It is frequently claimed that public expenditure is out of control. Claims are often based on the trajectory of federal entitlements spending, which will climb from 41 percent of the budget in 2013 to 60 percent in 2030; and a gross public debt that is almost 95 percent of GDP (*Economist*, 2013h, p. 29). Recent cuts from the *sequester* (procedures for automatic, forced cuts) derived originally from the Graham-Rudman-Hollings Act modifications of 1987 apportion half of the reductions to defense and the other half to nondefense programs, projects, and activities (Lee & Johnson, 1998, p. 238). The addition of tax rate increases has now reduced the deficit to 2.8 percent of GDP. Federal budget cuts are also important to the states and localities, which receive respectively about 30 percent and 4 percent of their revenues from federal grants. The states have a collective debt of about $90b and owe almost $6b to Medicaid consistent with their obligations under the cost-sharing formula. The problem with austerity mechanisms such as sequestration for programs and cuts in general is that this blunt response excludes cost-benefit and cost-effectiveness analyses and is taking place in a fragile economy with high unemployment and low growth. Many argue that fiscal deficits are only one deficit (e.g., others include the infrastructure deficit noted above) and that the most important goal of economic policy is to achieve growth, not simply budgetary balance (Summers, 2013, p. A16). Others suggest that increased growth of 1 percent more each year for the next ten years could reduce the debt/GDP ratio to a "comforting downward trajectory." This could be done without making cuts to a single program like Medicare or food stamps or without raising a single dollar from additional tax revenue (Lowrey, 2013, p. 5).

Thus, it is important to identify the components of the spending control problem and tackle the most important ones for economic growth and fiscal discipline. There are three drivers of spending trajectory problems. Viewed this way, the spending is not out of control from a treasury perspective. Rather, the growth is predictable but beyond revenue capacity to sustain it. Two of the three spending trajectory control problems focus on budget implementation and one focuses more on budget formulation: (1) overresponsiveness to special interests, (2) fiscal reporting systems that fail to provide timely and valid balances for decisions, and related to this, (3) cash management systems that are weak and unable to match spending and revenue availability during implementation. It might also be argued that spending trends are largely under control on a cash basis (current requirements) but not on an accrual basis (obligations).

Overresponsiveness to Special Interests

As indicated in the above discussion of fringe benefits at the state-local level, there are no soft options, only hard choices and tricky tradeoffs to be made to respond to the growing number of pensioners (45% more by 2035) who will gain access to social security and health care benefits (*Economist*, 2005, p. 35). The relevance of the issue here is as an explanation for spending growth at all levels of government. States have a collective $3.4t shortfall and municipalities are short $574b, with leaders such as Ohio and Colorado set to exhaust the assets in their pension funds by 2030 and 2022 respectively (*Economist*, 2010, p. 95). City workers such as teachers, firefighters, police and other civil servants have received dramatic increases in pension benefits from council decisions. Using an 8 percent return rate, cities such as New York, Chicago, and Los Angeles will exhaust their assets in their pension funds in 2012, 2019, and 2027 respectively (*Economist*, 2011b, p. 29). Nationally, the United States spends relatively less on pensions as a percentage of GDP compared to OECD countries: about 4 percent compared to 13 percent (Italy), 12 percent (France), or 10 percent (Germany). At the same time, pensioners as a percentage of workers in the United States are far fewer (34%) than in these countries: 71 percent (Italy); 50 percent (France); and 48 percent (Germany) (*Economist*, 2012c, p. 38).

The budgetary burden is serious, and the question is: What is driving it, beyond simple aging demographics? The first explanation is technical: overpromising pension benefits based on exaggerated estimates of returns on pension fund estimates at the state and local level. The case of Detroit's recent bankruptcy was noted above. The technical problem was also noted: actuarial calculations are often undiscounted or cash-based. To obtain taxpayer exposure to pension promises, future costs have to be converted to present value, or what they are worth in today's money. In other words, as noted in chapter 3, they should be using higher DRs, which would lower the present value of future promises (review Figure 3.7 above). Instead, using cash-based expected returns, states and localities come up with estimates around 8 percent instead of current bond yields of around 2 percent (*Economist*, 2010, p. 95). The distortion produces a cash-based rather than accrual-based pension fund deficit, which would be much higher. This makes it appear that public sector pensions can be delivered more cheaply (*Economist*, 2010, p. 96). For example, the accrued net present value of additional Medicare and Social Security promises grew by $2.9t in FY 2011. But under cash rules, it was not added to the deficit of $1.3t—a total of $4.2t (Lawrence, 2011). If treasury bond yields were used as the basis of pension liability discounting, total state pension liabilities would increase by 68 percent more than is currently reported (ibid.).

The second explanation is political pressure from interest groups. This answers the question of how so many pension experts could use the wrong accounting rules when standards would dictate using the discounted cost of borrowing (accrual) rather than the expected returns rule (cash). The answer would appear to lie in the coincidence of results and represented member interests. The most powerful forces for increased pension and fringe benefits have been groups such as: AARP, American Federation of State, County, and Municipal Employees (AFSCME), National Education Association (NEA), and the Service Employees International Union (SEIU). Their spending habits on advertising to defeat opposition to debt reduction at the expense of salaries and benefits is well known, for instance, $15m between June and August 2011 alone (Colarusso, 2011).

The important point is that pension spending trajectories are out of control because pension fund returns are cash-based and overestimated. Many other examples of politically driven spending that masks excessive costs of production that drive up deficits and debts can be cited. For example, Medicare repayment rules favor selection of more expensive drugs by doctors, but congressional rules prevent Medicare from negotiating better drug prices directly from drug companies as is done in countries such as the Netherlands and Britain. At the same time, Medicare reimburses doctors on the basis of average price plus 6 percent (Whoriskey & Keating, 2013, p. A1). This, together with rebates from the manufacturer (i.e., Genentech for use of Lucentis which cost $5.7b more [2009–2013] than the least expensive drug made by the same manufacturer) is an example of the perverse incentives that drive up health care costs and perpetuate inefficiencies. Continuation of rules such as these are likely a function of concentrated political power at the electoral district level, which makes hard choices and tradeoffs to control them difficult. The pressure for higher entitlements spending (and opposition to cutting the rates of growth or the amounts), in other words, is coming less from public sector than groups that represent its clients and its employees.

Weak Fiscal Accounting and Reporting Systems

In contrast with special interest–driven costs, deficits, and debt, databases and information systems are sound and have largely produced the information necessary to control and manage expenditures. "Budgeting is no better than the supporting information systems that provide the essential data for planning, formulating, implementing, controlling, and evaluating budgets" (Axelrod, 1995, p. 246). Budgetary accounting, reporting, and control systems have evolved from fragmented, weak, paper and pencil systems to computerized financial management systems (FMIS). Attention to the plumbing and architecture of PFM produced this important reform, which permeates all governments and is reinforced by data and research from GFOA, ICMA, and the World Bank's Web site (https://eteam.worldbank.org/FMIS) on the design and implementation of FMIS systems. If there were systemic problems, financial managers would be unable to receive signals when control over funds had broken down (e.g., internal control and audit; purchasing and treasury management); compare payroll costs with personnel rosters and timesheets (personnel); compare planned spending levels of obligations and costs incurred (accounting and reporting); contrast planned work units with work actually done (cost analysis); and provide financial analysis needed to predict the consequences of alternative course of action (performance budgeting) (Axelrod, 1995, p. 248). In general, FMIS systems now exist at all three levels of government that can generate this data and information.

The accounting information system is crucial for budget formulation and implementation. Accordingly, governments classify their revenues and expenditures into accounts for tracking and control purposes. This is the *chart of accounts* which is the heart of the budgetary accounting system (Coe, 1989, p. 20). With the exception of temporary operating and budgeting accounts established at the beginning of each fiscal year and closed at year-end, the rest of the budgetary accounting structure remains the same. Thus, it is critical that the annual budget codes match the rest of the chart of accounts.

A typical chart consists of four types of accounts (Coe, 1989, p. 20) (Figure 5.1 on page 180). Each account is coded and subdivided based on the particular information needs of the government. Some examples are provided below. Larger governments will have more complex decision needs and thus use lengthier codes and more detailed structures. For example, departments can be broken down into activities, cost centers, programs, and capital projects. In

Balance Sheet
   1. Assets
      Water and Sewer (Enterprise Fund)   31
      Customer Accounts Receivable   126
      2nd prior year   02

   2. Liabilities
      General Fund   10
      Taxes Collected in Advance   241
      No Further Explanation Needed   00

Budgetary and Operating Accounts
   1. Revenue accounts
      Debt Service Fund   20
      Taxes: Ad Valorem   301
      2012 Levy   89

   2. Expenditure accounts
      Fund (e.g. Electric Utility)   XX
      Department/Function (Maintenance)   XXX
      Object of Expenditure (Auto Supplies)   XX

Figure 5.1. The Chart of Accounts

linking inputs and outputs, accounting thus supports budgeting as a performance management tool.

Computerized accounting systems are also known as *general ledger* systems. Ledgers are simply collections of individual accounts. The thousands of daily transactions and source documents (e.g., purchase orders) that occur throughout government must be recorded first in *journals* or books of original entry by date and explanation. These transactions are recorded and classified according to purchases, payroll, and cash. They are summarized and posted to the *ledger* or book of final entry. The ledger contains the control accounts and is linked to subsidiary ledgers for payroll, operations (revenues and expenditures), receivables (e.g., property tax owed), and payables (e.g., accounts payable and bond payable ledgers) (Coe, 1989, pp. 34–35). Computerized FMIS systems enable posting and reporting to be done in real time. The amounts posted and reported enter into three types of financial reports: balance sheets, cash flow statements, and income or operating statements. These reports are based on transaction reporting during budget implementation. Figure 5.2 illustrates the relationship between budget formulation, implementation, accounting, and reporting.

As indicated, budgets are planned by objects of expenditures (OEs) based on forecasts and ceilings provided. The budget is approved by the legislature or council and entered into the general ledger system. Implementation is then tracked and summarized by reported entries for revenues, commitments and outlays. These figures are converted into three standard financial reports: (1) *income statements* (IS) or operating statements (OS), which report changes in revenues and expenditures over time (often two years); (2) *balance sheets* (BS), which report of assets and receivables as well as liabilities and payables for the year; and (3) *cash flow statements* of monthly and quarterly cash flows.

For expenditure control, it is critical that governments track cash inflows and outflows as well as debt obligations. General or governmental funds are generally accounted for on a *cash basis*, which means flow of funds, cash in-cash out. Proprietary funds, such as city enterprises such as airports and utilities, report on the commercial-type *accrual* basis, which means they attempt to reveal the full cost of programs and projects or the full amounts owed to the government

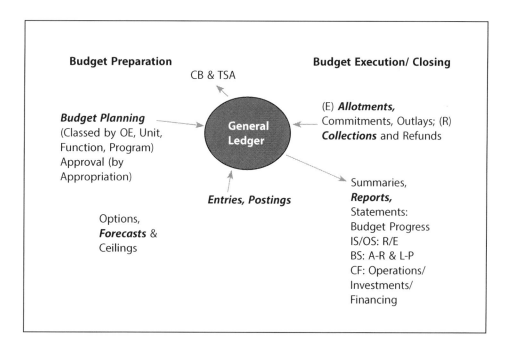

Figure 5.2. Public Financial Management Transactions Using IFMS Support.

(Axelrod, 1995, p. 254). On the revenue side, this can be problematic since some taxes may be accruable such as ad valorem property (at least until the 2009 financial, property and banking crisis) while others such as sales and fees are not known in advance and overestimated accruals could be used to produce phantom balances. For this reason, some governments use *modified accrual*—or rules that accrue expenditures but report only cash revenues (Coe, 1989, p. 19).

Given that calculation and disclosure of full costs for services and programs is not simple either, most governments rely on a third way to control budgetary outlays: *encumbrance accounting*. Few governments anywhere rely on solely on cash accounting since it would lead to constant financial crises. It is instructive for expenditure control to note the difference between cash and operating budgets prepared under encumbrance or modified accrual. Governments know in advance that they must pay salaries monthly, bills as they come due, place purchase orders, and award contracts throughout the year. To finance this, they receive revenues at irregular intervals depending on tax schedule payments, for example, quarterly property, monthly sales, monthly fees. On the expenditure side, they must obligate, commit, or encumber funds to lock them in. This system ensures that other unrecorded commitments are not made that lead to overspending and reveal a control problem. Table 5.1 provides an example of encumbrance or modified accrual accounting (Coe, 1989, p. 19), which is a standard feature of FMIS.

But, it wasn't always this easy. Integration of fragmented accounting and budgetary control systems began in 1975 in response to the New York City fiscal crisis. NYC was unable to determine the size or composition of its debt, estimate the amount it had in cash in its bank accounts, or reconcile its bank account balances with budgetary data. It led to the fiscal crisis of 1975 and the beginning of the IFMS reform movement. By 1980, NYC's IFMS enhanced budget management and control; signaled deviations in revenue collection and expenditures from plans and forecasts; tracked all changes in implementation

Table 5.1. Budgetary Control Using Encumbrance Accounting

	Transaction	Appropriation	Encumbrances	Expenses	Available Balance
1	Original amount	$200,000			$200,000
2	Purchase Order Issues	$20,000	$20,000		$180,000
3	Invoice Paid			$18,500	$181,500

by agency, program, project, and fund; and even accounted for expenditures on an accrual basis (1995:263). Most states and cities have similar systems with what are called core (e.g., accounting, general ledger, budgeting, cash management, debt management, and treasury payments) and non-core modules (e.g., personnel, purchasing, and capital projects). One problem with IT and FMIS systems is the danger of computerizing bad administrative systems. To avoid this, the IFMS concept has been expanded to enterprise resource planning (ERP) systems and combined business process re-engineering (BPR) with change management systems (Melbye, 2010, p. 36) to ensure that the new IT systems reflect the decision needs of the departments and governmental structures and budget calendar they must serve.

The process of installing ERPs often uncovers major design and performance problems in governmental organizations and systems that could constrain the effectiveness of the new FMIS. The normal silo problem of information hoarding must be meshed with systems of institutional incentives (e.g., reduced requirements to report irrelevant data and information) to report data for different PFM needs (Guess & Farnham, 2011, p. 95). The IFMS concept is that fiscal data from all units is reported in real time for the whole of government, from the lowest cost center in a department or project (e.g., school, hospital), which changes the daily cash position and financial condition of government recorded in the central treasury (i.e., treasury single account). This requires design of systems sensitive to departmental workloads and decision needs. Properly purchased and installed, IFMS can facilitate normative centralization (i.e., a central database and set of norms) with decentralized operational responsibility for programs, services, and projects.

Figure 5.3. How Not to Design IFMS. DILBERT © 2002 Scott Adams.

In short, if there are any expenditure control problems remaining, they can likely be traced not to the FMIS systems but rather to assumptions used on the data generated, such as the time periods, and the relevance of past fiscal decisions on the composition of budget baselines for purposes of determining deficits. Even with erroneous or unentered fiscal data, it is hard to game these systems to produce treasury checks that would constitute leakage. For example, through budget relativity (or budgetary alchemy) it is possible to use an accounting baseline for federal budgeting deficit-debt negotiations that assumes past tax cuts have already expired or been paid for—leaving a smaller amount to cut to achieve a lower Debt/GDP trajectory (Klein, 2012, p. A2). This is harder to do at the state and local levels since operating budgets alone must balance each year. Either way, the numbers are there from FMIS; the issue is simply which ones are being used for decision making.

Weak Allotments Control and Cash Management

Allotments

Budget implementation is critical to actual service, program and project results because it will differ from the approved budget. Allotments are made by the budget office (sometimes called *apportionments* or *allocations* of budget authority or appropriated funds to larger units and programs; and then *allotments* of funds to subunits) to agencies or departments. Table 5.2 indicates a sample allocation broken into allotments for four quarters.

Table 5.2. Breaking Appropriations or Allocations into Allotments

2160	Travel and Training	Proposal	Adjustment	OP Plan	Notes
2161	Travel	$238.00	$ (25.00)	$213.00	Reduce travel for conferences
2163	Travel and Conferences	543.00	(75.00)	468.00	Reduce attendance at conferences
2164	Memberships	145.00	(45.00)	100.00	Reduce supported memberships
Total	Travel and Training	926.00	(154.00)	781.00	

Consistent with this table, the operating plan is then apportioned by: timing (i.e., on a monthly, quarterly, or annual basis) and degree of departmental discretion (i.e., lump sum = high versus line item = low), Agencies and departments are used to implementing budgets within ceilings or position controls and reporting the transactions to the budget office (Axelrod, 1995:233). What is harder is any requirement to seek approval for each line item allotted to them—this is viewed rightly as overcontrol and weakens managerial discretion to deliver efficient and effective services. It is only at the end of the fiscal year, when all modifications of the original appropriations ceilings are accounted for (i.e., withheld funds, supplemental funds, transferred funds, reprogrammed funds, and unspent funds) that actual budgetary balance can be calculated (Axelrod, 1995:222).

During the year, the budget offices, departments, and legislative or council committees charged with budget implementation oversight engage in guardian versus spender conflict over the limits of discretion on spending changes. Departments often view appropriations as entitlements or contracts when they are merely provisional ceilings that must change with economic and political circumstances. Departments are forced to implement budgets by appropriations acts that often specify percentage limits on changes,for instance, dollar ceilings on transfers; or "no more than 5% of the appropriation may be transferred" [Axelrod, 1995, p. 230]). Conversely, legislative and council committees and subcommittees often try to micromanage and limit departmental requests to shift funds within an appropriation for different purposes than contemplated (*reprogramming*) or between accounting subdivisions (e.g., O&M to personnel) (*transfer authority*) (Mikesell, 2011, p. 201).

While conflict over budget changes during implementation is often contentious, the changes are all reported into the FMIS systems and accounted for. Minimal slippage or loss of budgetary control occurs because of weaknesses in allotments or cash management. Consistent with this conclusion, the five major activities in the allotments process are performed well in most state and local governments:

1. *Adjusting expenditure plans* in the wake of legislative actions on the budget: throughout the year economic conditions and forecasts change and departmental needs change (e.g., new and unneeded projects; failure of intergovernmental grants to materialize as planned) which requires that central budget offices work with the spending departments to develop revised spending plans for which new allotments will be required (next month; next quarter, etc.) (Axelrod, 1995, p. 224).

2. *Controlling outlays* through powers to rescind, defer, or cut expenditures. For example, in Illinois, departments must submit quarterly allotment plans to the state BOB, which reviews them and often focuses on low-priority programs to cut after which the governor can impound the funds (Axelrod, 1995, p. 227). This requires intense reporting and monitoring of revenue and expenditure trends and has become a major role for budget offices in volatile economic times to ward off fiscal crises. They assess rates of spending by departments (e.g., to prevent them from using up all their funds too early) and focus on overspending as much as underspending. The latter is a serious problem despite fiscal scarcity, caused by technical reasons such as: delays, management problems or absorptive capacity issues, and unforeseen difficulties that can require budget offices to spend in order to meet planned targets (1995, p. 228). They also set selected expenditure ceilings on departmental obligations and expenditures as well certain capital projects and programs. Another action based on monitoring to ensure that budgets are implemented without major surprises is to add earmarks for such items as salaries and equipment into departmental allotments. Budget offices might also add into allotments emergency reserve requirements for rainy day funds (e.g. the Texas Economic Stabilization Fund against deficits), disaster relief, and law enforcement (1995, p. 229).

A major tool for monitoring over and underspending to guide analyses of causes is variance analysis. There are two kinds:

a. *Departmental or Line-Item*: This is based on budget department review of regular reports of budget progress. The purpose is to ensure that no serious deviations from approved budgets have occurred and to guide corrective actions. The formula for variance analysis is the same as that for forecasting interyear trend differences noted previously (Guess & Farnham, 2011, p. 220):

$$\frac{Current\ Period\ Actuals(A) - Base\ or\ Plan(B)}{Past\ Period\ Expenditure\ or\ Revenue(B)} = Variance$$

Table 5.3 indicates the schedule of approved allotments to cover the annual budget plan in $000s.

Using these reported data, the budget office can calculate variance and analyze the patterns. For example, expected higher expenditures in March and September may be due to installments of debt charges on equipment, but that needs to be investigated. Using the actual figures, the budget office can determine if differences between planned and actual expenditures constitute normal

Table 5.3. Budget Line Item: Road Maintenance (Total Approved = $2m)

Month	Jan	Feb	Mar	Apr	May	June	July	Aug	Sept	Oct	Nov	Dec
Expected Expenditures (B)	120	120	260	120	120	120	130	120	270	350	130	130
Total Expenditures To date (A)	120	240	500	620	740	860	990	120	1390	1740	1870	2000
Percentage of Total	6	12	25	31	37	43	49.5	56	69.5	87	93.5	100

versus serious deviations from plan (McMaster, 191, p. 118) and then take actions in such noted forms such as: ceilings, earmarks, or cuts.

b. *Flexible Budgeting Variance*: Based on the *flexible budget* noted in chapter 3 for budget formulation, which shows the expected impacts of volume changes, this method provides management with more information than simple departmental or line-item variances for implementation review. This method allows a department to prepare a budget for one activity level and another for different volume levels; it also allows monitoring of both budgets by central budget offices to influence rates and amounts of outlays. We noted earlier the behavior of fixed and variable costs with greater output or volume. A 10 percent volume or activity level change will not translate neatly into a 10 percent cost increase. But more workload will consume more resources and increase costs by some factor, and managers need to know this. This can answer the question whether variances are due to spending more money to provide expected levels of service or spending more money to provide a greater level of service (Finkler, 2010, p. 290).

As indicated in Table 5.4 on page 188, flexible budgeting variance analysis can provide greater insights into expected expenditures for maintenance (B) by including volume, price, and quantity. Maintenance spending is a function of: (a) its *volume* or output requirements (e.g., road miles to be maintained that might be more than planned based on new problems discovered, or students that actually enroll in school); (b) *price or rate*—inflation may increase the price of pavement materials and supplies or other price-related costs necessary for performing maintenance; or the rate charged per unit may have changed (e.g.,

Table 5.4. Original Budget versus Flexible Budget: Maintenance for March

Budgeted Volume	X	Budgeted Quantity	X	Budgeted Price =	
—Actual Volume	X	Actual Quantity		Actual Price =	
50		2		2.6	260
50		4		2.5	500 (U)

hourly wage for labor; price of meals for a homeless shelter); and (c) *quantity* or use which indicates if more resources (e.g., number of school textbooks or textbooks/student) were consumed than planned—which is separate from their price (2010, p. 291).

Using the maintenance example, suppose the budget office wanted to examine March to see what caused the variance and suggest ways to deal with the obvious unfavorable variance for that month.

The variance analysis provides a red flag for quantity or resources consumed to produce the output (maintenance), which doubled from plan. At the same time, actual prices paid dropped slightly. Since this suggests that despite constant volume, the amount spent for resources doubled, it strongly suggests that efficiencies need to be found in purchasing cheaper materials or perhaps the maintenance function should be outsourced to a private contractor (which is common now).

3. *Responding to Unforeseen Developments in the Current Budget*: When faced with revenue shortfalls, unexpected workload increases (e.g., more transit riders during periods of high gas prices that demand more buses and trains, which requires overtime or more drivers and mechanics), recessions, manmade and natural disasters, judicial decisions that require expanded services, such as social services and prisons, existing appropriations are often inadequate in spite of stringent expenditure controls (Axelrod, 1995, p. 230). Budget offices respond with supplemental and deficiency appropriations and increased transfer and reprogramming discretion for departmental managers to shift funds to try and make ends meet.

4. *Responding to Changes in the Economy*: All three levels of government in the 2007-present recession and financial sector crises responded with expansive stimulus programs to generate employment and income: construction, acquisition of equipment, and additional income maintenance and unemployment

programs (1995, p. 231). Stimulus programs can either result from expansive use of the allotments process to shift funds around to try and stave off economic disaster and stimulate state and local economies; or they can be the result of new legislation such as the American Recovery and Reinvestment Act (ARRA) which authorized the maximum use of fiscal policy tools. Of the $862b that was to be spent over ten years for economic stimulus, $525b or 61 percent was earmarked for infrastructure. In G-20 countries, about 50 percent of stimulus program funds used during that period were spent for infrastructure and the rest for social safety nets/state aid and tax cuts (Baldacci & Gupta, 2009, p. 35). It appears in retrospect that more economic stabilization can be obtained by safety net and state-local grants to keep teachers, transit, health, and other workers on the job rather than focus on "shovel-ready" projects that may only produce large numbers of temporary jobs. While better CIPs that weight and score job-creation projects more highly during appraisal can help, the bulk of state and local grants ultimately depend on the federal government to use its allotment process to shift the funds downward. There is evidence that this happened, but given deficit and debt fixations, those funds have been spent and are unlikely to be replenished. Even though growth is returning (estimated at 2.4% of GDP for 2014), unemployment remains high at 5.6 percent.

5. *Controlling the Efficiency and Effectiveness of Programs and Projects*: The ability of the budget office to allot funds on the basis of program and project efficiency and effectiveness depends a lot on the technical capacity of the budget office itself. Some large city budget offices have this capability. Some medium-sized cities, such as Milwaukee, have this capability thanks to bold and innovative political as well as administrative leadership. Some large states and cities lack this capacity.

For example, the Boston I-93 rerouting and tunnel project was estimated to cost $2.8b and be finished in 1998. In fact, the "Big Dig" project finally cost $22b and was only completed in 2007! More commonly, large capital projects are funded from multiple levels of government and authority for oversight is shared. The $1b Dade County Metrorail project in the 1980s was financed by federal (77.3%), state (9.7%), and county (13.0%) funds. Construction and project management was largely the responsibility of Kaiser Transit Group. Because of poor management and shoddy construction, the county sacked KTG, hired some of its best staff, and took responsibility for project management and turned the project around. Throughout this drama, the state and federal agencies (UMTA now FTA) were passive partners and did not oversee the project in any detail (Guess, 1984, p. 580). Dade County finally exercised its allotment process to review and reallocate funds from a contractor to county transit officials, with major improvements in efficiency and effectiveness.

Conversely, where state or local budget departments lack data and information on efficiency and effectiveness and have few surplus funds to hire consultants to engage in program analysis, they can rely on internal audit agencies that have increasingly designated staff and budget resources to value for money or performance audits (Coe, 1989, p. 234). They do this on a rolling basis in some jurisdictions, focusing on a schedule of projects and programs to evaluate by sector and importance.

Cash Management

This PFM function includes both revenues and expenditures and seeks to avoid three dangers: (1) liquidity crises when the government runs out of cash to meet known and foreseen obligations; (2) failure to collect revenues owed to the government and deposit them quickly in government bank accounts; and (3) failure to invest funds that may not be needed for days, months, or years (Axelrod, 1995, p. 239). None of these dangers are serious enough to be a cause of expenditure control problems. Compared to the financial and banking sector liquidity crises of 2007 that threw the economy into the Great Recession of 2007–09, state and local cash management practices represent a model of fiscal rectitude.

1. *Avoiding Liquidity Crises*: The problem with government finances is that the flow of both revenues and expenditures fluctuates widely with seasonal, statutory, and economic factors. Budgets are rarely in balance during the year—they may be in deficit for a few months as salaries and contracts must be paid, followed by a surplus position as revenues flow in according to collections schedules. We have discussed revenue shortfalls due to recession and required allotment decisions to keep salaries paid and services delivered. At the federal level, recent cash management problems from about 2010 to 2014 have been due to self-generated crises of political deadlock in Congress. In addition to the 2013 federal government shutdown, their response has been: the crude across-the-board sequester; brinkmanship over debt ceiling renewals; and cancellation and default on contract payments that have cost the government additional penalty charges. All this has been disruptive to federal managers who had for many years enjoyed major cash management reforms, for example, the Cash Management Improvement Act of 1991, which produced an electronic payments and collection system; and improved daily, weekly, and monthly cash

flow forecasting techniques. Short-term cash forecasting and management based on the vicissitudes of congressional politics is much harder to do than simple revenue and expenditure forecasting for the annual budget (Axelrod, 1995:242). At the federal level now, it is much harder to predict politically driven rather than statutory, economic, and seasonal cash flow problems.

All levels of government have both clear policies and solid systems in place to provide information on cash on hand, outstanding commitments and obligations against the cash, and anticipated revenues and expenditures (Coe, 1989:121). These systems are informal (i.e., public financial managers with their counterparts in commercial banks) as well as formal, such as annually approved policies contained in budgets and IFMS or GFMIS systems. The 2014 Gaston County cash management/investment policy is indicated in Figure 5.4 on page 192.

GFMIS is a now-common, computerized data storage and terminology framework that facilitates information sharing across PFM functions. The cash management module works closely with the general ledger and accounting systems to ensure budget control. In 2008, the Government of Jordan (GOJ) began installation of a Government Financial Management Information System (GFMIS) system using Oracle EBusiness system (EBS) of integrated modules. It should be noted that Oracle is a Tier I system, meaning that was a comprehensive system with the broadest range of functional capability; other Tier I systems include: SAP, DB/2, and SQL (Dave Burna, in Melbye, 2010, p. 44). Like many GFMIS systems in use, the core purposes of this EBS system were to improve cash management, expenditure tracking, and financial reporting during budget execution. The EBS was required to cover the treasury single account and to support future reforms such as the planned program or results-oriented budget (ROB) system. There were nine modules: (1) general ledger or G/L, (2) accounts receivable or AR, (3) accounts payable or AP, (4) Procurement, (5) Cash Management, (6) Budget Allocation/Management, (7) Budget Preparation, (8) Projects, and (9) Positions/payroll. The two additional "functionalities" using Oracle Hyperion were (a) Cash Planning and (b) Cash Forecasting, which support cash management and cash spending in the Government of Jordan.

The first six GFMIS modules supported overall budget execution systems for improved fiscal discipline. The last three modules were integrated to support budget preparation systems. Prior to installation of EBS, the ministry of finance (MOF) found it hard to forecast cash flow because the accounting system did not consistently record budget commitments (or encumbrances). This led to wide fluctuations in cash flow estimates and actual cash requirements.

Financial Policies

Cash Management / Investment Policies

1. It is the intent of the county that public funds will be invested to the extent possible to reduce the need for property tax revenues. Funds will be invested with the chief objectives of safety of principal, liquidity, and yield, in that order. All deposits and investments of county funds will be in accordance with N.C.G.S. 159.
2. The Finance Director will establish a cash management program that maximizes the amount of cash available for investment. The program shall address at a minimum: accounts receivable/billings, accounts payable, receipts, disbursements, deposits, payroll and debt service payments.
3. Up to one-half (50%) of the appropriations to non-county agencies and to non debt-supported capital outlays for county departments can be encumbered prior to December 31. Any additional authorization shall require the County Manager's written approval upon justification. The balance of these appropriations may be encumbered after January 1, upon a finding by the County Manager that there is a reasonable expectation that the county's budgeted revenues will be realized.
4. The county will use a central depository to maximize the availability and mobility of cash for all funds that can be legally and practically combined.
5. Cash flows will be forecasted and investments will be made to mature when funds are projected to be needed to meet cash flow requirements.
6. Liquidity: No less than 20% of funds available for investment will be maintained in liquid investments at any point in time.
7. Maturity: All investments will mature in no more than thirty-six (36) months from their purchase date.
8. Custody: All investments will be purchased "payment-verses-delivery" and if certificated will be held by the Finance Officer in the name of the county. All non-certificated investment will be held in book-entry form in the name of the county with the county's third party custodian (safekeeping agent).
9. Authorized Investments: The county may deposit county funds into any Board approved official depository, if such funds are secured in accordance with NCGS-159 (31). The county may invest county Funds in: the North Carolina Capital Management Trust, US Treasury Securities, US Agency Securities specifically authorized in GS-159 and rated no lower than "AAA", and commercial paper meeting the requirements of NCGS-159 plus having a national bond rating.
10. Diversification: No more than 5% of the county's investment funds may be invested in a specific company's commercial paper and no more than 20% of the county's investment funds may be invested in commercial paper. No more than 30% of the county's investments may be invested in any one US Agency's Securities.
11. Allocation: Investment income will be allocated to each participating fund or account based on a fair and equitable formula determined by the Finance Director.
12. County staff will generate and review reports that show current investment holdings and will present this information to the Board of Commissioners at least quarterly or more frequently as deemed necessary by staff.

Figure 5.4. Gaston County 2014 Cash Management/Investment Policies.

For this reason, GFMIS specifications required that functionality for the cash flow module include: (1) projection of daily, weekly, monthly, and quarterly cash flows; (2) adjustment of the cash flow plan based on actual receipt and payment balances in the treasury's single account; (3) reconciliation of bank accounts with budgetary cash flows; (4) comparison of the cash flow plan with the operating budget; (5) generate "what-if" cash flow scenarios and cash forecasts; (6) production of monthly financial plans for: debt service, current, and capital expenditures; (7) support for design of cash limits for fiscal crises that included commitment balances as well as cash flows. These are typical requirements for a modern EBS cash management module and the installation of GFMIS has strengthened cash management in Jordan as elsewhere (Campbell & Guess, 2011).

2. *Failure to Collect Revenues and Pay Bills Timely*: A problem with many governments is that they fail to collect all revenues owed to them. A related problem is the failure to pay bills on time, resulting in penalties. Delayed payment of bills can be viewed as a problem—or as a short-term opportunity for the wrong purposes. Payment delays allow financing of short-term cash flow problems with arrears. Some governments even finance annual deficits with arrears! Ensuring that the FMIS monitors budget commitments, vouchers-issued and cash flows can help control this problem by indicating when the arrears arise (Diamond & Schiller, 1991, p. 164). The FMIS needs to ensure that payment orders are registered with the treasury or finance office and that internal controls indicate whether there are sufficient funds to actually pay the obligation; if not and checks cannot be issued by a certain date, the arrear should appear in the budgetary accounting system (1991, p. 163). The federal government often runs short of cash now and uses such cash management techniques for its intergovernmental grants as letters of credit to grantees (e.g., state or local governments), which does not count as debt but can be cashed by the grantee at its commercial bank (Axelrod, 1995, p. 242).

For cash management, an Oracle EBS revenue management module has the following functionality: (1) revenue collection from regional and local centers, and (2) a record of dishonored checks and recovery of amounts owed. The cash management module also links to the accounts receivable and accounts payable modules to reduce invoice processing time for payables and processing time of receipts for receivables. This strengthens cash management, saves funds, and indirectly provides budget financing revenues that were unrecognized and unavailable before.

Revenues lost due to slow invoicing procedures or not depositing receipts promptly can be determined by:

$$\text{Lost revenue} = \text{volume of late purchases x}$$
$$\text{prevailing interest rate x (\# days delayed/365)}$$

3. *Failure to Invest Idle Funds*: State and local governments face the problem of having idle funds in some or all of their accounts that can either remain in demand deposits or the current account and that pay no interest. Or they could allocate idle cash to time deposits that do pay interest (Axelrod, 1995, p. 243). Well-run governments routinely invest 99 to 100 percent of their idle funds at high rates of return and have earned billions of dollars each year from these short-term, often overnight investments (Coe, 1989, p. 116). States fix responsibility in treasurers and boards. The Wisconsin's Investment Board, for instance, manages the cash balances of all its funds as well as assets of the state retirement system; and local governments are free to participate in this pool (Axelrod, 1995, p. 244).

Local government treasurers and finance directors typically rely on either government securities dealers or commercial banks for their investment advice. Reliance on dealers for unsecured funds such as repurchase agreements "repos" (cash transferred by government to a dealer for security and the dealer's promise to repay the cash plus interest in return for the future return of the security). But in 1985, two securities dealers collapsed and left many governments with large losses (Mikesell, 2011, p. 682). This market remains uninsured and unregulated. Commercial bank investments, by contrast, are low risk and low return—but incrementally have gained lots of cash for local governments.

Selecting a Bank: Local governments select banks based on fees and services. The reason banks are used is that they can increase cash collections, control disbursements, reconcile accounts, and invest any available funds for fees. They typically invest the "float," which is the time between check issuance and deposit/clearance in the government's account, that is to say, lag time between mailing of the check (which is not much in 2014 with direct deposit) and its receipt by a vendor or payee (Coe, 1989, p. 136). To select a bank, the local government prepares a request for proposal or RFP for banks to bid on providing specified services. Local financial managers conduct interviews with managers and make their selection on multiple criteria: price or fees are most important. Governments pay this price either by (1) type of service (e.g., budgetary such as collection of fines/tolls, wire transfers, lockboxes, and deposits; credit such as financing lease-purchases, processing principal and interest for bond payments, and advising on debt management; sale of TANs, BANs, and RANs), or (2) leaving a minimum compensating balance in its checking account.

The following formula can be used to select a bank:

$$\frac{\text{Minimum bank monthly cost}/(1\text{-reserve requirement})}{\text{Compensating Balance (MCB)}} = \text{earnings allowance}$$

Suppose the First National Bank of Rockville City charged $12,520 and the thirty-day treasury bill rate is 3.0 percent. Suppose also that the bank is subject to an Eighty-five-day reserve requirement (a Federal Reserve required set-aside to cover potential banking crises). What is the MCB (Coe, 1989, p. 125)?

$$= \frac{12,520/(1\text{-}0.85)}{.03}$$

$$= \$354,733$$

Depending on the bank or state, it may be possible to negotiate a direct fee for services to avoid high MCB requirements.

Control of Government Finances: To ensure control, there should be only two consolidated or master accounts for budgets: revenue and expenditure plus subaccounts for inflows and outflows for bonds via special funds. Within this control structure, the finance department is able to deposit overnight all its surplus revenues in its *zero-balance/concentration account* at the bank. This account maintains no balance and is a mechanism to minimize idle balances (Coe, 1989, p. 122). The bank's exposure would be only one day's receipts plus any secured certificate of deposit (CD) investments used to increase investible cash balances. It is important that the government ensure that its CDs are collateralized or secured. Should a bank fail, those assets pledged by the bank to back the CDs ensure that the public funds are not lost. On the other hand, if the collateral loses market value (i.e., collateralized mortgages) then the CD loses value and the government would lose the money (Mikesell, 2011, p. 681). It is therefore critical that state-local finance managers ensure that the collateral is solid, in other words, not toxic mortgages mixed in with sound mortgages and rated AAA by agencies. Finance managers should know how to monitor and obtain information (either from financial advisors or in-house expertise) on the composition of its debt as part of due diligence and regular financial condition reviews.

Cash Management in Denver: In the early 1980s, cash management was not functioning well in Denver. The city had forty-five bank accounts with shared control between the city treasurer and other officials which also had signature authority over the accounts. The bank accounts had not been reconciled with budget accounts in many years and substantial idle balances existed in the different bank accounts that had not been invested efficiently at the highest return because the amounts were too small.

The new CFO in 1984 closed all accounts and opened two new consolidated ones: revenue and disbursement. Both accounts were bid out competitively and placed in only one commercial bank. The city bought an encoding machine and encoded the checks received for various payments to specific accounts to which the CFO wanted the funds deposited. The checks were delivered to the bank early enough in the day so that they were able to use the funds by the next day which increased the investible cash balance significantly.

Payments into the account were made by warrant (an option to purchase shares of bank stock at a predetermined price), which allowed funding of the account the same day that the warrant/draft cleared. That permitted the use of a zero-balance disbursement account. Denver also selected a bank based on service fees rather than balances on deposit—which they believed to be the superior option. With a higher investible cash balance from good relations with the bank, they were easily able to pay the fees and have substantial funds left over for spending or reinvestment. After regular transfer of surplus funds to the annually appropriated expenditure account, the CFO invested it in both: (1) short-term overnight repo instruments for liquidity, and (2) long-term to match future cash requirements.

Bond proceeds from project financing (Denver did not use short-term instruments such as TANs or BANs for cash flow borrowing) were deposited in a separate account to comply with the bond indenture (legal terms of the security for debt—usually liens on property and/or income of the issuer) (Moak, 1982, p. 353). Denver had thirty-two separate accounts with legal ownership or a strong policy claim to these surplus funds. So, the new CFO consolidated them into three investment accounts. Investments could now be made at lower cost and higher amounts to maximize rates of return, for instance, greater than $1m T-bill investments avoided the "haircuts" charged by brokers and dealers on investments of less than $1m. The terms "consolidation" or consolidated account used by the CFO in the early 1980s is now called a "treasury single account" and a common requirement for sound municipal (as well as national) cash management. He also set up an accounting system that tracked all inputs and allocated interest from investments to the thirty-two separate bond-related city accounts. In this system, a portion of the investment manager's salary and office expenses were paid for by imposition of an "investment management charge" on non–general fund accounts (i.e., proprietary and fiduciary). By 1986, the increase in investible balances and efficiencies generated a net $2m in interest income to the general fund. Mayor Federico Pena used this positive cash management as evidence of professional leadership in his 1987 campaign and won reelection (Briggs, 2011).

Questions

1. Referring to Table 5.1 on page 182, what is the available balance? What explains the difference between the $20k order encumbrance and the $18,500 expense? How would you find out?

2. Rockville City plans to order supplies every quarter of the year (Finkler, 2010:71:2–22). It uses an *operating budget* based on a *modified accrual* method that tries to match revenues and expenses that incur in providing a service to the same fiscal period; the *cash flow budget* looks similar but only records expected cash payments and receipts. Here, Rockville expects to receive the supplies in the quarter after they are ordered. It expects to use them the quarter after that and pay for them the quarter after that. For example, if it orders supplies in Q1, it will receive them in Q2, use them in Q3 and pay for them in Q4. The city pays salaries in the quarter that the employees work.

   The City earns its income tax revenues equally throughout the year. However, it receives substantially more cash in April, when the tax returns are filed. It plans to borrow $35k on a twenty-year, 89 percent annual note, on the first day of Q4. Interest will be paid once each year at the end of Q3.

   The City prepares its operating budget following the unique rules of modified accrual accounting used by governments. Under these rules, expenses are recorded when the city receives goods or services and becomes legally obligated to pay for them. It does not matter if they have been used or not. Also, cash inflows or proceeds from long-term loans are treated as if they were revenues. Using the information from Table 5.5 on page 198, prepare an operating budget and a cash budget for Q4 only. Assume the city has $300k in cash when Q4 starts.

Table 5.5. Operating versus Cash Flow Budgets in Rockville City

	Jan–March	April–June	July–Sept	Oct–Dec	Total
Supply Orders	$300,000	360,000	390,000	330,000	1,380,000
Salaries	600,000	750,000	825,000	720,000	2,895,000
Income Tax Cash Receipts	600,000	600,000	1,200,000	600,000	3,000,000

3. Rockville City Elementary School spent $90k for textbooks for the Fall 2013 semester. They had expected to have a total enrollment of four hundred students who would each have needed four textbooks at a cost of $55 each. Using the formula to calculate flexible budget variance for price, quantity, and volume, calculate their textbook expense variance. Is it favorable or unfavorable? Why?

4. As part of its treasury management program, Rockville City buys a T-bill with a face value of $100k for $96k (i.e., at a discount from face value). The bill matures in 182 days. What is the yield? Use this formula:

$$\text{Yield} = \frac{\text{Selling Price—Purchase Price}}{\text{Purchase Price}} \times \frac{360}{\#\text{days}}$$

References

Allan, I. J. (1996). Evaluating alternative revenue sources. In Rabin et al., *Budgeting: Formulation and execution; Workbook* (2nd edition); *Data Sourcebook* (2nd edition). Athens, GA: Carl Vinson Institute of Government.

Allen, R., Hemming, R., & Potter, B. H. (Eds.). (2013). *The international handbook of public financial management*. New York: Palgrave Macmillan.

Anton, T. J. (1966). *The politics of state expenditure in Illinois*. Urbana: University of Illinois Press.

Axelrod, D. (1995). *Budgeting for modern government* (2nd edition). New York: St. Martin's Press.

Baldacci, E., & Gupta, S. (2009). Fiscal expansions: What works. *Finance and Development*, 46(4) (December).

Bell, M. E. (2012). Real property tax. In Ebel, R. D. & Petersen, J. E. (Eds.), *The Oxford handbook of state and local government finance* (pp. 271–300). New York: Oxford University Press.

Berne, R., & Schramm, R. (1986). *The financial analysis of governments*. Englewood Cliffs: Prentice-Hall.

Blackman, E. (2013). E-mails. March 5 & 24.

Briggs, T. (former CFO, City of Denver) (2011). E-mails. October 30.

Campbell, L., & Guess, G. M. (2011). Jordan: GFMIS post implementation review. Amman: DAI/USAID Fiscal Reform Project, November, 48 pp.

Chan, J. I. & Zhang, Q. (2013). Government accounting standards and policies. In Allen, Hemming, & Potter (Eds.). *The international handbook of public financial management* (pp. 742–767). New York: Palgrave Macmillan.

Chen, G. G., Forsythe, D. W., Weikart, L. A., & Williams, D. W. (2009). *Budget tools: Financial methods in the public sector*. Washington, DC: CQ Press.

Chu, K-Y., & Hemming, R. (1991). *Public expenditure handbook: A guide to public policy issues in developing countries*. Washington, DC: International Monetary Fund.

City of Milwaukee, Budget and Management Department. (2003). *Plan and budget summary 2003*.

Coe, C. K. (1989). *Public financial management*. Englewood Cliffs: Prentice-Hall.

Colarusso, L. (2011). Debt crisis ad blitz. *The Daily Beast*, August 2.

Cooper, M. (2010). An incinerator becomes Harrisburg's money pit. *The New York Times*, May 20, p. A4.

Dannin, E., & Cokorinos, L. (2012). Infrastructure privatization in the new millennium. In Ebel & Petersen, *The Oxford handbook of state and local government finance* (pp. 727–756). New York: Oxford University Press.

DeBonis, M. (2013). Existing CFO saw sonnets behind bond ratings, budgets. *The Washington Post*, p. B1.

Delaney, J. (2013). A fund to jump-start the economy. *The Washington Post*, November 22, p. A14.

Dener, C., Watkins, J., & Dorotinsky, W. (2011). *Financial management information systems: 25 years of World Bank experience on what works and what doesn't*. Washington, DC, World Bank.

Diamond, J., & Schiller, C. (1991). Expenditure arrears. In Chu & Hemming, *Public expenditure handbook: A guide to public policy issues in developing countries* (pp. 159–164). Washington, DC: International Monetary Fund.

Dunn, W. N. (2008). *Public policy analysis: An introduction* (4th Edition). Upper Saddle River, NJ: Pearson Prentice-Hall).

Ebel, R. D., & Petersen, J. E. (Eds.). (2012). *The Oxford handbook of state and local government finance*. New York: Oxford University Press.

———, & Ha T.T. V. (2012). Introduction: State and local government finance in the United States. In Ebel & Petersen (Eds.), *The Oxford handbook of state and local government finance* (pp. 1–45). New York: Oxford University Press.

Eckersley, J. (2013). Will higher taxes on rich derail California's economic comeback? *The Washington Post*, February 18, p. A4.

The Economist. (1999). Are stadiums good for you? March 17, p. 19.

———. (2002). Promise now, bill your children. June 16, p. 82.

———. (2003). *2003–2008 Capital Improvements Plan*.

———. (2005). A brighter future for pensions. December 3, p. 35.

———. (2008). The cracks are showing. June 28, p. 36.

———. (2010). A gold-plated burden. October 16, p. 95.

———. (2011). Illinoyed. December 3, p. 38.

———. (2011b). Blood on the table—money in the bank. July 9, p. 29.

———. (2012a). Brownian motion. January 17, p. 25.

———. (2012b). Too much risk, not enough reward. March 17, p. 23.

———. (2012c). Brazil's pension system: Tick, tock. March 24, p. 38.

———. (2013a). Too much of a good thing. February 23, p. 30.

———. (2013b). A little faster, George? March 9, p. 15.

———. (2013c). Making nice. December 14, p. 35.

———. (2013d). Skid row. February 23, pp. 29–30.

———. (2013e). Those pension blues. December 7, p. 29.

———. (2013f). The Texas budget: Too much of a good thing. February 23, p. 30.

———. (2013g). Commerce and conscience. February 23, p. 71.

———. (2013h). The America that works. March 16, p. 13.

———. (2013i). America's competitiveness. March 15, p. 14.

———. (2013j). D (for dilapidated) plus. April 6, p. 34.

———. (2013k). Deficit-reduction disorder. February 9, p. 29.

Finkler, S. A. (2010). *Financial management for public, health and not-for-profit organizations* (3rd edition). Upper Saddle River, NJ: Prentice-Hall Pearson.

Fisher, R. C. (2007). *State and local public finance* (3rd edition). Mason, OH: Thomson South-Western.

Fox, W. F. (2012). Retail sales and use taxation. In Ebel & Petersen (Eds.), *The Oxford handbook of state and local government finance* (pp. 406–429). New York: Oxford University Press.

Francis, Norton (2012) "Revenue Estimation" in Ebel & Petersen (Eds.), *The Oxford handbook of state and local government finance* (pp 497–519). New York: Oxford University Press.

Gifford, J. L. (2012). Transportation finance. In Ebel & Petersen, (Eds.), *The Oxford handbook of state and local government finance* (pp. 594–624). New York: Oxford University Press.

Glover, M. (1994). *A practical guide for measuring program efficiency and effectiveness in local government*. Tampa: Innovations Group.

Government Management Daily. (2013). Judge overturns voter-approved pension change. December 24. www.daily@govmanagement.com.

Guess, G. M. (1988). Budgetary cutback and transit system performance: The case of MARTA. *Public Budgeting and Finance*, 8(1) (Spring), pp. 58–69.

———. (1985). Role conflict in capital project implementation: The case of Dade County Metrorail. *Public Administration Review*, 45(5) (September/October).

———, & Farnham, P. G. (2011). *Cases in public policy analysis* (3rd edition) (2000, 2nd edition). Washington, DC Georgetown University Press.

———, & Todor, C. (2005). Capital programming and budgeting: Comparative local government perspectives. In Rabin (Ed.), *Encyclopedia of public administration and public policy* (pp. 1–9). New York: Marcel Dekker.

Halsey, A. (2012). U.S. water and sewer systems tapped out. *The Washington Post*, January 3, p. A1.

Heller, P. S. (2013). Assessing a government's non-debt liabilities. In Allen et al. (Eds.), *The international handbook of public financial management* (pp. 638–661). New York: Palgrave Macmillan.

———. (1991). Operations and maintenance. In Chu & Hemming, *Public expenditure handbook: A guide to public policy issues in developing countries* (pp. 52–59). Washington, DC: International Monetary Fund.

Hemming, R. (1991). Transfers to public enterprises. In Chu & Hemming, *Public expenditure handbook: A guide to public policy issues in developing countries* (pp. 75–81). Washington, DC: International Monetary Fund.

Johnson, F. S., & Roswick, D. L. (1991). Local fiscal capacity. In Petersen & Strachota (Eds.), *Local government finance* (pp. 177–199). Chicago: GFOA.

Kincaid, J. (2012). The constitutional frameworks of state and local government finance. In Ebel & Petersen (Eds.), *The Oxford handbook of state and local government finance* (pp. 45–83). New York: Oxford University Press.

Klein, E. (2012). It's hard to make all the numbers add up in budget physics. *The Washington Post*, December 22, p. A2.

Kory, R. C., & Rosenberg, P. (1984). In Matzer (Ed.), *Practical financial management: New techniques for local government*. Washington, DC: International City Management Association.

LaClair, E., & Machado, J. (2011). Forecasting volume, and break-even analysis: The Centerville Animal Control Program. Assignment for PUAD 633 Public Financial Management Class, 2011, at American University, George M. Guess, professor.

Lane, C. (2013). Big bloat on campus. *The Washington Post*, January 1, p. A15.

Lawrence, B. (2011). The dirty secret in Uncle Sam's Friday trash dump. *The Washington Post*, December 28, p. A14.

Lee, R. D., & Johnson, R. W. (1998). *Public budgeting systems.* (6th edition). Gaithersburg, MD: Aspen.

Lehan, E. A. (1991). Organization of the finance function. In Petersen & Strachota (Eds.), *Local government finance* (p. 33). Chicago: GFOA.

———. (1981). *Simplified government budgeting*. Chicago: Municipal Finance Officers Association.

Lewis, C. W., & Walker, G. (1984). *Casebook in public budgeting and financial management*. Englewood Cliffs: Prentice-Hall.

Liner, C. D. (1996). Projecting local government revenues. In Rabin, Hildreth, & Miller (Eds.), *Budgeting: Formulation and Execution; Workbook* (2nd edition); *Data Sourcebook* (2nd edition). Athens, GA: Carl Vinson Institute of Government.

Listokin-Smith, S. (2012). Public employee pensions and investments. In Ebel & Petersen (Eds.), *The Oxford handbook of state and local government finance* (pp. 843–871). New York: Oxford University Press.

Lowrey, A. (2013). The low politics of low growth. *The New York Times*, January 23, p. 5.

Mackenzie, G. A. (1991). Price subsidies. In Chu & Hemming, *Public expenditure handbook: A guide to public policy issues in developing countries* (pp. 60–67). Washington, DC: International Monetary Fund.

Marlowe, J. (2013). Capital budgeting and spending. In Ebel & Petersen (Eds.), *The Oxford handbook of state and local government finance* (pp. 658–682). New York: Oxford University Press.

Mathers, E. (2009). Hunkering down under the big sky. *Public Management*.

Matzer, J. (Ed.). (1984). *Practical financial management: New techniques for local government*. Washington, DC: International City Management Association.

McMaster, J. (1991). *Urban financial management: A training manual*. Washington, DC: World Bank.

Melbye, D. (Ed.). (2010). *The ERP book: Financial management technology from A to Z*. Chicago: GFOA.

Michel, G. R. (2001). *Decision tools for budgetary analysis*. Chicago: GFOA.

Mikesell, J. L. (2014). *Fiscal administration, analysis, and applications for the public sector* (9th edition) and (2011, 8th edition). Boston: Wadsworth Cengage.

Milbank, D. (2013). Economy's biggest boat anchor? Congress. *The Washington Post*, December 19, p. A2.

Miller, M. (2013). California dreamin'. *The Washington Post*, April 6, p. A13.

Moak, L. L. (1982). *Municipal bonds: Planning, sale, administration*. Chicago: Municipal Finance Officers Association.

Montgomery County (MD) Office of Management and Budget. (2011). *FY12 approved operating budget and FY 12–17 public services program*. Rockville, MD.

Nachmias, D. (1979). *Public policy evaluation: Approaches and methods*. New York: St. Martin's.

Neels, K., & Caggiano, M. (1996). Pricing public services. In Rabin et al., *Budgeting: Formulation and execution*; *Workbook* (2nd edition); *Data Sourcebook* (2nd edition) (pp. 173–174). Athens, GA: Carl Vinson Institute of Government.

Newman, K. (2013). In the South and West, a tax on being poor. *New York Times*, March 10, p. A5.

Nourmohammadi, N. (2011). WMATA: Problem escalators to Get needed repairs. *Washington Times*, November 2, p. A-5.

Petersen, J. E., & Ciccarone, R. (2012). Financial markets and state and local governments. In Ebel & Petersen (Eds.), *The Oxford handbook of state and local government finance* (pp. 682–727). New York: Oxford University Press.

Petersen, J. E., & Strachota, D. R. (Eds.). (1991). *Local government finance*. Chicago: GFOA.

Posner, P., Lewis, T., & Laufe, H. (1998). Budgeting for capital. *Public Budgeting and Finance*, 18(13), pp. 11–24.

Powdar, J. C. (1996). *The operating budget: A guide for smaller governments*. Chicago: GFOA.

Pressman, J. L., & Wildavsky, A. (1984). *Implementation* (3rd edition). Berkeley: University of California Press.

Rabin, J. (Ed.). (2005). *Encyclopedia of public administration and public policy*. New York: Marcel Dekker.

Rabin, J., Hildreth, B. W., & Miller, G. J. (1996). *Budgeting: Formulation and execution*; *Workbook* (2nd edition); *Data Sourcebook* (2nd edition). Athens, GA: Carl Vinson Institute of Government.

Rabin, J., & Lynch, T. D. (1986). *Handbook on public budgeting and financial management*. New York: Marcel Dekker.

Rein, L. (2010). Streetcar effort may go down to the wire. *The Washington Post*, April 6, p. C1.

———. (2010b). A major sore point for the Silver Line. *The Washington Post*, April 22, p. B1.

———. (2013). No-bid Medicare's sticker shock. *The Washington Post*, March 5, p. A16.

Rivlin, A. (2012). Foreword. In Ebel & Petersen (Eds.), *The Oxford handbook of state and local government finance* (pp ix–xi). New York: Oxford University Press.

Robinson, M. (2013). Performance budgeting. In Allen et al. (Eds.), *The international handbook of public financial management* (pp. 237–259). New York: Palgrave Macmillan.

Schultz, J. (2005). *Follow the money: A guide to monitoring budgets and oil and gas revenues*. New York: Open Society Institute.

Sjoquist, D. L., & Stoycheva, R. (2012). Local revenue diversification: User charges, sales taxes, and income taxes. In Ebel & Petersen (Eds.), *The Oxford handbook of state and local government finance* (pp. 429–463). New York: Oxford University Press.

Spiotto, J. E. (2012). Financial emergencies: Default and bankruptcy. In Ebel & Petersen (Eds.), *The Oxford handbook of state and local government finance* (pp. 756–783). New York: Oxford University Press.

Strachota, D. (1994). *The best of government budgeting: A guide to preparing budget documents*. Chicago, GFOA.

Sullivan, P. (2013). Arlington halts bus stop construction. *The Washington Post*, p. B4.

———. (2013b). Arlington gets no rest from critics of bus stop. *The Washington Post*, March 25, p. B1.

Summers, L. (2013). The growth plan we need. *The Washington Post*, February 11, p. A16.

Sun, L. (2008). Cash strapped Metro needs millions in repairs. *The Washington Post*, March 27, p. B4.

Toulmin, L. M., & Wright, G. E. (1983). Expenditure forecasting. In Rabin & Lynch, *Handbook on public budgeting and financial management*. New York: Marcel Dekker.

Turque, B. (2013). Concrete tests faulted. *The Washington Post*, March 27, p. B1.

———, & Bui, L. (2013). Council debates schools budget. *The Washington Post*, March 14, p. B2.

U.S. Department of Transportation (USDOT). (1986). *Financial management for transit: A handbook*. Washington, DC: USDOT, Report 1-86-10.

Valente, C. F., & Valente, M. (1984). Evaluating financial condition: City of Smithville. In Lewis & Walker, *Casebook in public budgeting and financial management* (pp. 300–309). Englewood Cliffs: Prentice-Hall.

Vincent, W. (2013) Arlington's runaway streetcar. *The Washington Post*, December 8, p. D2.

The Washington Post. (2013). Keep an independent CFO. February 14, p. A16.

The Washington Post. (2013a). 15 cents a gallon. December 27, p. A20.

Wildavsky, A. (1986). *Budgeting: A comparative theory of budget processes (Revised Edition)*. New Brunswick, NJ: Transaction Books.

———. (1984). *The politics of the budgetary process* (4th edition). Boston: Little, Brown.

Whoriskey, P., & Keating, D. (2013). Expensive drug costs Medicare billions. *The Washington Post*, December 8, p. A1.

Zorn, P. W. (1991). Public employee retirement systems and benefits. In Petersen & Strachota (Eds.), *Local government finance* (pp. 369–393). Chicago: GFOA.

Index

Accounting information system, 179

Accrual based accounting, 175, 182, 197

Actionable problem, 142

Actuarial present value (APV), 111

Administrative feasibility, 53

Affordability analysis, 155–156

Allotment, 9, 175, 181, 184–186, 175, 189–190

American Society for Civil Engineers (ASCE), 131

Apportionment, 184

Arlington County (VA), 167–169

Arrears, 74, 97, 120, 193, 200

Assessment ratio, 62–63, 81

Australia, 130

Average costs, 68–69

Averaging or proportionate change, 73–76

Balance sheet, 113, 118, 180–181

Baltimore County (MD), 54

Bank selection for cash management, 194

Bankruptcy, 50, 62, 80, 130, 156, 175, 177, 204

Baseline, 15, 18, 23, 43, 60, 104–105, 116, 184

Betterment districts, 161–162

Borrowing authority, 9

Break-even analysis, 101–103

Budget authority, 9, 36, 53, 184

Budget calendar, 8, 10, 87, 183

Budget classification, 18, 21, 36, 44

Budget composition or shares, 27, 105, 139

Budget function, 8, 10, 105

Budget process, xii, xv, 1, 8–9, 19, 61–62, 85–87, 183

Budget reform, 139

Budget request, 51, 103–105, 107, 119, 122, 139, 142, 164

Build operate and transfer (BOT), 159

Business process re-engineering (BPR), 183

Canada, 19, 39, 72, 130, 133

Capital budget, 43–44, 74, 94–95, 97, 114–115, 120, 129–132, 139, 145, 149, 151, 154, 156, 160–163, 193, 200

Capital expenditures, 22, 36, 119, 131, 171, 173

Capital improvements program (CIP), 43, 67, 132, 138, 150, 157, 200

Capital leases, 160

Capital needs assessment, 139–140, 158, 162

Capital program, 2, 43, 47, 122, 130–131, 137–139

Capital project, 139, 142, 144–145, 152, 154–155, 163, 179, 183, 186, 189

Cash based accounting, 181–182

Cash flow statement, 180–181

Cash management, xvii, 9–10, 175, 177, 183–185, 196–197

Certificate of deposit (CD), 195

Charges, 27, 47, 50–52, 58–59, 64–66, 81, 114, 119, 132–133, 158, 186, 190, 204

Chart of accounts, 179–180

Chicago Transit Authority (CTA), 19

Comprehensive Annual Financial Report (CAFR), 118

Contract bidding systems, 163

Cost center, 97, 99, 179, 183

Cost effectiveness, 87, 135

Cost-finding, 96

Costs v expenditures, 40, 66

Cost-volume pricing, 95–100

Cross-walking, 39

Current services budget, 21, 105, 130

Dade County (FL), 189–190, 201

Data v information, 19, 107

Debt burden, 49, 119–121, 131, 161

Decentralized expenditure authority, 22

Deferred maintenance, 115, 131

Defined benefits plan, 86, 110, 114

Defined contribution plan, 86, 110, 114

Demand for services, 15, 31, 52, 58, 67–68, 70, 72, 87, 108

Detroit (Michigan), 50, 80, 86, 175, 177

Direct cost pricing, 66–67

Discount rate, 111–114, 134, 147, 149–150, 164

Discounted benefit cost ratio (BCR), 147–149, 152, 164

Discounting, 114, 134, 136, 145, 147, 178

Discretionary funds, xii, 9, 53, 97

Economies of scale, 67, 69

Efficiency, 140, 147, 150, 156, 172, 175, 189, 190, 201

Encumbrance accounting, 182

Enterprise resource planning (ERP), 19, 27

Entitlement authority, 94, 176, 178, 185

European Union (EU), xi, 114, 130

Evaluating revenue sources, 54–61

Expenditure control, 175, 181–182, 184, 188, 190

Expenditure trends, 18, 80, 186

Explicit producer subsidies, 117, 119

External auditor, 18

Facilities condition database, 139–140, 150

Fargo (ND), 133

Fees, xii, 15, 22, 27, 29, 64–65, 76, 81, 115, 119, 129, 143, 156, 157, 159–160, 173, 186, 194, 196

Fiduciary funds, 27, 114, 119

Financial capacity, 140–141

Financial management information system (FMIS), 12, 14, 156

Financing options, 154–162

Fiscal condition, 2, 15, 86, 120

Fiscal reporting system, 176

Fiscal space, xiii, 15

Fiscal transparency, xiv, 2–3, 14, 19, 23, 44, 66, 119, 135

Fixed costs, 67, 82, 96, 99, 101–103, 108, 126

Flexible budgeting, 102–103, 187–188

Fringe benefits including pensions, 108–114, 119, 177, 178

Full cost pricing, 67–68, 70

Functional budget classification, 31, 36, 38, 98, 172, 173

Gallatin County (MT), xvii, 64, 98, 101, 150

Gaston County (NC), xvii, 2–3, 15, 17, 23–24, 29, 30–32, 36, 38, 54–55, 122, 191–192

General fund, 19, 22–23, 54, 65, 80, 83, 1–6, 117–118, 141, 180, 197

General ledger, 175, 180–181, 183, 191

Generally Accepted Accounting Practices (GAAP), 27, 111–114

Germany, 72, 177

Government Accounting Standards Board (GASB), 111, 114

Government Finance Officers Association (GFOA), 10, 19–20, 23, 59, 89, 107, 133, 177

Government financial information systems (GFMIS), 14, 123, 175, 191, 193

Grants, xii, xviii, 8, 15, 23, 53, 61, 65, 85, 93, 108, 115, 150, 152, 155, 158–159, 162, 168–170, 176, 175, 187, 193

Guaranteed debt, 160

Harrisburg (PA), 155–156, 200

Idle funds, 194

Income-based pricing, 71, 72, 101

Incremental budgeting, 1, 21

Infrastructure deficit, 131, 176

Infrastructure trusts, 162

Insolvency, 86

Inspector-general (IG), xiv, 9

Integrated financial management system (IFMS), 163, 181–183, 191

Inter-fund transfers, 19, 116–117, 119

Internal audit, xiv, 107, 137, 190

Internal control systems, 136

Internal rate of return (IRR), 147, 149

International City/County Management Association (ICMA), 59, 105, 107, 111, 133, 179

Inventory controls, 163

Invoicing procedures, 194

Journal, 118, 180

Keystone XL pipeline, 143

Land use plans, 133

Ledger, 118, 175, 180–181, 183, 191

Linear regression, 73, 76–80

Liquidity crisis, 10, 15, 190, 196

Local economic development, 61, 74, 143

Make-buy analysis or decision, 98, 101, 142, 160, 165

Mandatory expenditure, xii

Marginal analysis, 101

Marginal costs, 68–71, 82, 95, 116

Marginal productivity curve, 98–99

Market value, 62–64, 120, 143–144, 195

Medium-term expenditure framework (MTEF), 169–173

Merit goods, 166

Metropolitan Atlanta Rapid Transit Authority (MARTA) (GA), xviii, 72–73, 97

Miami (FL), 117, 149

Millage rate, 62, 64, 81

Milwaukee (WI), 10–13, 19, 21, 23, 25, 31, 36, 40, 44, 61–63, 87, 89, 94–95, 108, 122, 126, 138, 140141, 149, 156–157, 161–162

Ministry of finance (Jordan), 191

Monetary project benefits, 143

Monopoly, 65–67, 70, 130

Montgomery County (MD), 19–20, 22–23, 27, 31, 43–44, 45, 47, 149, 163

Municipal development banks (MDBs), 161–162

Natural monopoly, 66–67, 70
Net present value (NPV), 147–150, 164
Netherlands, 178
Nominal property tax rate, 62, 81
Non-guaranteed debt, 161

Object of expenditure classification, 2,
    12, 21–27, 29, 40, 47, 86, 91, 107, 108
Operating statement, 19, 181
Operations and maintenance (O&M), 2,
    36, 97, 114–116, 119, 128, 132, 146,
    151, 163–164, 166, 170–171, 185
Oracle EBusiness system (EBS), 191, 193
Outcomes, 20, 40–41, 86, 89, 91, 93,
    107, 126
Outputs, 20, 40, 68, 86, 89, 93, 107–108,
    180

Pay-as-you-go funding, 158–159
Pay-as-you-use financing, 160–162
Penalty prices, 71
Performance measures, 88–94, 98, 100,
    104, 108, 126, 140
Performance Service Agreement (PSA)
    (UK), 93
Pittsburgh (PA), 74
Political Culture, 51
Politicizing project benefits, 134–135
Price elasticity of demand, 58, 69
Primary project benefit, 98, 143
Private public partnerships (PPP), 159
Procurement, 136, 150
Productivity, 10, 31, 40, 54, 67, 88,
    98–100
Program budget classification, 31, 36, 39,
    86, 93
Property tax assessment, 61–64
Property tax bill, 62
Proposition 13 (California), 50, 52, 58,
    59, 64

Proprietary funds, 19, 27, 116, 181
Public enterprise, 72, 160
Public financial management (PFM), 10,
    12, 14, 40, 44, 114, 169, 171, 183,
    190–191
Public goods, 65

Ratios, 16, 18, 23, 88, 101, 107–108,
    111, 115, 120, 164
Real or inflation adjusted value, 18, 59,
    76, 94–95, 105–106, 144, 149, 171, 187
Receipts deposit, 193–195, 197
Rehabilitation, 23, 101, 114, 130–132,
    136, 139, 151, 154, 158, 163, 170, 173
Reporting burden, 139
Reprogramming authority, 40, 139, 185,
    188
Reserve funding, 110
Revenue adequacy and stability, 52
Revenue budget, 60, 73
Revenue collection, 10, 54, 83, 119, 182,
    193
Revenue diversification, 52
Revenue forecasts, 60, 72–74, 81
Revenue policy, xv, 51–53
Running costs, 22, 97, 144

Sales tax, 15, 49–50, 52, 58, 60–61,
    72–73, 173
Salt Lake City (Utah), 31, 39, 40, 120
San Diego (CA), 74
Sequester, xii, 53, 122, 155, 176, 190
Short-term debt, 160–161
Social Impact Bonds (SIBs), 103–104
Strategic v. operational level decisions,
    2, 154
Subsidies, 19, 22, 66, 70, 72, 86, 116–
    119, 136, 158, 170–171, 173
Subsidy pricing, 66, 71
Switzerland, 72

Tax expenditure, 7, 36, 119
Tax increment financing (TIF), 161–162
Transfer authority, 185
Transfers, 9, 19, 22, 97, 116–117, 119, 129, 170, 173, 185, 194
Treasury single account, 183, 191, 196

Undiscounted payback, 145–146

Variable costs, 67–70, 82–83, 96, 101–103, 126, 144, 187

Variance analysis, 9, 186–188

Washington, D.C., 2, 12, 43, 50, 81, 91, 132–133, 136, 140, 159
Weighting and scoring method, matrix or framework, 152–154
Workload measures, 87

Zero-balance or concentration account, 195
Zero-based budgeting, 97

Made in the USA
Monee, IL
28 August 2024

64778250R00134